The Politics of Necessity

Critical Human Rights

Series Editors

Steve J. Stern ❦ Scott Straus

Books in the series **Critical Human Rights** emphasize research that opens new ways to think about and understand human rights. The series values in particular empirically grounded and intellectually open research that eschews simplified accounts of human rights events and processes.

In the mid-1990s, South Africa underwent a remarkable transition from an apartheid state to a multiracial democracy. This book raises key questions about what that democratization has achieved and what democracy itself means. Most discussions of democracy and democratization focus on liberal political rights and procedural matters. That is, the standard questions are: Is the playing field fair? Are elections competitive? Are civil society institutions, including the media, free to operate in their societies? Elke Zuern argues that this focus on civil and political rights, as well as on procedural matters, misses a fundamental set of issues related to equality and material well-being. Many people in poor societies expect democracy to bring with it improvements in their standards of living, including income, health, housing, and education. Zuern contends that the fight against apartheid was rooted in such concerns for social and economic rights, and that current dissatisfaction with the postapartheid regime stems from its failure to address these substantive issues adequately. Reflecting a deep engagement with South Africa, *The Politics of Necessity* also speaks to the situation in other countries of Africa as well as in parts of Latin America. In challenging narratives that concentrate exclusively on one category of rights, this book prompts us to consider what rights are fundamentally human.

The Politics of Necessity

Community Organizing and Democracy in South Africa

Elke Zuern

The University of Wisconsin Press

Publication of this volume has been made possible, in part, through support from the ANONYMOUS FUND OF THE COLLEGE OF LETTERS AND SCIENCE at the University of Wisconsin–Madison, and from the EVJUE FOUNDATION, INC., the charitable arm of *The Capital Times*.

The University of Wisconsin Press
1930 Monroe Street, 3rd Floor
Madison, Wisconsin 53711-2059
uwpress.wisc.edu

3 Henrietta Street
London WCE 8LU, England
eurospanbookstore.com

5   4   3   2   1

Library of Congress Cataloging-in-Publication Data
Zuern, Elke, 1968–
The politics of necessity: community organizing and democracy in South Africa /
    Elke Zuern.
        p.   cm.—(Critical human rights)
        Includes bibliographical references and index.
        ISBN 978-0-299-25014-0 (pbk.: alk. paper)
        ISBN 978-0-299-25013-3 (e-book)
1. South Africa—Politics and government—1989-1994.   2. South Africa—Politics
    and government—1994-   3. Community organization—South Africa.   4. Basic
    needs—Government policy—South Africa.   5. Poverty—Political aspects—South Africa.
    I. Title.   II. Series: Critical human rights.
DT1971.Z84   2011
322.4´30968—dc22
2010011579

Copublished with University of KwaZulu-Natal Press
Customers in South Africa, Botswana, Namibia, Lesotho, Zimbabwe, and Swaziland should order from University of KwaZulu-Natal Press at www.ukznpress.co.za.

To
BERTA and **ROBERT ZUERN**,
for your love and support

Contents

Illustrations

Preface

This book investigates the creation of democracy from the perspective of the ordinary people who helped to bring it about by organizing, protesting, and demanding a wide range of rights. The initial idea for the project developed during my work interviewing volunteers with the Wits/Vaal Regional Peace Secretariat in mid-1994, just after South Africa's historic democratic elections that brought Nelson Mandela to the presidency. I was struck by the great contrast between the stories that these volunteers told and those that I had read in both journalistic and academic texts on South Africa's transition. Many popular accounts described the creation of nonracial democracy as a miracle. In-depth analyses of the transition often suggested that the real work was done by elites during the on-again, off-again negotiations that began even before Nelson Mandela was released from prison. Neither the image of a miracle nor that of elites ironing out the details of the new democracy captured the experiences of these volunteers. They found themselves on the front lines of the struggle for democracy, standing as peace monitors between rival political parties, working to prevent violence from erupting, and trying to minimize it when it did occur. They often could only enter tense areas in armored vehicles dubbed "doves," named so because of the Peace Secretariat's logo, a blue dove, emblazoned on the side of the vehicles. For these volunteers, as for so many other South Africans, the creation of a democratic regime in South Africa was not the miraculous product of elite actions but rather the result of a long and ongoing popular struggle.

Since 1994, I have followed the work of many community organizations, from the older township-based civics to newer social movements. As a PhD student, I conducted preliminary fieldwork in South Africa in 1995 and then returned for the year in 1997. The most important insights that I gleaned came from the many interviews that ordinary South Africans granted me. It was through these interviews that I began to develop an understanding of how people living in the impoverished townships created by apartheid viewed the struggle for democracy, their sacrifices, their achievements, and the short-comings of their new system. These interviews also placed an important check on many of the models of democratic transitions that I had read before engaging in fieldwork. I was frequently struck by how poorly those models matched the realities described by the people I interviewed. Not only were many of the broader understandings of how transitions happen incorrect, but, as I was to learn, they led researchers to ask the wrong questions. I began with questions about how people believed their country had achieved democracy but learned that I needed to ask what democracy was and what people were actually strug-gling for. I have been very fortunate to return to South Africa regularly since 1997. These annual visits offered me an opportunity to see the changes that occurred from one year to the next and to continue interviewing the people who sought to be part of ongoing political processes in their local commu-nities. Their answers to my many questions and their rephrasing of these ques-tions form the basis of this book.

The struggle for the overwhelming majority of the people I interviewed is a struggle for human rights and democracy, but not in the way in which mainstream western approaches most often employ these terms. Liberal de-mocracies such as the United States and prominent international human rights organizations tend to focus on civil and political rights while sidelining socio-economic rights. This narrow view that ignores the fundamental indivisibility of all human rights is a legacy of the cold war and the triumph of capitalism. During the cold war, the United States could point to its respect for civil and political rights and demonstrate the general absence of those rights in the Soviet Union. A focus on socioeconomic rights would have complicated the argument of straightforward U.S. supremacy. Since the end of the cold war, the ideology of neoliberalism has worked to perpetuate this partial attention to human rights by defining freedom as the focal point in rights-based discus-sions. Within this framework, the state engagement required to ensure socio-economic rights is often presented as limiting fundamental civil and political freedoms. South Africans have directly challenged this approach by arguing that freedom can only be realized when civil, political, *and* socioeconomic rights are protected and enforced.

This book traces the struggles of community organizations and social movements in South Africa and compares their experiences to those of popu-lar actors in other transitioning societies. In so doing, it fills a gap in the litera-ture on democracy, social movements, and material inequality. Numerous texts have addressed questions of democratization in African states (e.g., Ake,

Democracy and Development in Africa; Bratton and van de Walle, *Democratic Experiments in Africa*; for South Africa: Alexander, *An Ordinary Country*; Sisk, *Democratization in South Africa*; Wood, *Forging Democracy from Below*), and many others have investigated the power of movements across the globe in effecting regime change (e.g., Goodwin, *No Other Way Out*; Schock, *Unarmed Insurrections*; Tilly, *Contention and Democracy in Europe, 1650–2000*). Relatively few have followed the impetus of this book: to investigate the key interactions between popular movements and states in the production and critique of democracy as it is fought for, established, and institutionalized. Those that have pursued these questions have tended to focus on Latin American cases studies (e.g., Avritzer, *Democracy and the Public Space in Latin America*; Foweraker and Landman, *Citizenship Rights and Social Movements*; Paley, *Marketing Democracy: Power and Social Movements in Post-Dictatorship Chile*). Although this book is centered on the South African experience, it investigates the lessons offered comparatively, by engaging other African as well as Latin American histories of mobilization during and after political and economic transitions.

Two central methods are employed in this study: the comparative method and process tracing. Comparisons are made across time and space. Within South Africa, the experiences of community organizations are compared from the late apartheid period, to the extended period of negotiations to end formal apartheid, to postapartheid democracy. During the three decades from 1979 to 2009, many existing organizations have folded, and new ones have been created. Some have managed to survive despite the dramatic changes occurring around them. To illuminate the lessons of these organizations, the experiences of popular actors in South Africa are briefly compared to those in other African and Latin American countries. These comparisons do not form in-depth case studies. They present an opportunity to consider the broader implications of the South African findings and to further develop arguments concerning the connections between protest and democracy. Process tracing is employed within the South African case to demonstrate the mechanisms that bring about shifts in perceptions, actions, and organizations.

In order to limit the analysis without sacrificing the insights it offers, the in-depth investigation of grassroots politics and protest in South Africa focuses on the African townships around four major metropolitan areas: Johannesburg, Ekurhuleni (East Rand), Tshwane (Pretoria), and Nelson Mandela Bay (Port Elizabeth). These four metropolitan municipalities are based in areas where the African National Congress (ANC) has faced little challenge from opposition parties and where civic organizations have been consistently active. In Johannesburg the areas addressed in this study include townships in Soweto (Dobsonville, Zola, Moraka, Meadowlands, Orlando West, Diepkloof, and

Kliptown) as well as numerous zones in Alexandra; in the Vaal region, south of Johannesburg: Sharpeville, Sebokeng, Bophelong, Boipatong, and Evaton; in the East Rand, the townships of Katlehong, Thokoza, Vosloorus, KwaThema, and Wattville; outside Pretoria: Mamelodi and Soshanguve; in the Port Elizabeth area: Kwazakele and New Brighton as well as Uitenhage, Cradock, and Grahamstown in the Eastern Cape. Movements in Cape Town and Durban (the two remaining major metropolitan areas not covered in the earlier research) are also included in the postapartheid period. For each time period, the local organizations chosen were among the most vocal and influential in the country. They attracted the greatest media attention for their work and their challenges to the state, the regime, and the ruling party.

The primary data upon which arguments are based include archival records, court transcripts, nongovernmental organization (NGO) project reports, survey research, newspaper sources, and well over two hundred interviews conducted during the first fifteen years of South Africa's experiment with nonracial democracy. From 1994 to 2009, I interviewed civic and social movement leaders from the local to the national level. I also conducted interviews with local government leaders and members of NGOs and other community organizations. Several interviewees chose to remain anonymous due to the politically sensitive nature of our discussion; when I have cited them, they are simply defined by their general job description and their broader geographic area. Together, these interviews conducted both on and off the record provide key insights into how civic and social movement participants and others perceived the work and the role of local associations over time. They demonstrate how a range of ordinary people viewed the transformation process as a whole. As South African politics shifted, so did the opportunities and challenges for its new citizens. Many respondents were interviewed on more than one occasion, often as they moved from work with local organizations to government or private business. As a result of their changing roles, many were willing to keep talking only if our discussions were off the record.

Acknowledgments

This book would not have been possible without the contributions of many South Africans who shared their experiences of struggle and their expectations for democracy. Mzwanele Mayekiso first introduced me to civic organizers and members in Alexandra and beyond. As the interviews snowballed, so did my debts. Donovan Williams, Mike Tofile, Ntsokolo Daniel Sandi, Maynard Menu, Emmanuel Tseleii, Ali Tleane, Philemon Machitela, Mandla Mazibuko, Vuyisile Moedi, Aubery Nxumalo, Mlungisi Hlongwane, Lucas Qhakaza, Jabulani Tshabalala, Trevor Ngwane, Ashraf Cassiem, and Max Ntanyana, among many others, were all incredibly generous with their time. The political studies department at the University of the Witwatersrand (Wits), the Centre for Civil Society at the University of KwaZulu-Natal, and the Centre for the Study of Democracy at the University of Johannesburg all provided institutional homes at different points in this project. Historical Papers and the South African History Archive at Wits, as well as the Robben Island Museum Mayibuye Archives at the University of the Western Cape, provided an incredible bounty of original documents from the apartheid period. The South African Media Service at the University of the Free State provided newspaper clippings from 1979 to the late 1990s. Over the years, Rupert Taylor, Tom Lodge, Phillip Frankel, Shireen Hassim, Jeremy Seekings, Imraan Valodia, Richard Ballard, Sakhela Buhlungu, Ashwin Desai, Sophie Oldfield, Patrick Bond, Stephen Greenberg, Anthony Egan, Steven Friedman, Leila Patel, David Moore, Peter Alexander, and Luke Sinwell have all shared ideas and helpful advice. Adam Habib has always offered generous support and ample opportunities for debate.

In Johannesburg, I found a home away from home and a wonderful friend, Samantha Yoewart. She graciously cleaned out her study again and again as I kept returning to Johannesburg for just one more research visit. Sam talked me through more puzzles and contradictions than I care to remember, smoothing over the rough bits with coffee, wine, and whiskey. Her family, Bill, Tinks, Tessa, Doon, Al, and Mandy, welcomed me into their family. Naveen Naidoo, who first suggested Sam take me in, has been incredibly supportive from the beginning and has remained a true friend.

In the United States, Columbia University, Amherst College, and Sarah Lawrence College provided both intellectual and material support for this research. At Columbia, Tony Marx, Chuck Tilly, Ira Katznelson, Mahmood Mamdani, Linda Beck, and Ron Kassimir provided a wonderful mixture of critique and encouragement. Special thanks go to Chuck Tilly, who passed away before this book was completed, for always providing speedy comments and creating a welcoming and engaging intellectual home in the Contentious Politics seminar. Amherst College offered crucial time away from full-time teaching with an Andrew W. Mellon Postdoctoral Fellowship and, a few years later, a Karl Lowenstein Fellowship. Pavel Machala, Amrita Basu, Uday Mehta, Austin Sarat, Tom Dumm, and Anston Bosman talked through ideas and offered helpful comments. At Sarah Lawrence College, Robert Desjarlais, Jamee Moudud, Frank Roosevelt, Shahnaz Rouse, the late Ray Seidelman, Mary Porter, Barbara Kaplan, Geoffrey Danisher, Lillian Ho, Kristy Staniszewski, and Rosemary Weeks supported this project in many different ways. I have benefited enormously from discussions with my students both in class and outside. Allison Ferrier, Eleanore Hyde, Cody Trojan, Jennifer Campbell, and Katherine Graham provided crucial help as incredibly able research assistants.

In New York and beyond, Sean Jacobs, Jessica Blatt, Jacqueline Klopp, Jose Antonio Lucero, Maria Elena Garcia, Marybeth MacPhee, Ebenezer Obadare, Anne Pitcher, John Krinsky, Vince Boudreau, Sun-Chul Kim, Roy Licklider, Zehra Arat, Stephen Ellman, and Penny Andrews critiqued and inspired my work. Invitations to speak at the Africa Workshop at the University of Michigan, Ann Arbor; the South Africa Reading Group, New York Law School; the Seminar on Human Rights at Columbia University; the AIDS and Civil Society Reading Group at CUNY; and the Comparative History of Ideas Program at the University of Washington all offered stimulating discussion and critical feedback. Martin Murray, Michael McDonald, and Heinz Klug provided extremely helpful comments on the full manuscript. Gwen Walker, Sheila McMahon, and many others at the University of Wisconsin Press transformed a stack of papers into a finished book, and Bob Schwartz created a comprehensive index.

Finally, Sumedha Senanayake, my partner and best friend, defender of a far wider range of rights than those covered in this book, and graphic-design emergency specialist, provided the love and support to sustain me through this project. I can't imagine this journey without him.

Abbreviations

AbM	Abahlali baseMjondolo
AAC	Alexandra Action Committee
ACO	Alexandra Civic Organization
ADESS	l'Association pour le Développement de la Sous-Préfecture de Sakété (Sakété District Development Association)
AEC	Anti-Eviction Campaign
AIG	American International Group
AJSS	l'Association de la Jeunesse de la Sous-Préfecture de Sakété (Sakété District Youth Association)
ANC	African National Congress
APF	Anti-Privatization Forum
AZAPO	Azanian People's Organization
BC	black consciousness
BDP	Botswana Democratic Party
BLA	Black Local Authority
CEDC	community economic development center
CKGR	Central Kalahari Game Reserve
COSAS	Congress of South African Students
COSATU	Congress of South African Trade Unions
CP	Conservative Party
CRADORA	Cradock Residents' Association
DA/DP	Democratic Alliance/Democratic Party
ESKOM	Electricity Supply Commission
EZLN	Ejército Zapatista de Liberación Nacional (Zapatista Army of National Liberation)
GEAR	Growth, Employment, and Redistribution
GDP	gross domestic product

HDI	human development index
HSRC	Human Science Research Council
IDASA	Institute for Democracy in South Africa
IFP	Inkatha Freedom Party
LPM	Landless People's Movement
MEC	member of executive council
MK	Umkhonto we Sizwe
MOSOP	Movement for the Survival of the Ogoni People
MPAEC	Mandela Park Anti-Eviction Campaign
MST	Movimento dos Trabalhadores Rurais Sem Terra (Landless Rural Workers Movement)
NAFTA	North American Free Trade Agreement
NARCO	National Association of Residents and Civic Organizations
NICC	National Interim Civics Committee
NGO	nongovernmental organization
NP/NNP	National Party/New National Party
PAC	Pan Africanist Congress of Azania
PEBCO/PEPCO	Port Elizabeth Black Civic Organization/Port Elizabeth People's Civic Organization
PRI	Partido Revolucionario Institucional (Institutional Revolutionary Party)
PWV	Pretoria Witwatersrand Vereeniging
RDP	Reconstruction and Development Program
RSA	Republic of South Africa
SACP	South African Communist Party
SAIRR	South African Institute of Race Relations
SANCO	South African National Civic Organization
SAPA	South African Press Association
SCA	Soweto Civic Association
SDU	self-defense units
SECC	Soweto Electricity Crisis Committee
SIH	SANCO Investment Holdings
SPD	Soweto People's Delegation
SRDI	SANCO Research and Development Institute
TAC	Treatment Action Campaign
TCLSAC	Toronto Committee for the Liberation of Southern Africa/ Toronto Committee for Links between Southern Africa and Canada
TPA	Transvaal Provincial Authority

UDF	United Democratic Front
UNDP	United Nations Development Program
VCA	Vaal Civic Association
WCAEC	Western Cape Anti-Eviction Campaign

The Politics of Necessity

South Africa

International Boundary
Provincial Boundary
★ National Capital
● Provincial Capital

0   100   200   300 Kilometers
0   100   200   300 Miles

ZIMBABWE

BOTSWANA

MOZAMBIQUE

Musina

LIMPOPO

Polokwane

Modimolle

NAMIBIA

Rustenburg

Mbombela

Pretoria

Mafikeng

MPUMALANGA

NORTH
WEST

Johannesburg

Emalahleni

GAUTENG

Vereeniging

SWAZILAND

Vryburg

Klerksdorp

Standerton

Kroonstad

KWAZULU-
NATAL

Upington

FREE
STATE

Bethlehem

Ulundi

Kimberley

Ladysmith

★
Bloemfontein

LESOTHO

Pietermaritzburg

Springbok

NORTHERN
CAPE

De Aar

Durban

Port Shepstone

Calvinia

Victoria West

Middelburg

Umtata

Vanrhynsdorp

Queenstown

EASTERN
CAPE

Beaufort
West

Bisho

Saldanha

WESTERN
CAPE

East London

Cape Town
★

Worcester

Swellendam

Mossel Bay

Port Elizabeth

Place names as of September 2010

(map by Sumedha Senanayake)

Introduction

n the early 1980s a flier proclaiming "Asinamali Masinhlanganeni [We are poor—let us unite] . . . Organise or be
homeless" called upon local residents to form a civic association in an impoverished community in the Vaal region, south of Johannesburg. In another
township, this one outside Durban, protesters donned red T-shirts, which
loudly and simply proclaimed, "Land! Housing!" once again demanding that
basic needs must be addressed. These are just two examples of an uncountable
number of placards, fliers, and T-shirts produced in South Africa defining the
reasons for protest in poor townships created and undermined by the system
of apartheid. In a country marked by stark injustices that were repeatedly met
with large-scale protests, these two calls to action are unremarkable in many
respects, except that they span more than two decades of dramatic political
change. While the Vaal Triangle flier was produced in 1983, at the height of
apartheid, the T-shirts were produced, the smaller print on the shirts noted, as
part of the "Kennedy Road Year of Action 2005," more than a decade after the
creation of nonracial democracy. The establishment of a formal system of
democracy did not transform the basic demands of these protest movements.

In South Africa, as elsewhere, material needs and stark inequalities often
serve as the basis for popular protest. Protesters draw attention to the daily
struggles of ordinary people to demand public action and to call for broader
domestic and international support for their cause. As they make their demands, the protesters, where effective, construct a popular understanding of
material necessities, but while their immediate demands, such as those for land
or housing, are unmistakable, the deeper implications of their actions are often
overlooked. Protests organized around socioeconomic struggles are a product
of shared perceptions of injustice. This injustice is not only economic but also
political. Those taking to the streets have been unable to or do not believe that

they can effectively address their demands through the formal institutions of the state. They charge the state, whether it is run by an authoritarian or a democratic regime, with a failure to recognize and uphold what they believe to be their rights. In doing so, they seek to bring about change in the political system.

Regardless of the system of rule, interactions between protesters and states offer clear indicators of the democratic content of a regime and offer the possibility for its redefinition. Potential protesters weigh their actions depending on their expectations as to whether state officials will recognize their right to protest and if so, which forms of protest action will be allowed. As protesters organize and mobilize, they also work to delineate, implicitly and explicitly, their ideal system of rights and their understandings of what democracy should be. If protests grow powerful enough, they can work to redefine a regime as governments seek to resist, reform, or accommodate opposition demands. Through these interactions between ordinary people and the state, protests draw attention not only to the material hardships people raise but also to the political marginality of those who feel the need to engage in protest. In this way, they work to illuminate both socioeconomic and political inequalities.

The link between material demands and democratic rights that many South African protesters spanning the decades have emphasized stands in sharp contrast to the way in which protests are often represented in the popular media and by the governments against which they mobilize. Protests aim to challenge, and by doing so, to destabilize authority, to force power holders to change their priorities. It is most often this potentially destabilizing impact of protest as well as the specter of violence that governments stress and the news media cover. Governments around the world often blame "agitators" for growing protest activity, suggesting that most participants are uninformed followers. Newspaper, television, and radio news reports often define actions as spontaneous protests or riots, suggesting disorder and a lack of clear grievances and demands. They frequently draw disproportionate attention to any act of violence whether against physical property or against persons, even in cases where the overwhelming majority of participants engage in nonviolent actions. These perceptions are often misleading and may dangerously, as many toppled governments later realize, underestimate the unity, commitment, and potential power of popular mobilization. Ordinary people are rarely blind sheep; although they may not be fluent in all the debates that their protests generate, and they may have important differences with protest leaders, they also have clear reasons for choosing to join a protest. Even when protests are not well organized, rapidly growing actions often generate support due to shared grievances against the actors and institutions deemed to be broadly responsible for the hardships people face.

Social movements face a wide range of challenges in organizing and mobilizing (Goodwin and Jasper 2004). Arguably, a more democratic regime should provide more options for protesters to engage in peaceful actions by legalizing marches and creating multiple avenues for the presentation of demands to decision makers. A regime that formally guarantees the right to protest will not, however, necessarily make it easier for activists to generate large-scale protests than a regime that represses dissent. The rise of protest movements is a product of multiple factors that are not determined by regime type. These factors include the effective framing of grievances by potential protest movements (Is there a clear reason for *us* to protest?) (Melucci 1985, 1989; Snow et al. 1986; Touraine 1981), the perceived opportunity for protest (Might protest *now* help to address our grievances?) (Castells 1983; McAdam 1996; Tarrow 1994), and the resources on which potential movements might draw (*Whom* do we know? *What* kinds of protest action might work?) (McAdam 1982; McCarthy and Zald 1973; Tilly 1978, 1986).

Although nondemocratic regimes recognize fewer rights than formal democracies, the violation of civil and political rights under oppressive regimes can serve as a basis for rallying domestic and international support for protesters. When nondemocratic regimes seek to constrain popular actors through strategies ranging from verbal threats to detention, torture, and extrajudicial killings, they present tremendous challenges to any opposition but also lend new legitimacy to their struggle. Newly democratic regimes, in contrast, offer at least formal recognition of civil and political rights. While an authoritarian regime may threaten violence against protesters, a democratic regime is more likely to seek to delegitimize protest through subtler means. Protesters may be presented as endangering democracy, threatening instability, and, most powerfully, betraying the nation. This does not mean that democratic states will not use force against protesters; they may. But democratic regimes tend to have a wider range of tools at their disposal than their authoritarian counterparts. For one, democratic regimes can fall back on the claim that since citizens' civil and political rights are formally recognized, protest is no longer necessary; citizens should now use legal means to pressure the state. Those who do not, state officials may well suggest, are hooligans, malcontents, or subversives. Although any transition from authoritarian rule to some form of democracy will bring about dramatic change, the formal establishment of a democratic regime will not give all citizens equal access to the state. As a result, it does not automatically signal an end to protest or the rights-expanding potential of contention.

The last few decades have been marked by dramatic shifts in national political contexts with the creation (or re-creation) of formally democratic regimes in Southern Europe, Latin America, and Eastern Europe as well as much of

Asia and Africa. Although electoral democracy formally guarantees civil and political rights, it does not necessarily alleviate the central material concerns that led many protesters into the streets under authoritarian rule. The expansion of democracy over the last several decades has, in fact, been marked by the persistence of high and even increasing rates of economic and, with it, social inequality (Bermeo 2009). Freedom House has charted the expansion of liberal democracy around the world: from 66 electoral democracies in 1987 to 116 in 2009; from 44 countries classified as "free" in 1972 to 89 in 2009 (2010).[1] At the same time, domestic income inequality has risen in new democracies as diverse as Argentina, South Africa, and Uruguay (*Economist*, November 3, 2003; Leibbrandt et al. 2010; UNDP 2009), and as expected, it has risen even more dramatically in the former communist states of Eastern Europe (Heynes 2005). It has remained exceedingly high (defined here as a Gini coefficient of 50 or more on a scale of 0 to 100) in countries such as Brazil, Chile, Ecuador, Botswana, and Namibia. Older democracies are also not immune; income inequality has increased markedly in the United States since the late 1970s (U.S. Census Bureau 2001).[2] Although income inequality is often difficult to measure, particularly in the poorer countries on the African continent, it is clear that democracy, while offering the promise of greater political equality, has not mitigated the global and domestic economic pressures that have increased inequality in the majority of countries measured worldwide (Cornia and Court 2001 as cited in Leysens 2004, 1–2; International Monetary Fund 2007, chap. 4).[3] This inequality, as the World Bank (2001) has stressed, undermines the poverty-reducing potential of economic growth. Growth, in turn, will not necessarily mitigate inequality.

Despite high and even growing income inequality in many new democracies, discussions of the expansion of democracy tend to sideline debates regarding socioeconomic inequality by focusing almost exclusively on civil and political rights. Struggles to tackle these forms of inequality are, in contrast, often perceived as potentially antidemocratic, threatening basic civil rights such as property rights. While social movement activists most often focus on protest actions, in the streets and on the front lines, those who focus on democratization tend to prioritize state procedures and formally guaranteed rights. The former tend to prefer noninstitutional processes, investigating innovations that successfully draw popular and media attention to the demands of the marginalized, while the latter seek to focus on existing institutions and processes of formal institutional change. Both discussions, however, fundamentally concern the meaning of citizenship and the status and protection of fundamental rights. This disjuncture between analyses of social movements and debates concerning democracy undermines attention to their fundamental interaction. It is the active engagement between citizens and their governments that defines both the political regime and the very content of citizenship. Although movements and the new democracies or the potentially democratizing states within which they operate often represent two distinct and distanced political camps, one cannot be understood without the other.

Democracy and Inequality

The argument that economic inequality undermines democracy is hardly new. Support for this contention comes from a wide range of sources, from the South African protester on the street to the *Economist* (November 3, 2003), which has argued: "Income inequality goes hand in hand with unequal access to good things such as education, health and political power—inequalities that violate basic principles of democracy." Writing in the early 1800s, Alexis de Tocqueville argued, in the opening paragraph of *Democracy in America*, for the central importance of a general "equality of social conditions" for the establishment of American democracy (Tocqueville [1835] 2003, 11).[4] He noted: "It would be impossible to imagine men [*sic*] forever unequal in one respect, yet equal in others" (66). This simple lesson unfortunately does not receive the attention that it deserves. The United States presented such an attractive model for Tocqueville's understanding of democracy because he assumed class mobility and low levels of economic inequality. In Tocqueville's idealized understanding of the United States, citizens had similar opportunities to participate and influence political outcomes. This is what made democracy work.

If these assumptions of low levels of economic inequality and high levels of mobility do not hold, durable inequalities (Tilly 1998) develop whereby inequality in one realm reinforces that in another. In contrast to an ideal situation of an "equality of social conditions," durable inequality consistently provides a wide range of benefits to the same group of people, starkly limiting social mobility. Racial and ethnic distinctions, for example, may determine economic opportunities. Economic inequalities, in turn, reinforce political inequality, offering the wealthy the means to effectively "buy their way out of democratic processes" (Tilly 1998, 224). In apartheid South Africa, state-defined racial categories formed the basis for extreme political and economic inequalities. As a result of colonialism, segregation, and apartheid, South Africa has one of the highest levels of income inequality today, but it is only one of twenty-five countries with exceedingly high income inequality; all, except one, of these states are in Latin America or Africa (UNDP 2009).[5] This suggests that, despite their differences, those Latin American and African states with extreme levels of income inequality face a number of similar challenges in establishing democratic systems that protect the rights of all citizens.[6] Due to the difficulties of collecting comparable data in many African countries, there is much more information available about inequality in Latin America.

In 2004 the World Bank defined economic inequality in Latin America as "extensive," "pervasive," and "resilient" (2004, 1). It noted: "Inequalities with respect to education, health, water, sanitation, electricity, and telephony are also typically large and correlated with differences in income" (2004, 2). Although the authors argued that existing surveys did not offer the data to scientifically prove the impact of this extensive income inequality on power in the state, they noted a wealth of historical and sociological data that demonstrates the close correlation between the two. Since the return of democracy across the region, income inequality has actually increased, rising in the 1980s and 1990s. In the early years of the new millennium, countries with relatively low inequality, such as Uruguay, have generally seen their inequality levels increase. Brazil, which formerly had the highest levels in the region, has reduced income inequality, but in Bolivia and Colombia, which previously had the second and third highest levels, inequality has remained stubbornly persistent.[7] Although there has been a reduction in some Latin American countries, it is not widespread or robust enough to signal a clear trend (Gaspirini, Cruces, and Tornarolli 2009; UNDP 2009). Across Latin America, high levels of inequality have had stark consequences in many countries, not only reducing growth and potentially destabilizing states but also allowing elites to corrupt politicians, undermine judicial processes, and "run roughshod over constitutions and contracts" (Karl 2000, 155). Interestingly, inequality and support for existing democratic regimes seem to be negatively correlated: surveys demonstrated the greatest support for democracy in Uruguay (when it had the lowest inequality in the region) and the least in Brazil (when it had the highest) (Karl 2000, 155–56).[8]

Over half a century ago, T. H. Marshall offered an idealized scenario in which the development of citizens' rights would address inequality as part of the natural progress of democracy and the development of capitalism. Looking at Britain, he charted a process that began with civil rights ranging from the right to free speech to the right to own property, then extended to political rights including the right to vote, and finally included social rights beginning with public education (Marshall and Bottomore 1992). In this way, the equality of citizenship would mitigate the inequalities of social class as the enfranchisement of an increasing proportion of those living within the state would change the character of social policies to more broadly benefit all citizens.[9] Although appealing in its simple functionality, Marshall's rendering of British history is remarkably free of conflict. It suggests that the elite classes stood idly by as their power and influence in state and society were dramatically reduced. Most historians would beg to differ. While Marshall assumed an almost automatic and linear process, history, in Britain and elsewhere, has repeatedly demonstrated that the expansion of rights is uneven and consistently occurs through contentious processes, at times involving open conflict (Tilly 2004).

Contrary to Marshall's idealized scenario, the expansion and protection of a wide range of rights are a product of ongoing struggle in all states. The creation of formally democratic regimes does not guarantee that citizens' civil, political, and social rights will be upheld. Latin American democracies in the 1980s and 1990s, for example, alarmingly suggested an alternative pathway to that defined by Marshall in which political rights were expanded by the state while civil rights were not realized and social rights actually contracted. In Marshall's conception formal citizenship, which is a product of membership in a political community defined by the state, and substantive citizenship, which includes civil, political, and social rights, were linked (Holston 1999, 168); membership in the community was sufficient to grant citizens their rights. But formal citizenship neither requires nor guarantees substantive citizenship. People may be holders of state-issued documents confirming their citizenship, but this does not mean that they have access to the full set of rights that their democracy formally guarantees.

Neoliberalism, which places great emphasis on the protection of private property and works to limit the reach of the state, has driven a deep wedge between formal and substantive citizenship. This phenomenon has created what Deborah Yashar has dubbed "neo-liberal citizenship regimes," which offer the promise of political rights such as the right to vote while reducing access to civil and social rights by pressing governments to reduce the responsibilities of the state (Yashar 1999, 80; Dagnino 1998). The rights associated with substantive citizenship are effectively privatized. This leaves what might best be termed an "empty" form of citizenship in which the ideal of an efficient and orderly state and society is used by those in power to criminalize the unruly and disruptive actions of political actors who demand the recognition and expansion of their rights (Lukose 2005; Hassim 2009). A dramatic example of this weak enforcement of legally mandated rights is illustrated in Brazil, where the phrase "'Go look for your rights' (*Vai procurar os seus direitos*)" has been employed when conflicts occur (Caldeira and Holston 1999, 707–8). It implies that the claimant would need to go to great ends to enforce her formal rights and may well be better off seeking alternative means or simply forgetting about the abuse that has occurred.

Marshall observed a period of history in which the role of the state grew as many states increased their interventions in the market to expand social welfare programs for citizens. In sharp contrast, the new democracies of Latin America, Eastern Europe, and Africa have come into being in an age of reduced state intervention. This embrace of free markets is aptly demonstrated by the loan conditionalities established by the World Bank and the International Monetary Fund in the 1980s and 1990s. One need not engage in debates concerning the impact of structural adjustment reforms and the extent of subsequent policy revisions in order to recognize that these new democracies were faced with the challenge of expanding citizenship, at the same time that states were expected to reduce their role in providing for their citizens. This fundamental contradiction has made the development of citizenship rights as envisioned by Marshall increasingly difficult, if not impossible. It has hollowed out our understanding of citizenship (Murray 2008). As a result, democracy risks becoming irrelevant if democratic governments are unable to address these contradictions and the growing inequalities that they produce (Oxhorn 2003, 58).

This book investigates the ways in which social movements address the threat of the irrelevancy of democracy through their struggles. Many of the movements presented here do not define themselves as movements for democracy; for this reason their actions are often understood as exclusively focusing on material demands, and their role in local struggles for democracy is often overlooked. The focus here is not on how movements form, for these questions have received a great deal of attention elsewhere, but rather on how existing community-based movements attempt to affect the inequality of political, civil, and socioeconomic rights through their complex and changing interactions with political parties and the state. The outcomes of these interactions are examined in a range of regime types, demonstrating how movements may be demobilized by the expansion of political rights, even without a corresponding expansion in economic and social rights. In sharp contrast to Marshall's largely conflict-free progression of rights, this study offers an analysis of contention and an uncertain future. It focuses not on singular movement victories or failures but on the broader contention they generate and the state responses they provoke. These responses range from repression to cooptation to the incorporation of movement demands. None necessarily suggests victory or failure for the movement or its goals. Each does, however, provide important clues regarding the shape and content of the regime and the prospects for democracy.

The Politics of Necessity

From apartheid to democracy, South African movements have drawn connections between material necessities, stark inequality, and basic rights. Through popular protest they have constructed their understandings of what democracy must entail. South Africa under apartheid offers one of the clearest cases of cumulative inequality: poverty, race, and a complete lack of political rights all overlapped. Like Brazil (and the United States among advanced industrialized states), South Africa has long stood out for its high levels of income inequality.[10] Similar to those in Brazil, South African survey respondents have expressed high levels of dissatisfaction with their democracy. In the Afrobarometer surveys conducted from mid-1999 to mid-2001 in twelve largely English-speaking African countries that had undergone some degree of political and economic reform, South Africans expressed the highest levels of dissatisfaction with their democracy (44 percent of respondents were "unsatisfied with democracy"), followed by Malawi and Zambia (Bratton, Mattes, and Gyimah-Boadi 2005, 83).[11] This is particularly striking when contrasted with external perceptions of South Africa as one of the strongest and most vibrant democracies on the continent. Countless analysts have lauded the rights and freedoms enshrined in South Africa's new constitution; Freedom House (2010) has given South Africa high scores for both political rights and civil liberties. In South Africa, in contrast, less than half of the survey respondents defined themselves as "very satisfied" or even "fairly satisfied" with democracy in 2008 (Afrobarometer 2009b). Since 1999 this dissatisfaction has increasingly been seen on the streets. During the 2004/5 financial year, almost six thousand protest actions took place across the country (Atkinson 2007, 58). In 2009, protest actions once again reached new heights as citizens demonstrated their frustration with the government by marching, submitting petitions, and at times destroying government property (Sinwell et al. 2009). Clearly those who praise the extent of South Africa's democracy are missing something to which both the survey respondents and the protesters wish to draw attention.

South African respondents stood out across the surveyed African countries in that they expressed more substantive understandings of what a democratic regime should entail by including socioeconomic conditions in their definition of democracy.[12] They also demonstrated a greater readiness to engage in protest actions. This led Michael Bratton, Robert Mattes, and E. Gyimah-Boadi (2005) to suggest that South Africa may be exceptional as a product of its apartheid past and its recent liberation. However, if one approaches the case of South Africa with an eye to the experiences of Latin American states, South Africa appears as much less an outlier. Growing dissatisfaction with democracy and high levels of protest action, often in response to poor living conditions and services, seem to be correlated with a perception of relative deprivation and high levels of inequality. In fact, given South Africa's significant political and economic reforms as well as its urbanization, processes that all African countries are struggling with in different ways, the South African experience may well be an indicator of challenges that other states and societies will increasingly face. Just as apartheid was an extension of the broader politics of colonial rule rather than an exception (Mamdani 1996), South Africa's current challenges and its citizens' discontent are a product of severe inequities that are felt across the continent and around the globe.

Over a decade after the African National Congress (ANC) came to power, addressing the material poverty of the majority remains a stark challenge. Government development indicators show persistently high unemployment rates. According to the narrow definition of unemployment, which includes only job seekers who looked for work in the four weeks before the survey, unemployment declined slightly from a high of 31.2 percent in early 2003 to 25.3 percent in mid-2010 (SSA 2010, xii). In the broad understanding of unemployment also presented in government indicators, 36 percent of South Africans remained unemployed in 2010 (*Economist*, August 23, 2010).[13] South African survey data from 1993, 2000, and 2008 show a substantial increase in inequality, both within the population as a whole and within the African population (Leibbrandt et al. 2010).[14] In 2009 the government reported that income inequality still had not been reduced despite years of economic growth (RSA, Presidency 2009, 25).[15] Although the indicators do show some growth in the incomes of the poor, the rich have gained at a faster rate.

Poverty remains pervasive. Government indicators report only a slow decline in poverty since 1993. By 2008, 22 percent of the population (the "hard core" poor) continued to live below the very low international poverty line of $1.25 a day, or R283 per month (RSA, Presidency 2009, 27).[16] Afrobarometer's 2008 survey offers indicators of "lived poverty": 42 percent of adult respondents said they "went without" food at least once in the past year (down only 1 percent from 2004); 36 percent said they went without clean water (the same as 2004); 52 percent went without electricity (up from 47 percent in 2004); 53 percent went without a cash income (down from 60 percent in 2004) (Afrobarometer 2004, 2009b). While stark, these numbers may still underreport indicators of lived poverty, due to the difficulty of reaching the country's poorest citizens (*Cape Times*, March 11, 2005). They do, however, demonstrate the impact of state interventions: the decrease in people without a cash income is a product of the increase in social grants, and the increase in people without electricity is at least in part due to disconnections for nonpayment.

These grim realities are a product of South Africa's past as well as its present. A few statistics, while offering a partial and vastly incomplete picture of the brutality of apartheid, demonstrate the great challenges that postapartheid governments have faced. In 1946 white per person income was more than ten times that of African income (L. Thompson 2000, 156). Between 1960 and 1983, an estimated 3.5 million people were forcibly removed from their homes and communities to the overcrowded and impoverished "homelands" far from urban centers and jobs. In 1975–76 an astounding 381,858 Africans were arrested for violating the pass laws, which were designed to keep them out of white areas where they sought to find work. Even after a considerable increase in the number of African children enrolled in school by 1978, the apartheid government still spent ten times more per white student than it did for each African student (L. Thompson 2000, 193–96). The legacies of racial discrimination in education and job opportunities, the removal of so many people from their homes and communities, and the impact of a migrant labor system that separated families are profound and daunting. As Jeremy Seekings and Nicoli Nattrass argue: "No other capitalist state (in either the North or South) has sought to structure income inequalities as systematically and brutally as did South Africa under apartheid" (2005, 2).

These hardships have led to what is termed here a "politics of necessity," where engagement in the public sphere is defined in an environment in which many struggle just to get by: to feed their families, to maintain a home, and to obtain basic access to health care, education, and paid work. In certain circumstances, these needs lead to community organizing and concerted efforts to bring material and broader demands to the attention of government. The politics of necessity is not exclusive to South Africa. In their discussion of Latin American social movements, Sonia Alvarez and Arturo Escobar have referred to a "politics of needs" mobilizing popular struggles (1992, 320). In Mexico City, Miguel Díaz-Barriga found a discourse of *necesidad* among urban movements; grassroots activists defined their goals in terms of necessities that included land, education, and basic services such as electricity, potable water, streets, and medical clinics (1998, 257). Around the globe, the absence of what people locally define as basic necessities can translate into movements that work to bring the private struggles of marginalized individuals and silenced communities into the public discourse with potentially profound implications for democracy.

Social Movements, Inequality, and Democracy

Social movements have played a fundamental role in drawing attention to injustices and discrimination under a range of regimes. Their mobilization can lead to the extension and expansion of rights and work to address different forms of inequality, but this process, even when it is successful, is never automatic (Tilly 1993–94). First, movements may have exclusionary and antidemocratic goals (Fatton 1995). Second, as the civil rights struggle in the United States clearly demonstrated, even peaceful protest may be met with violence and repression on the part of the state, and often prolonged struggle is necessary to extend basic rights to all citizens (McAdam 1982). Violence may also originate from those struggling to be heard, whether as a product of frustration and anger or as strategy. The relationship between social movements and the extension of democracy is therefore not a simple positive correlation in which one seamlessly reinforces the other. The potential impact of movement activity on democracy can occur at three levels. An effect at one level must not translate into an effect at another (McAdam, Tarrow, and Tilly 2001, chap. 9). At the level of the individual, movements can work to empower people to consider alternative futures, to engage their government, and to demand formal access to the state (Appadurai 2004). The experience of participating in movement organizing can form the basis for engaged citizenship. At the level of a community, social movements serve as experiments in deliberation and debate as participants establish rules in their interactions with one another, determine who will serve as representatives, and decide on the content of that representation (Avritzer 2002). At the level of the state, social movements draw attention to demands that challenge the state and its citizens to engage them and to determine if and how they should be met (Tarrow 1994).

The politics of necessity can be a force for the expansion of democracy; it can also expose its retreat. Through an analysis of community-based struggles, this book examines both the formal development of a democratic system and popular discourses of what democracy should entail. Four central arguments motivate the discussion of community-based movements in South Africa and their comparison to mobilization and organization in other African and Latin American states. First, the politics of necessity is not only about material needs. Those who frame their demands in protest often begin with and emphasize basic material necessities, but their demands also include the right to be heard, to have a voice, to be consulted, and to become full members of the political community. Through different periods of movement activity in South Africa, protesters not only presented demands but also defined their identity, as persons who deserved equal and substantive citizenship, as community members who were being neglected by those negotiating on their behalf, whether appointed or elected, and as marginalized citizens who sought to become full members of their political community. Struggles against apartheid at the community level commonly began not with demands to end apartheid but with demands to address basic material needs, be they cheaper bus fares or more affordable housing. Over time, these demands became increasingly politicized as protesters called for the expansion of political rights and a change in regime.

This expansion of demands has been documented in South Africa and beyond, but the mechanism whereby it occurs is underexplored and often assumed rather than explicated. Through a focus on civic leaders' "conscientizing" efforts, this work seeks to fill the gap. Leaders with experience in organizing beyond their local communities worked to link the material needs voiced by residents to a lack of broader rights and therefore to encourage rights-based demands aimed at the national state rather than local authorities. As part of this process, organizations developed new understandings of what democracy must entail as a product both of leaders' arguments and of popular resistance to excessive direction from leaders. These democratic ideals emphasized both more-participatory and more-substantive concerns than prevailing national and international definitions. By engaging in popular actions, protesters demonstrated their active participation in a broader political community and worked to redefine the very nature of that political community. Ironically, this mobilization, while eliciting some positive change for local communities, has been more likely to increase formal and national political equality through the expansion of political and civil rights and regime democratization than to directly address the underlying reasons for protest, material inequality and poverty.

Second, successful advances in political rights often work to demobilize existing movements even as the underlying socioeconomic concerns that led to their mobilization persist. Great attention has been given to the rise of movements but significantly less to their decline and its impact. As part of any process of transition, those who wish to continue to participate in the process must adapt to changing conditions. Movements that have concentrated on challenging a particular law, actor, or system face great difficulties in redefining themselves once that entity realistically presents itself as transformed. New regimes, in turn, work to rein in the protest that has led to their creation. As they work to enforce the new rules of the game, they engage in a process of disciplining by requiring actors to work through the new formal procedures and submit to the rules established by state institutions. In contrast to the leadership-centered mechanism encouraging the shift to rights-based demands, the process of demobilization is a product of institutional reorganization and disciplining. This reconstruction of power reduces the participation of a wide range of actors who worked to bring about change, even where that change is toward democracy. Social movement leaders respond to new opportunities that draw them away from movement activity, whether into government or into the private sector, and ordinary participants shift their focus in the hope that engaged participation will no longer be as necessary as during the struggle to achieve democracy. Those who remain active in existing movement organizations seek to respond to new opportunities, which at times results in counterintuitive outcomes.

These influences along with the need that many people express to "get on with their lives" lead to at least a temporary decline in movement activity. The broader impact of this reduction in movement activity is significant not just for the movement organizations but also, more importantly, for the broader networks of people who relied upon the channels they offered for communication, organization, and some forms of representation. The decline of a range of existing movements with the extension of political rights may paradoxically leave ordinary citizens with fewer means for bringing their concerns to those in power, until a new cycle of mobilization begins. This is particularly problematic in the extended period during which a newly democratic regime works to establish effective institutions to receive and consider citizen input. Where governments are less capable and motivated to improve access and representation, these problems will persist. In this way, while the expansion of political rights offers greater formal opportunities and political equality, it may also reduce existing avenues for marginalized communities to effectively demand reductions in other forms of inequality.

Third, contention is a potentially productive asset in multiple-regime environments. Although most studies focus on mobilization under one regime, it is important to understand the functions of contention both in destabilizing authoritarian regimes and in expanding democracies. This factor is significant because the destabilizing and potentially democratizing aspects of mobilization necessarily work in tandem and cannot be understood in isolation regardless of the regime within which they mobilize. In the struggle to end apartheid, protest against the state played a fundamental role in bringing about the transition. At the societal level, within what is commonly referred to as a singular opposition movement, there were clear tensions between the need for unity and the demands of different interests, arguments, and ideals. The multiplicity of voices challenging the authoritarian state was far greater and arguably more important than any history traced back from the perspective of its victors would reveal. Popular participation, central to the power of mass-based movements, along with disagreement and debate provide the mechanisms to empower large numbers of citizens to engage state policies.

After democratic elections had been held and movement activity declined, the discourse of unity to overcome adversity received increasing support from civil society actors who wished to strengthen the new South African government. Within five years, however, a new wave of mobilization began, led by postapartheid social movements. As state actors resisted the new movements' material demands, a new cycle of contentious action unfolded, and protesters made increasing calls for an expanded framework of rights. This present contention can only be understood by drawing on the history of past struggles and exploring the postapartheid interactions between those formerly united in the antiapartheid struggle. While the authoritarian state sought to silence those who would oppose it, the new democratic state is often similarly disinclined to listen to those who challenge its development paradigm. Both regimes are guilty of what James Scott (1998) has termed "seeing like a state," working to technocratically, bureaucratically, and when necessary forcefully establish its vision of a productive, developed society while minimizing the distraction of contentious movements. Under apartheid, repression was brutal, stark, and extensive. Under the democratic state, although citizens' rights are frequently violated as they seek to engage in protest actions, there are legal mechanisms for redress. Those without significant resources are, however, generally unable to access the courts to demand their rights. Under both regimes, considerable contention exists among competing movements and between movements and the state. It is through this contention that rights are demanded, expanded, or restricted.

Finally, most academic analyses of democratization employ liberal and procedural definitions of democracy that focus on civil and political rights. Democratization is generally understood as an extension of a process of political liberalization and is most commonly measured according to a relatively minimal procedural definition focusing on institutions and freedoms. This approach is taken for the sake of parsimony, clarity of analysis, and comparability across cases. But it stands in stark contrast to the understandings of democracy that often inspire ordinary people to protest against their nondemocratic regimes. For these actors, socioeconomic rights are central to democracy's success and potentially to their support for a democratic government. By focusing on popular concerns, this book redefines democracy, from a procedural to a substantive understanding, from a focus on civil and political rights to a recognition of the indivisibility of all human rights, including socioeconomic rights. Democracy is not a set of institutions but a process of continued contestation in which popular organizations play a central role in both challenging and strengthening democratic norms.

Viewed in this way, the most significant danger to a democratic regime is a popular loss of confidence in a democracy that fails to guarantee a full set of rights to all citizens. Many theorists of democratic transitions and consolidation have focused on the danger of military coups or popular uprisings that lead to the overthrow of government (Gunther, Diamandouros, and Puhle 1995), but these have proven to be relatively infrequent. A much broader challenge to democracy is the slow undermining of the legitimacy of its institutions as ordinary people lose faith in what their democracy actually offers them and become alienated from a regime, institutions, and processes that fail to fully include them because of the barriers erected by poverty and inequality. The greatest danger in most countries is not a revolution or a coup but rather an increasing lack of participation and support. In South Africa, liberal democracy is often challenged as a system that meets the needs of the wealthy at the expense of the poor. These concerns expressed by ordinary South Africans echo those raised by Tocqueville well over a century ago. If inequalities become cumulative and durable, the very basis of democracy is destroyed.

Each of these arguments runs counter to often-repeated and idealized understandings of how democracy is established. In the rhetoric of liberal democracies such as the United States, established democracies should seek to support peaceful institutional processes to strengthen democracy worldwide (USAID 1998). According to this idealized conception, new democracies would be created through negotiation between the leaders of nondemocratic regimes and a well-organized opposition party and civil society actors (O'Donnell and Schmitter 1986). This negotiation process would not involve excessive protest, violence, or great instability. It would be completed by elite actors and not involve the distraction of popular demands focused on socioeconomic rights. Many of the policies of the U.S. government for promoting democracy abroad implicitly build on such idealized frameworks. They also draw upon modernization theory, which suggests a smooth, linear path toward economic and political development, as well as romanticized histories of civil society effectively institutionalizing a new system. This book challenges the assumption that rights will evolve without political conflict. Instead, it engages the messiness of politics to address both the idealized visions of civil society and the threat-based portrayals of social movements. In following the arguments of ordinary people, it includes socioeconomic rights as central to democracy and investigates how regimes might live up to such expectations. This approach allows us to more clearly see the great challenges that all democratic regimes face and to begin to consider how to support those who offer innovative ideas to address these challenges.

Structure of the Book

Chapter 1 ("Community Organizing in South Africa") discusses the incredible rise of civic organizations, commonly known as "civics," a particular brand of township community organization in South Africa. Based on archival documents, court transcripts, and interviews with activists over more than a decade, this chapter tells the story of the formation of key civics, the process of their expansion, their relationship with the exiled ANC, and their interactions with the apartheid state. From Soweto to Port Elizabeth and the Vaal Triangle, civics pioneered new methods of resistance, and their successes and failures served as models for others as they sought to challenge apartheid local-government authorities without being crushed by the state.

Chapter 2 ("Material Inequality and Political Rights") details the construction of a rights-based discourse in South Africa and builds on Arjun Appadurai's notion of the "capacity to aspire" for local communities. This chapter discusses the conscientizing work of community leaders under apartheid as well as ordinary residents' demands to be heard. It illuminates the stark consistency in protesters' demands from apartheid to the postapartheid period and discusses the postapartheid shift in relations between state and nonstate actors. This phenomenon is demonstrated by the rise of postapartheid movements such as the Soweto Electricity Crisis Committee and its approach in demanding better and more affordable services. The chapter concludes with a comparison of the South African findings to an analysis of the expansion of rights through movement activity in Brazil, Chile, Mexico, and Spain.

Chapters 3, 4, and 5 each present in-depth analyses of the central relationship between protest and democracy at different moments in South Africa's recent history. Chapter 3 investigates the role of democratic principles in township organizing against apartheid and raises a question: is democratic organizing possible under a repressive regime? Chapter 4 examines the context of the formal transition and considers to what extent local organizations play a role in and are empowered by the formal creation of a democratic system. Chapter 5 focuses on the interplay between a newly democratic regime and social movements and considers whether protesters are defending or challenging democracy by taking to the streets. In each chapter, the experiences of community organizations and social movements in South Africa form the basis for the development of arguments concerning the interaction of protest and democracy. In order to expand and check these arguments beyond the South African case, each chapter also briefly engages two secondary comparative examples, one from the African continent and a second from Latin America. These examples, many of which offer most different cases, demonstrate both the strengths and the limitations of the central arguments developed in each of the chapters.

Chapter 3 ("Power to the People!") focuses on the twin goals of liberation and democracy that the South African civics pursued under apartheid. Although the tactics of achieving liberation and democracy are often presented in opposition, this chapter demonstrates how the two worked together. South Africa's democratization process was popularly understood as a process of liberation. This simple fact is central to understanding the interests of many who participated in the struggle. It also differs dramatically from the models of democratization that analysts most often employ, for it includes not only political and civil rights but also socioeconomic demands for greater equality. Chapter 3 concludes with a comparative discussion of two very different and influential cases, the Zapatista movement in Mexico and the Movement for the Survival of the Ogoni People in Nigeria. Each movement worked to connect material demands and political rights but achieved different degrees of success. This comparison allows for a discussion of the limitations of civic-led movements.

Chapter 4 ("Disciplining Dissent") discusses the daunting challenges faced by the civics as a result of the introduction of democracy and their informal alliance with the new ruling party. This chapter illuminates the process of institutional disciplining that occurs in the new regime and probes the difficult interactions among former comrades who find themselves on opposite sides of unfolding debates concerning community services and representation. Interviewees repeatedly point to the personal as well as political toll that these conflicts take on those who continue to engage in community activism. As the new democracy centralizes power and seeks to develop a technocratic developmental state, discourses of loyal and disloyal opposition flourish. Each of these trends produces negative consequences for poor township residents who seek to critically engage policy-making processes. The chapter concludes with an illuminating comparison, once again, to two very different cases: Benin and Chile. In both instances, local community organizations operating under different party and state structures experienced many of the same challenges as those confronting South Africa's civics.

Chapter 5 ("Contentious Democracy") focuses on the actions and development of the so-called disloyal opposition in South Africa. This chapter begins with a discussion of dissident actions within the existing civic structures and their impact. In response to the rather dramatic co-option of the formerly independent civics and popular frustration with local government and the state's economic reforms, social movements in South Africa experienced a resurgence in the late 1990s. This chapter focuses on the different strategies that these movements pursued and the role of disruption and destabilization that all movements employ. Movements defined by the state as "ultraleft" and antisystem such as the Western Cape Anti-Eviction Campaign and Abahlali baseMjondolo have faced significant restrictions and even repression. But their actions did not differ as dramatically from those of other movements as the antisystem label would suggest. Even the co-opted civics began to employ some of the most successful strategies of the so-called ultraleft. Chapter 5 closes with a discussion of two contrasting cases, Botswana and Argentina, to consider the impact, respectively, of very low and extremely high levels of contention in new democracies. These cases offer the opportunity to explore whether the politics of necessity might lead to the downfall of democracy.

The final chapter ("Substantive Democracy") returns to a central question: what is democracy? It compares dominant academic understandings of democracy with those expressed by South African protesters. This chapter also draws on Afrobarometer survey data from nineteen countries across the continent to demonstrate the fundamental disconnection between the goals assumed by much of the democratization literature and those voiced by ordinary people. On the African continent, many protesters struggling for democracy are also fighting for liberation. This ideal includes not just the attainment of civil and political rights but also the enforcement of socioeconomic rights. It demands independence from the dictates of more-powerful states. The distinction between formal democracy as espoused by many liberal democracies and liberation as understood by popular actors helps to explain why academic analysts and ordinary people on the street often offer such dramatically different assessments of democratic regimes. This underlines a simple but often overlooked truth: in order to understand the prospects for democracy, we must pay greater attention to the ordinary people who help bring it about.

1

Community Organizing
in South Africa

South Africa is widely known for its history of popular struggle. Thousands took to the streets in waves of protest that spanned more than four decades of apartheid rule. Several of these protest actions are well known internationally, such as the 1960 antipass demonstration that ended with the Sharpeville massacre and the 1976 student-led Soweto uprising, but the majority have not been widely remembered as individual events. Instead, they are generally understood as part of a broad but singular struggle led by the ANC (Baines 2007; Bozzoli 2004). This dominant post-apartheid narrative obscures the many, often competing organizations that fought apartheid and gives the ANC too much credit in orchestrating mass mobilization. The politics of resistance were never so singularly organized or so unified.

Women's, worker, youth, civic, religious, and other organizations mobilized people across the country. In doing so, they defined their own goals and methods of struggle. Although the ANC has played a crucial role over almost a century of South African politics, its victories should not be read backward to argue that it therefore organized and led all significant resistance to apartheid. It did not lead the 1960 Sharpeville antipass protest or the 1976 Soweto uprising. ANC cadres did, however, support the formation and growth of local organizations and worked to popularize and expand local methods of struggle. ANC leaders identified opportunities presented by local actors, the state, and the international community and worked to encourage and support many of them. Despite its strengths, the ANC was not able to control or at times even to effectively lead the struggle against apartheid. There were far too many actors for any single organization to simply direct their actions.

Among the many organizations that developed during the struggle against apartheid, one stood out for its challenge to local government: the civic. Rather than defining themselves as representatives of a particular segment of the population such as workers, women, or youth, local civics claimed to represent all people living in a particular geographic area. By presenting themselves as the "true" representatives of a township or set of townships, they directly challenged the legitimacy of local government. Where they were strong, the civics developed alternative forms of governance and addressed issues ranging from domestic disputes to schooling and crime.[1] Because of their prominent position as community advocates, the civics offer a unique view into the processes by which ordinary people worked to challenge structures of power. Their experiences also provide key insights into the interactions between local organizations and a national opposition movement and later governing party.

The ANC has often sought to appropriate the history of the civics and to suggest that the first civics were formed under its direction. As we will see in this chapter, this is not true. The early civics did, however, include many ANC members and supporters in their ranks, and by the mid-1980s, the overwhelming majority endorsed its nonracial approach. After the unbanning of the ANC in 1990, many civics folded into a larger organization allied to the ruling party. Existing civics that maintained their independence and the new civics that were formed as autonomous organizations were seen by many in the ANC as a potential threat. As a result, despite the dramatic expansion of political rights and the ANC's transition from liberation movement to ruling party, a surprising range of civic actions from the late 1970s are still being employed more than three decades later. The history of the civics therefore opens a window to a deeper understanding of present-day contentious politics.

State and Opposition under Apartheid

The first township-based civics formed in opposition to the gross injustices of apartheid. At the time, repressive legislation controlled almost every facet of daily life. Every South African was classified by the state into a racial category and treated according to the laws pertaining to that race.[2] Support of communism, broadly defined, was made illegal.[3] "Tribal" authorities were created for the various state-defined groupings of Africans, without their consent.[4] These so-called Bantustans were then presented as the "original" homelands of the African people. Those determined to "belong" in a certain area were resettled there regardless of whether they wanted to go or whether they had ever been to the place. All Africans over the age of sixteen outside the Bantustans were required to carry a passbook at all times; failure to do so resulted in imprisonment.[5] Marriages and even sexual relations across racial groups were prohibited.[6] Passive resistance was made illegal.[7] Separate and unequal amenities were established for the different racial groupings. Africans were subject to a grossly inferior curriculum for primary and secondary education and denied access to elite, "white" universities.[8] Certain jobs were reserved for certain races, and strikes were illegal for black workers.[9] Public meetings of over twelve persons were subject to government control.[10]

The pillars of apartheid legislation were put in place in the 1950s. In the following decades, the state sought to crush all black opposition. In 1960, police fired into an antipass demonstration in Sharpeville organized by the Pan Africanist Congress (PAC), a political movement that had broken away from the ANC the previous year.[11] In the aftermath of the Sharpeville massacre (Frankel 2001),[12] both the ANC, which had operated legally within South Africa for almost half a century, and the PAC became banned organizations. Both went underground and soon established military wings. By the 1970s, the ANC, which once had a strong presence in many urban townships, was virtually nonexistent as a domestic political force (Barrell 1992).[13]

The black consciousness movement, which championed the unity and empowerment of black people on their own terms, grew to fill the void left by the banning of the multiracial ANC (Biko 1978; Marx 1992). Angered by the government's mandate that Afrikaans (the language of the ruling minority) be the language of instruction for arithmetic and social studies classes and inspired by black consciousness (BC) ideology, students under the banner of the South African Students' Movement organized a mass protest in Soweto on June 16, 1976. Police opened fire on the young protesters near Orlando High School, leading to the death of two, including twelve-year-old Hector Pieterson, whose lifeless body was captured in a now-famous photograph.[14] The police response to unarmed students provided the spark for unrest, which spread across the country. An estimated one thousand protesters died in the following months as the government sought to crush resistance (Karis and Gerhart 1997, chap. 6; Lodge 1983, chap. 13; Mashabela [1987] 2006).

As a result of the Soweto uprising, pictures of apartheid brutality were featured in newspapers around the world. The South African government suffered from growing political estrangement and even international isolation. At the same time, it faced mounting economic challenges at home. In an attempt to adapt to these changing conditions, Prime Minister Botha unveiled the Total Strategy doctrine, which called for a greater centralization of power in the executive and gave the security establishment an increased role in policy making (Murray 1987; Price 1991). As part of its attempt to perpetuate white rule, the government also moved from a general policy of viewing all Africans as temporary residents in white South Africa to an acceptance that many actively employed Africans would remain permanent residents of urban areas. Black trade unions were also legalized, provided that they registered with the government (Lodge 1983). These policy changes allowed a small space for increased organization in the wake of the repression that had followed the 1976 uprising. At this time, various types of residents' committees already existed in the African townships, but their reach was limited. These groups were mostly organized around single-issue campaigns such as the detention of local youth, the education crisis, or crime. Most became inactive as the specific issue they targeted was either addressed or shown to require much more than localized mobilization. This was about to change.

Contrasting Civic Strategies—Soweto and Port Elizabeth

Toward the end of September 1979, a group of prominent Sowetans dubbed the Committee of Ten held a two-day conference with the theme "Soweto—an Introspection."[15] The committee originally formed following the Soweto uprising to provide leadership for the community. It was an adult response to a youth-led rebellion, but it had failed to meet its objectives because in the words of Dr. Nthato Motlana, "we tended to cater only for the educated elite instead of organizing the masses" (*Rand Daily Mail*, September 25, 1979, 4). By 1979, committee leaders were responding to their group's shortcomings as well as the successes of a more localized, popularly driven organization. Earlier that year, a bus accident in Diepkloof, part of Greater Soweto, led residents to form a crisis committee to raise money for the families of the deceased. The great success of this effort led to the formation of a more permanent community group, the Diepkloof Civic Association, to continue to address the "bread and butter" needs of the community (SCA n.d., 1). This local structure served as the model for a Soweto-wide civic whose motto stressed the importance of basic material necessities and self-empowerment: "More services to ourselves, through ourselves and with ourselves" (*Rand Daily Mail*, September 22, 1979, 2).

Shortly after the launch of the Soweto Civic Association (SCA), a similar organization was launched in Port Elizabeth, the Port Elizabeth Black Civic Organization (PEBCO). The Port Elizabeth civic, like its Sowetan counterpart, was built on local structures, such as the more informal civic groups in the townships of Zwide and Kwaford outside the white city of Port Elizabeth. Both the Sowetan and the Port Elizabeth civic organizations were noteworthy for their determined resolve to fight for greater rights for their communities. A reporter commented that "people [were now] accepting that they will suffer, and even die, for change to take place in this country" (*Post*, September 25, 1979, 8). At PEBCO's opening meeting, its leader, Thomazile Botha, boldly remarked in his speech: "We are bonafide residents of South Africa and we are prepared to die in South Africa" (*Post*, October 10, 1979, 3). The leaders of both groups repeatedly stressed the fact that their organizations were concerned with civic matters and were not political parties, but admitted that some civic matters are by definition also political (for SCA, see *Sunday Times*, September 23, 1979, 10; for PEBCO, see *Eastern Province Herald*, October 16, 1979, 3). At meetings of both groups, calls were repeatedly made for the resignation of town councilors and other officials serving on the "dummy bodies" of apartheid such as the community councils and homeland governments. The SCA and PEBCO tested the limits of state acquiescence to independent African township organization. One, however, offered a more direct challenge than the other.

Though the SCA and PEBCO developed under the same regime and expressed generally similar aims, important differences between the two illustrate a range of civic strategies. The SCA was led by an older, more conservative group of middle-class leaders; its chairman, Nthato Motlana, was a medical doctor. PEBCO, in contrast, was led by a young, charismatic, working-class leader. In its first few months, it was able to continuously draw larger crowds and attract greater media attention than the SCA. An estimated eight thousand people attended PEBCO's first mass rally. The Port Elizabeth civic, through its leader, was also particularly effective in attracting workers and students, who tended to represent the most militant sectors of the township population. It received unprecedented media attention for a local township organization. From mid-October to mid-November 1979, widely read regional newspapers catering to a white audience ran almost daily articles on the formation of the civic and the large attendance at its meetings. Headlines read: "New Black Voice Must be Heard," "Black Civic Meeting Draws Big Crowd," "Strong Support for New PE Civic Body," "A New Force Emerges," and "2,000 Join on First Day" (*Weekend Post*, October 13, 1979, 12; *Eastern Province Herald*, October 25, 1979, 4; *Post*, October 28, 1979, 19; *Eastern Province Herald*, November 8, 1979, 14; *Evening Post*, November 12, 1979, 2). While the SCA's stance toward local government authority was confrontational, PEBCO's stance was overtly militant.

By January 1980, PEBCO boasted four thousand card-carrying members (*Financial Mail*, January 11, 1990, 97).[16] Because its publicly stated goals, in contrast to those of the SCA, more directly challenged the apartheid system, and because it mobilized so many people, it was viewed by the state as a clear threat. PEBCO reached a high point of its early power and influence in the beginning of January. On the sixth of that month, it held a mass meeting, attended by an estimated ten thousand people, where plans were made for a peaceful demonstration against the demolition of the Walmer location (an African township) to coincide with the visit of George Mossison, deputy minister of cooperation and development. The government preempted PEBCO's planned actions by canceling the visit to the township and detaining three leaders including Botha. In the following month, a public meeting was called to plan actions to protest the detention of the leadership. Once again the government was able to derail PEBCO's plans, this time by releasing the leaders but then banning them from public life (*Daily Dispatch*, February 26, 1980, 5; March 14, 1980, 1).

By detaining and then banning the outspoken leaders, the apartheid government gained a major victory in its attempt to control the development of civic organizations in South Africa's townships. As the state realized that its actions, from the detention of local leaders to public events hosted by key government officials, offered PEBCO a platform to raise its demands, it worked to quickly remove these opportunities without conceding to any community demands. By banning the leaders, the state made it incredibly difficult for them to continue to organize civic actions. The charismatic Botha had been crucial to PEBCO's early success; the organization depended heavily on his populist appeal. After his release under banning orders, he was unable to return to his work at Ford Motors. He tried but failed to make a living by selling fruits and vegetables and subsequently fled South Africa.[17]

After Botha's departure, tensions among leaders within PEBCO exploded, almost destroying the emerging organization. The new acting chairman represented a more conservative group of leaders, more closely resembling the SCA under Motlana. Some members, particularly students and workers, began to complain about a lack of mass meetings, and the newspapers discussed PEBCO's organizational crisis rather than its strength. During the next few years, the civic was seriously weakened by continued state repression and leadership disputes. By 1982 it was once again holding mass rallies, though its campaigns were hampered as leadership disputes continued.

While the SCA did not generate the same high level of press and public attention that PEBCO achieved in early 1980, the SCA's leadership continued to gain support in Soweto. The *Star*, a prominent English-language

Johannesburg-based newspaper, conducted a survey of three hundred Soweto residents. The most striking finding was the clear support for Dr. Motlana. Questioners asked how respondents would vote in either a two-way race between Dr. Motlana along with the Committee of Ten versus the current community council or a three-way race that included the relatively conservative Zulu cultural organization, Inkatha, led by Chief Mangosuthu Buthelezi.[18] In both mock elections, Dr. Motlana and the committee won an overwhelming victory with 73 percent of the poll in a two-way race and 69 percent of the poll in a three-way race. While the committee's support was slightly stronger among the so-called more militant groups including the young and men, a solid majority in every category of age, gender, income, and ethnic group favored it (*Star*, November 14, 1980, 3, 17). Despite the broad support it received, the early SCA still did not effectively include ordinary Soweto residents in its decision-making processes, and this lack of widespread community involvement thwarted several of its planned actions (Molefe, interview, July 16, 1997). A rent boycott in the early 1980s, for example, never included more than 5 percent of the community (Lodge 1983, 355), and an attempted bus boycott against the Putco bus company's 1981 fare increase also failed to meet even modest expectations (SAIRR 1981, 251).

Unlike PEBCO's early leaders, the SCA's leaders were not banned, which allowed them to continue their civic work. In this way, the SCA's relatively conservative approach was more effective as a long-term organization-building strategy under conditions of state repression, but PEBCO was more successful in generating popular mobilization until the state crackdown. This contrast demonstrates a common challenge for social movement organizations: how aggressively should they confront state power? If an organization provokes harsh state repression including significant detentions and violence, it may well be crushed. Intermediate levels of repression can allow an organization and with it a broader movement to grow as state-based restrictions and violence work to anger residents and can encourage their participation as long as joining does not seem futile (Goldstone 1998). But as the case of PEBCO illustrates, intermediate levels of repression can also weaken organizations by provoking disputes over strategies and leadership. Another pitfall for movement organizations is to focus too heavily on working within the confines prescribed by the state. This applies to both authoritarian and democratic regimes. Frances Piven and Richard Cloward (1979), writing of U.S. movements in the 1930s and 1960s, lament the excessive concern that leaders placed on strengthening organization to the clear detriment of mobilization and ultimately the movements as a whole. Similarly, many activists critiqued the SCA's early leadership for their shortcomings in mobilizing local residents.

In South Africa, the leaders of the SCA and PEBCO made different choices regarding organization and mobilization and thereby offered important lessons for other organizations. They also established important firsts in township organizing.[19] The SCA claimed the title as the first townshipwide umbrella civic structure designed as an advocate for local residents. PEBCO supporters claimed another important milestone as the first civic to inspire thousands to mobilize and provided a model for incorporating a broad range of residents into a future national democratic movement. Both organizations developed out of a history of collective action and demand making against local municipalities. In the following months and years, the civic model spread, and the new organizations worked to toe the line between the demands of organization and those of mobilization to avoid the setbacks suffered by the SCA and PEBCO.[20]

Expanding the Civic Struggle

In 1983 the government unveiled a new plan designed to protect apartheid by granting minor concessions. In the process of trying to win over greater numbers of formerly disenfranchised residents, it provided both the spark and the fuel for broader opposition activity within South Africa. The National Party (NP) government proposed a new constitution that would establish a consociational system of limited power sharing within a tricameral parliament including populations labeled by the state as Indian and coloured. The three separately elected chambers (a white House of Assembly, a coloured House of Representatives, and an Indian House of Delegates) would each preside over the "own affairs" of their group but would together decide "general affairs" such as finance, defense, and law and order. The white chamber maintained an absolute majority, and Africans were completely excluded from these decision-making institutions. Two-thirds of white voters supported the new constitution in a referendum, and it was scheduled to come into force in 1984 (L. Thompson 2000, 225).

Changes in local government for Africans were also slated. African local authorities were now to be given greater powers to make them similar to the local authorities for the defined Indian, coloured, and white communities.[21] In reality, however, the minister of cooperation and development maintained the final say over all African local affairs, and financing for these local authorities was limited. Rental payments still went to the regional administration boards, so the local councils were expected to finance their operations largely with the profits from service fees, sorghum beer sales, and local fines (SAIRR

1983, 255). As the South African economy experienced its second consecutive year of negative growth, proposed government resources to upgrade the townships and build more homes were also reduced. At the same time, drought caused increased suffering in rural areas, particularly the impoverished homelands. Growing numbers of Africans migrated to urban townships, putting even greater pressure on the limited resources and housing stock. This encouraged the construction of illegal shacks, which the government promised to demolish.

In opposition to the new consociational system and the continuation of apartheid rule, a national front committed to the creation of a democratic South Africa was launched.[22] The United Democratic Front (UDF) was supported by 565 organizations at its inception, the vast majority of which had been formed since 1979. The groups represented students, workers, women, religious and political interests, and ordinary township residents. The civics, which had by now spread to townships across the country, made up a sizable bloc of 82 organizations (Lodge 1989; Seekings 2000) The theme for the UDF launch was "unity" under the slogan "UDF unites—Apartheid divides" (UDF 1983).[23] The state responded by attempting to limit the success of the UDF campaign by using tactics ranging from misinformation to the banning of meetings, detaining and even killing organizers. Despite state repression, the UDF championed opposition to the regime. A UDF campaign to discourage participation in the 1984 elections for both the coloured House of Representatives and the Indian House of Delegates was a success, with less than 20 percent of eligible voters actually voting (Collinge 1986, 253). Local civics, such as the SCA, worked to encourage Africans to boycott local elections for the new town councils. As a result, only 21 percent of all registered township voters voted in their council elections and as few as 5 percent of eligible voters voted in Soweto (SAIRR 1983, 258–59; Sparks 1990, 332).[24]

Shifting Identities

Civic structures proliferated across the country as a product of the increased organizing encouraged by the UDF. Unlike many of their predecessors, most of the newer civics immediately and directly challenged the apartheid state. In 1983, for example, several organizations were formed to oppose the upcoming council elections as well as new rent increases.[25] The UDF also worked to support existing organizations by bringing together activists from different areas to share ideas, and SCA leaders helped establish new civics in the Vaal, Ratanda, and Kagiso.

Vaal Civic Association flyer (1983)

The majority of these new civics quickly affiliated with the UDF. A leader from the Eastern Cape, who had been active with the civics since the late 1970s, explained: "The civics were very close to the UDF . . . so close as to be very much common in . . . their approach [and their] problems" (Kobese, interview, August 6, 1997). As the UDF mobilized greater numbers of South Africans, the civics blossomed; when the UDF was later banned, so were many civics. Some civic leaders, such as Popo Molefe, were also UDF and underground ANC activists and encouraged organizations to follow the ANC's charterist ideology based on the inclusive nationalism of the Freedom Charter adopted by the ANC and its allies in 1955 (Seekings 2000).

For a number of older civics, particularly the SCA and PEBCO, growing support for the Freedom Charter and the ANC generated considerable internal debate.[26] In the past, Motlana, Botha, and other leaders had frequently stated their support for the Azanian People's Organization (AZAPO), a legal political organization within the BC tradition that competed with the banned ANC for support. Dr. Motlana stated: "On the broader question of political rights, we liaise with other organizations, especially with AZAPO and almost all our members are members of AZAPO and we encourage this" (*Sunday Tribune*, November 16, 1980, 30). Although support for AZAPO was traditionally weak in Port Elizabeth, PEBCO also received some support from AZAPO, and Botha publicly endorsed the organization. Neither the SCA nor PEBCO received direct support from the ANC in the early years of their organizations, but once Botha fled into exile, he joined the ANC.

By 1984, new leaders had emerged in both Soweto and Port Elizabeth who moved their organizations away from past practices. The 1984 SCA annual general meeting became a forum for ideological debate that ended with many BC activists leaving the organization and a new team of ANC supporters taking over. The new leadership felt that the old BC approach was too intellectual and would not appeal to the majority. Pat Lephunya, the former secretary of the SCA, argued: "The Soweto Civic was basically at that stage, a grouping of individuals unconnected to the masses . . . when we took over in 1984" (Lephunya, interview, July 24, 1997). The new leadership embarked on a yearlong program to convert the structures into "a true people's organization." The non-elected Committee of Ten was officially dissolved, and an elected executive committee took its place. In Port Elizabeth, civic leaders also worked to change their organization's emphasis on BC ideology to one of nonracialism. A new constitution was to be drawn up, and the Port Elizabeth Black Civic Organization was to change its name in order to remove the word "Black" from its title. This process stalled, however, and although a new cadre of leaders did take over, the group was not called the Port Elizabeth People's Civic Organization (PEPCO) until the late 1980s (*Eastern Province Herald*, November 7, 1983, 2). An ANC supporter and early activist in PEBCO who worked to reduce the focus on black consciousness was nevertheless saddened by the process that led to the constitutional change and the loss of BC leaders. He recalled, "It was a very, very cruel process. We lost the best people in terms of articulation and theorizing around the state of our situation, but nevertheless we had to take that route" (Tofile, interview, August 5, 1997).

In each of these cases of transformation, ANC cadres spurred the movement toward the principles of the Freedom Charter and the UDF. These changes reflected a broader shift in South Africa's urban townships as charterism had steadily gained ground since the late 1970s (Seekings 2000, 35–40). In 1976, at the time of the Soweto uprising, the ANC was virtually absent as a domestic force, while BC was at its height. Ironically, the uprising strengthened the ANC while dramatically weakening the BC movement. To end the uprising, the state cracked down on BC organizations and their supporters, and police beat the founder of the movement, Steve Biko, to death in detention. As thousands of young men and women fled the townships and crossed South Africa's borders, the ANC in exile received the largest influx of new supporters in its history. By the early 1980s, some of these young activists were returning to South Africa after receiving political and military training. Around the same time, a number of older activists imprisoned by the apartheid government after the 1960 Sharpeville massacre were released (Price 1991, 166). This two-pronged influx of ANC cadres into the townships occurred as Umkhonto we Sizwe (the ANC's military wing, MK) staged several dramatic attacks on seemingly impenetrable apartheid government targets (Barrell 1990). As a result, the ANC's visibility increased dramatically, and a growing number of organizations, including the civics, pledged their allegiance to the Freedom Charter.

Leaders involved in both PEBCO and the SCA's transformation openly admit that the ANC influenced their discussions about the change in guiding ideology. They insist, however, that this shift was in no way forced on an unwilling community but was rather part of a wider movement taking place in the townships as the ANC and its nonracial stance gained greater popularity. Many scholars have argued that the ANC encouraged the development of civics (Seekings 1992a, 218). While this is certainly true, it is important to remember that the ANC did not form the civics or determine their goals or methods of struggle. The early civics were formed under the influence of BC, and even later civics were not led by the ANC in exile. In the words of one civic leader, UDF activist, and ANC member, the civic was not "an ANC child" (Lephunya, interview, July 24, 1997). The perception of ANC ties to the civics was often stronger than the reality. Just as few white South Africans would argue today that they supported apartheid, many township dwellers are eager to demonstrate their connections to the now triumphant ANC. Like the UDF, the ANC's focus was national, not local. Local civics allied to the UDF most often had no reason to disabuse people of the notion that they were also closely connected to the ANC.[27] They generally benefited from this perception and used it to gain wider respect as the ANC's popularity continued to grow (Shubane and Madiba 1992).

The formal shift away from black consciousness was largely a political reorientation. It signaled the appeal of the ANC and the strategic power of its call for inclusiveness. BC was crucial not just to the early civics but to the broader struggle against apartheid by empowering black South Africans to organize in their own communities and to challenge the disempowering rhetoric of the apartheid state. In this way, it provided an important first step for the broader mobilization that followed (Marx 1992). Rather than turning away from the successes of BC, the UDF and the ANC built on them while also working to encourage people and organizations to adopt a more inclusive nationalism. Similarly, individual civics continued to draw on the ideals of black empowerment to mobilize residents even as they aligned themselves with the UDF and the ANC.

The Vaal Uprising

As civic and other forms of organizing spread in the early 1980s, so did protest. The most widespread black civil unrest since the 1976

Soweto uprising occurred in 1984 (SAIRR 1984, xvii). The town councilors, who under the 1977 Community Councils Act had been given the task of diffusing growing discontent, proved incapable of doing so. Township residents were well aware that true power lay not with their local councilors but with the administrative boards that oversaw them and commonly referred to the councils as "stooge organizations" or "dummy bodies."[28] Although the councilors were at times willing to forgo rental increases or allow the proliferation of shacks, the administrative boards ultimately forced them to take a hard line to increase rents and often to demolish "illegal" shacks. These rental increases were justified, in part, by the argument that they would be used to pay for considerable improvements in township infrastructure. But these improvements almost always failed to materialize, thus aggravating local discontent. The councilors were also part of a patronage network. They controlled the allocation of housing and business sites and thereby determined who might set up profitable businesses within the townships.

In August 1984 the Lekoa town council, which administered the townships of Sebokeng, Sharpeville, Boipatong, Bophelong, and Zamdela (all in the Vaal Triangle), announced service charge increases for state-owned and privately owned dwellings. At this time, the average rent in the Vaal was the highest for Africans anywhere in the country (SAIRR 1984, 71). From 1980 to 1985, average income had grown slightly in all other areas of the large, industrial Pretoria Witwatersrand Vereeniging (PWV) region but actually fell in the Vaal Triangle by roughly 5 percent. Over 30 percent of residents were estimated to be living below the rather conservative minimum living level (Bureau of Market Research, as reported in Seekings 1988, 75). By April 1984 over half the households under the Lekoa town council were in arrears for rent and service charges due to a simple inability to pay (Seekings 1988, 69). At the same time, the newly elected councilors were reaping the benefits of their monopoly on liquor stores, beer halls, and shops in the area.

Attendance at meetings of the Vaal Civic Association (VCA) had been relatively low since its formation in late 1983, but the rent hike spurred interest in the organization. On August 25 the VCA, along with the SCA, the Sharpeville Anti-Rent Committee, the Vaal Women's Organization, the Congress of South African Students (COSAS), AZAPO, and the UDF held a mass meeting. At this meeting, they decided to call for a September 3 stayaway to coincide with the implementation of the new constitution. People were told to boycott shops, garages, and taxis owned by community councilors, and shopkeepers and other businesses were requested to remain closed for the day. The organizations also resolved that the new rents would be ignored. On August 26, 1984, the VCA held another meeting at the Anglican church in Boipatong, where residents agreed that the rental fees should be reduced and that the councilors should resign. The meeting then resolved to march on Monday, September 3, to deliver a list of grievances to the town council. On the night of September 2, youths erected barricades between the Bophelong township and Vanderbijlpark (a conservative white city), and Reuben Twala, the captain of the Bophelong soccer team, was killed by the police.[29] His death led to a running battle between township residents and the police (Sparks 1990, 337).

On Monday an estimated 60 percent of workers and almost all students (many of whom were already participating in school boycotts) stayed at home (SAIRR 1984, 71). VCA leaders and an estimated nine thousand supporters began gathering at five o'clock to march to the council offices. The marchers, however, were unable to bring their demands to the council offices. As the leaders walked in front of the procession, a small group of protesters left the march to go to the home of Sharpeville deputy mayor Sam Dlamini to call on him to resign and join their march. An argument ensued, and Dlamini shot a member of the group. The group retaliated by killing the deputy mayor. News of the killing quickly spread and worked to fuel hatred and fear. As the march continued, the leaders of the VCA and others were met by police in armored vehicles, who fired at them with shotguns, rubber bullets, and teargas.

A growing insurrection soon engulfed five townships in the Vaal. By the time the rioting had been quelled, four councilors had died, and property worth an estimated R9.5 million (over $6 million) had been damaged or destroyed, largely by arson.[30] When the VCA called for a meeting the following weekend to attempt to find a peaceful way to meet local demands and stop the violence, the meeting was banned, as were all other meetings scheduled for that weekend. This step effectively sabotaged local organizations' efforts to calm the situation. According to police, residents went on a rampage after the meetings were banned. By the end of September, four councilors resigned from the Lekoa and Evaton councils. Between September 3, 1984, and the end of the year, at least 149 people were killed; the overwhelming majority were ordinary township residents (SAIRR 1984, xvii).

In the aftermath of the uprising, twenty-two people were charged with treason as well as terrorism, subversion, and murder.[31] Almost all the defendants at the resulting Delmas treason trial either held office within the VCA structures or had attended one of the founding meetings of the VCA. Three— Popo Molefe (SCA), Mosiuoa Patrick Lekota, and Moses Chikane—were UDF leaders. The state would allege that the Vaal uprising "was a well-planned and effectively executed operation to paralyze public transport, attack and set arson to the buildings of the Black Local Authority and Administration Board and to intimidate and even kill councilors and effect their resignation.

The aim was to obliterate the Lekoa town council" (Delmas 1988, 891). None of the accused was alleged to have committed the murders himself but each was accused of being part of a conspiracy that led to the murders. Regarding the VCA, the state argued: "The VCA was in fact a small group of political activists which given the right issue at the right time, had the ability to activate the masses" (Delmas 1988, 732). The state made numerous contradictory arguments, asserting on one hand a lack of influence on the part of the VCA, and on the other, that leaders of the VCA had effectively manipulated entire township communities. It argued: "A large number of Lekoa witnesses had never heard of the VCA before the riots. . . . We conclude therefore that the VCA was neither democratic nor representative. . . . Never before have so many been manipulated by so few" (Delmas 1988, 734).

The defense responded to the state's allegations by claiming that the VCA acted in response to local residents' concerns and that the violence that occurred was not of their doing and beyond their control. Transcripts of testimony from countless witnesses described meetings of residents held by the VCA and other organizations, the desperation expressed at these meetings, and the attempts of the civic to organize nonviolent forms of protest such as the failed effort to deliver demands to the council offices on September 3. The uprising occurred, they argued, not as part of a planned explosion but out of frustration and anger. It was, like the Soweto uprising, led mainly by youth. Leading VCA and UDF members argued that they learned of the violence only after it had begun. A VCA leader later remarked: "Our position was that the community must show their anger, but they must not kill anybody or burn anybody's property. [This was] very hard to enforce" (Mokoena, interview, August 29, 1997).

Civic leaders interviewed just days after the uprising repeatedly asserted that violence was not in their best interest since it would quickly lead to state repression and the banning of formerly legal organizations (Swilling n.d.). As studies of earlier English and French rebellions reveal (E. P. Thompson 1971; Tilly, Tilly, and Tilly 1975), crowds do not need to be motivated by rabble-rousing leaders to take action. Popular conceptions of the injustice of elite actions are at times sufficient to provoke violence. Among residents of the Vaal townships, there seemed to be a broad consensus on what were considered legitimate and illegitimate targets (Swilling n.d.). Of the approximately 230 damaged buildings only a few were not public property or the property of councilors or former councilors. The destroyed buildings included six black administration offices, police quarters, liquor outlets, beer halls, and various councilors' shops. Councilors and their relatively excessive property were widely perceived as symbols of oppression, even as residents disagreed about what should rightly be done to them.

After the Vaal uprising, protests and violence spread across much of the country including Soweto, Port Elizabeth, the East Rand, Grahamstown, Cradock, and Uitenhage (SAIRR 1984, 65). Within four weeks, more than sixty people died in South Africa's townships, and thousands were arrested. Over R30 million ($20 million) worth of property was destroyed (SAIRR 1984, 71–72). From September 1984 to May 1985, 109 councilors were attacked (Lodge 1991, 76); by February 21, 1985, at least 45 town councilors had resigned (SAIRR 1984, 167). As part of the Delmas treason trial, the state attempted to demonstrate that the UDF and UDF-affiliated organizations (including the civics) had planned and carried out subversive and violent actions. All in all, the state investigated organizations operating in thirty-one areas of unrest; only seven did not have some form of civic association.

In each of these areas, the state attempted to demonstrate how the actions of the civics along with youth and other groups "organized and intimidated [and engaged in] violence and riots." The alleged subversive actions undertaken by civics included opposing rent increases, calling for more houses to be built, participating in the UDF Million Signatures Campaign against the elections, calling on people not to vote, calling on councilors to resign, advocating civil disobedience, and opposing forced removals. In the final judgment, the court found insufficient proof that the civic organizations did in fact organize violence. In Alexandra, for example, the court ruled: "There is no proof that Alexandra Civic Association had anything to do with the violence in Alexandra" (Delmas 1988, 519). In the case of Soweto, the court noted that a series of civic workshops had actually been used to teach participants to organize to address daily problems and channel the discontent of the people into nonviolent forms of protest.[32]

The chain of events that occurred in Duduza are fairly indicative of processes in other townships where civic leaders lost control of events that they had initiated. On February 17, 1985, the Duduza Civic Association organized a meeting to discuss housing and sewerage problems. Speakers from the civic association, the UDF, workers' organizations, youth organizations, and other civics gave short speeches concerning the conditions in the townships and the expected role of the state in addressing them. After these speeches, audience members spoke from the floor, arguing that there had been too much talk and something needed to be done. One woman suggested that the night-soil buckets (the result of the lack of a sewerage system) should be brought to the local administration offices so that the township manager "would feel the smell" (Delmas n.d., S6.8, 3). Though the woman suggested taking this action on the next day (Monday), several people at the meeting called for immediate action and urged residents to get their buckets. This led to a mass exodus from the church where the meeting had taken place. Civic leaders were unable to formally close the meeting as they normally would. As a large number of residents, most of whom were between fifteen and thirty years old, ran with their buckets toward the administration offices, the police panicked. When a youth was shot in the leg by a policeman, the officer was quickly identified by others, who then went to burn his house. This incident led to a cycle of violence in which more police officers' homes were burnt, more youths were injured, and one child was shot dead (Delmas n.d., S6.8).

During the Delmas treason trial, civic leaders repeatedly presented evidence of their attempts to create democratic structures to encourage resident participation in their organizations and to develop nonviolent methods of pressing their claims. They offered examples such as the Vaal march and the Duduza public meeting as evidence of their inability to quell or, at times, even channel overwhelming anger aimed at local authorities. Despite the testimony of many community leaders and residents as well as the poor and contradictory evidence in support of the state's case, the court ruled that the organizers of the September 3 march must have known that it would lead to violence. Three UDF leaders—Molefe, Lekota, and Chikane—were found guilty of treason with the intent of overthrowing the government with violence. Seven leaders of the VCA were found guilty of terrorism for their role in the events leading up to the riots. The UDF leaders were jailed, but six of the VCA leaders were released with restrictions including a two-year prohibition against attending any public meeting of more than twenty people, issuing press statements, serving in any organization, or participating in any protests (SAIRR 1988–89, 571–72).

Instead of quelling the protests, the state response to the Vaal uprising only fanned the flames of rebellion. In township after township, from Tembisa and Katlehong on the East Rand to Grahamstown and Cradock in the Karoo, councilors' homes, shops, vehicles, and beer halls were set on fire. Councilors were threatened with violence if they did not resign; some were attacked and even killed.[33] Schools were burned, police vehicles were attacked with stones, policemen's homes were destroyed, and police were often attacked and sometimes killed. Contrary to the state's claim in the Delmas treason trial, there was no correlation between organized civic activity and council resignations. The correlation instead was between popular unrest, reaching far beyond the civics, and resignations. What the state failed to accept was that the uprising in the Vaal, which then spread across the country, was an explosion of anger against the apartheid system.

The state banned all indoor meetings in twenty-one magisterial districts, including most of the PWV area districts (SAIRR 1984, 72). Outdoor meetings not of a sporting nature had long since been banned. On October 23, a seven-thousand-strong police and army force was deployed in the Vaal townships of Sebokeng, Sharpeville, and Boipatong (SAIRR 1984, xxi). In Sebokeng, soldiers spaced at fifteen-foot intervals stood guard on the main streets (Murray 1987, 254). Troops were also deployed in Soweto, Joza (Grahamstown), and the townships of Port Elizabeth. The state response, in short, was further repression. As the body count continued to rise in the townships, it was clear that the overwhelming majority of deaths occurred at the hands of the security forces. As police and councilors fled the townships, resentment toward apartheid state functionaries continued to grow, and the cycle of protest and violence continued. Because almost all other events were banned, funerals became a center for protest that often led to more violence.

Civic Persistence

From 1979 onward, the civics worked to expand the political space made available to them by state reforms. By doing so, they created further opportunities not only for civic organization and mobilization but also for other local and national actors. They were hardly uniform, however, and even the best organized could not control the growing uprising that was to spread across the country. Speaking of the UDF in 1985, Popo Molefe argued that the national movement was "trailing behind the masses" (Seekings 2000, 121). Although the civics, in contrast to the UDF, were locally based organizations, they too, as the unfolding of the Vaal uprising shows, were often eclipsed by local events beyond their control. What had begun as a carefully planned march and boycott developed into a running battle with police and resulted in a harsh clampdown on all local opposition activity.

Beginning in mid-1985, a partial state of emergency was declared. This was a result of both the failure of past state attempts to restore "order" in the townships and a reflection of the growing influence of civic and other popular organizations. On June 12, 1986, just four days before the tenth anniversary of the Soweto uprising, for which massive nationwide protests had been planned, a nationwide state of emergency was declared. This state of emergency was renewed annually for the next four years. Just prior to the declaration of emergency, thousands were detained in security sweeps through African townships. Within one year, 26,000 people were detained, with the largest numbers recorded in Soweto and Port Elizabeth (Webster 1987, 142–47; Lodge 1991, 87–88). Nationwide repression dealt a severe blow to civic organization and the many programs and initiatives begun by civic leaders. In February 1988 the government banned the UDF and sixteen other organizations including PEBCO, the SCA, the VCA, and two other civics.[34]

During the 1980s the trajectory of individual civics was determined by a host of factors including the strength of their local leadership, their engagement with broader networks of activists through the UDF, and the degree of state repression that they faced. This is evident from the early days of the SCA and PEBCO and also their later revival as leading civics. After the Vaal uprising, organizations in the Eastern Cape, particularly Port Elizabeth, experienced a dramatic resurgence. PEBCO gained new energy when two recently released prisoners from Robben Island (where Nelson Mandela and other ANC leaders were held), Edgar Ngoyi and Henry Fazzie, joined its executive committee in late 1984. PEBCO then once again played a leading role in organizing in the Eastern Cape (Lodge 1991, 69–73). This lasted for almost two years until repression under the state of emergency took its toll.

In contrast to the significant successes of civic organizing in other parts of the greater Johannesburg region, the SCA retained a relatively low profile in the early 1980s. It was not until after the state of emergency had taken hold across most of the country that the SCA once again rose to national prominence. This renewed importance was in part a product of the ebb and flow of leadership but also a result of Soweto's unique position as South Africa's largest conglomeration of African townships. Because of its size, Soweto proved more difficult for civics to organize than smaller, singular townships. It was also more difficult for the police to control. Although the formation of the UDF had removed several strong Sowetan organizers from local politics, the state of emergency brought many others to Soweto, where it was easier to hide and keep working. The state of emergency also forced the SCA to improve its capacity to include large numbers of residents in its campaigns. In the mid-1980s it once again became a leading actor in the fight against apartheid (Shubane 1991). In the late 1980s, after the SCA had been restricted from legally organizing, leaders formed the Soweto People's Delegation (SPD), which began the first negotiations to restructure apartheid local government for a post-apartheid democratic state.

Despite their sharp downturn with the state of emergency, the civics have persisted as an organizational form for more than three decades. Even after a national organization of civics was formed in 1992, local organizations have pursued a range of approaches and have achieved widely ranging degrees of success. Just as the majority of civics had become charterist organizations by the early 1980s, after 1990 the majority allied with the ANC. The late 1990s then saw the blossoming of a new set of independent civics that joined a resurgence of social movements to return to many of the demands made by the earlier civics.[35] Despite the dramatic changes from apartheid to formal democracy, many of the lessons from the 1980s continued to be relevant in inspiring both more and less radical organizations.

2

Material Inequality and Political Rights

During a 1999 protest in Westcliff, outside Durban, local government councilors told angry residents that their housing demands were unreasonable. Ashwin Desai chronicled the exchange that followed: "[A councilor:] Why were Indians resisting evictions and demanding upgrades? Indians were just too privileged. One elderly aunty, Girlie Amod, screamed back: 'We are not Indians, we are the poors.' . . . Bongiwe Manqele introduced her own good humored variant, 'We are not African, we are the poors'" (Desai 2002, 44).

This refrain of "the poors" suggests a postapartheid identity focused on economic hardship crossing the racial and ethnic divisions that apartheid worked to entrench. Although race remains an extraordinarily powerful category and apartheid-era urban planning still divides poor communities, the potential impact of any broader organizing around poverty cannot be overstated. An estimated 1.4 billion people worldwide were living in poverty in 2005, surviving on less than $1.25 a day (Chen and Ravillion 2008). In South Africa, just short of one-quarter of the population would be classified as living in poverty according to this very low measure (RSA, Presidency 2009, 27); many others struggle to get by with little more. This adds up to an enormous potential constituency of "the poors."

Since the late 1990s, South Africa has seen growing mobilization in many poor communities as new organizations have grown out of past experiences of civic organizing around material concerns. The names of several of the movements underline their focus: the Soweto Electricity Crisis Committee (SECC), the Landless People's Movement (LPM), the Anti-Eviction Campaign (AEC), and the Anti-Privatization Forum (APF). Participants have repeatedly defined themselves as both poor and in need of a greater say in the public sphere. In this way, they work to connect their material struggles to demands for more-democratic governance. These demands and the number of people who could potentially participate in making them are the root of the power, and perhaps the threat, of the politics of necessity.

The material basis of struggles around access to electricity, land, housing, and other basic necessities has received important attention. In his discussion of "the poors," Desai, like other analysts following him, emphasizes the stark shortcomings of South Africa's postapartheid democracy and offers crucial insights into the definition and creation of a broader movement. But, he deals with only part of a complex process. His work does not consider the ways in which these struggles impact (rather than just reflect) the state of governance. It does not address how material struggles might affect demands for and the construction or strengthening of a democratic system. Some may respond to this challenge by arguing that democracy is irrelevant when people must struggle to acquire the basic necessities of life and therefore should not be the focus of analysis. This book argues, however, that democracy offers the potential not only to rein in discriminatory state actions but also to give people a greater say in government policies and priorities. Democracy ideally works to reflect the needs and concerns of its citizens, to constantly revise and reinvent itself and thereby to create a stable but open system of rule. Although no existing regime meets this ideal, formal democracy provides an important, though not uncomplicated, opening for engaged citizens to influence their government. Célestin Monga stresses this point by arguing that Africans have not generally perceived democracy "as a cultural fetish used to disguise famine, misery, and suffering" as some have claimed. It is, instead, seen "as a means of expressing citizenship, confiscated and perverted by decades of authoritarianism" (1996, 10).

Organizing collective action (whether to address material or other concerns) requires the mobilization of participation and voice. These processes are also necessary but not sufficient for the functioning of any democratic system. Popular mobilization to achieve voice is not automatic. It requires a certain degree of agreement about the cause of people's hardship and a crucial change in responses to that hardship. Piven and Cloward define a threefold process in cases of successful mobilization: a shift in popular consciousness whereby previously powerful institutions lose their legitimacy, an expansion of popular claims for greater rights, and the achievement of a "new sense of efficacy" for participants (1979, 4). Although a lack of anti-government protest should not be read as a signal of popular support for public institutions, some popular consensus regarding the diminished legitimacy of key institutions is crucial to any movement for change. Such a shift in sentiment offers the potential to empower those who were previously silent to make demands for greater rights. Put another way, people move from either active consent or public silence to critical voice. In voicing their demands, they begin to frame their identity as a collective actor. In Westcliff this new collective actor was defined as "the poors."

Protests draw attention to the nature of inequality and pull broader communities into a public debate about state exclusions. Social movements work to build on these demands and popular understandings of justice to construct frames that provide a vehicle for increased mobilization and claim making (Oberschall 1996; Snow et al. 1986). When this collective consciousness raising and resistance moves beyond the sharing of frustration to repeated demands for greater rights, it potentially increases what Arjun Appadurai (2004) has termed "the capacity to aspire. This capacity goes a step further than the greater efficacy that Piven and Cloward suggest. Appadurai's notion describes a process of empowerment whereby people not only begin to believe their actions matter but also feel emboldened to imagine a more promising future and ways to realize it. By challenging existing understandings and widely accepted forms of discrimination, movements work to expand debates involving the application of basic rights and provide "alternative blueprints for democracy" (Alvarez, Dagnino, and Escobar 1998, 1). This process of claim making connects material concerns to broader demands for rights, translating a call for lower bus fares or access to land into a reimagination of community. The capacity of citizens to voice demands and their aspirations to challenge their marginalization offers the potential to redefine representation and the very meaning of democracy.

The importance of material demands as part of movements for greater democracy is evident across a wide range of cases. Movements such as the Zapatistas in Mexico and indigenous struggles in Bolivia, Ecuador (Lucero 2008), and Peru (García 2005) have worked to make long-standing forms of domination visible (Melucci 1998), to raise the voices of marginalized and excluded communities, and to give new meanings to existing debates. These indigenous actors have been joined by a broad range of movements representing the rural landless (M. D. Martins 2000), urban favela residents (Gay 1994), and many others. Regarding African popular movements in the early 1990s, Claude Ake argues: "The democracy movement in Africa . . . expresses the desire of ordinary people to gain power and material improvement" (1993, 240). In countries such as Zambia, Ghana, and Côte d'Ivoire, popular demands for democracy developed out of growing opposition to the stark material consequences of structural adjustment policies (Abrahamsen 2001).

In their analysis of protests and democratic transitions across sub-Saharan Africa, Michael Bratton and Nicolas van de Walle found that economic protest often propelled a movement for democracy. Although the severity of an economic crisis did not predict the level or even the advent of protest, the authors conclude that the number of structural adjustment loans a government accepted "strongly and positively correlated with popular protest" (1997, 133). Protest actions are clearly connected to the perceived legitimacy of the target actor or institution. When governments accepted numerous adjustment loans and the attached conditions, not only did their implementation cause considerable material hardship, but the governments' power and legitimacy also eroded in the eyes of many citizens, who perceived their leaders as unable or unwilling to resist the pressures of international financial institutions. This reduced legitimacy, coupled with the experience of increasing material hardship, offered an incentive for many to increase their engagement in the public sphere.

Hardship on its own does not bring about protest, but once people broadly dismiss general misfortune as the source of their problems and frame grievances to connect their struggles to the actions of broader institutions, this process opens the door for rights-based demands. Although numerous scholars have underscored the material basis for a wide array of struggles for democracy, the process whereby immediate material claims expand to include explicit demands for political and civil rights has remained opaque. This chapter focuses on the central mechanism of this transformation by investigating the role of leaders in "conscientizing" citizens by linking local material demands to national political processes. This process of consciousness raising works only when it incorporates and builds on the interests of local movement participants. The broadening of claims and aspirations are also strongly affected by the response of the state (or other target for change). When immediate demands are met, at least in part, the state may be able to defuse the development of broader claims and demobilize an incipient movement. When local officials resist demands, determined mobilizers will be pressed to address the broader power structure and possibly expand their movement. When repression is harsh and thorough, claim making may become difficult or impossible, but this repression may also further delegitimize the state, offering new opportunities for other movements. In any case, movement leaders encourage the capacity to aspire when they successfully demonstrate the connections between people's suffering and the broader political or social system. The following discussion compares the interaction of material and democratic demands during two dramatically different periods: the height of apartheid and the decade after its demise.

The Material Basis of Civic Organizing

General conditions in the African townships across South Africa have always been poor. In Soweto, a 1979 survey administered by the Institute of Urban Studies at Rand Afrikaans University found that 50 percent of all houses were "too small for satisfactory living conditions" (SAIRR 1979, 416). Estimates of the number of people living in four-room houses ranged from seven to twenty-nine people (Human Awareness Programme 1981, 4). Unemployment within the African population stood at roughly 25 percent (SAIRR 1979, 196–97). That same year, the Soweto, Dobsonville, and Diepmeadow community councils (together comprising greater Soweto) announced an average 100 percent increase in rent and service charges, with increases as high as 200 percent in some areas. After the repression following the Soweto uprisings in 1976, many residents had simply been too afraid to defy the state, but the shock of the rent increase made many reconsider their inaction. The Committee of Ten launched the SCA to address basic material concerns, including rent issues, inadequate housing, poor facilities, unpaved roads, lack of electricity and proper lighting, and high transportation costs. In Port Elizabeth, PEBCO was created to respond to similar concerns, including rent hikes, excessive service charges and water accounts, bus fares, forced removals, and inadequate housing. Although some issues, such as the forced removals, were long-standing grievances in Port Elizabeth, recent sharp increases in rate charges offered a spur to action.

More-radical township activists criticized the civics, arguing that basic material concerns addressed to local government offices should not be the focus of struggle. To such criticisms, the SCA's Motlana responded: "Some people say we shouldn't bother ourselves over civic matters as there is no liberation through civic matters. Every journey begins with the first step. We have to start somewhere" (*Post*, September 29, 1980, 2). Both the SCA and PEBCO expanded their demands as their organizations grew. As they worked with their supporters to develop a broader consensus regarding the role of government in creating the material conditions that led to their suffering, their demands extended beyond local rental fees and service charges to a call for the removal of all restrictions on urban Africans. In both the more careful approach of the SCA and PEBCO's bolder stance, civic demands began with particular material grievances but evolved to include, and eventually prioritize, broader demands for civil and political rights as well as representative and participatory government.

Township residents often began participating in local civic organizations through their attempts to address basic material concerns such as the allocation of washing times among residents of a yard sharing a single tap. Rising fees for poor services encouraged many more to attend civic meetings to see what the civic might offer. Mbulelo Goniwe, the nephew of state-assassinated civic leader Matthew Goniwe, described the material realities of apartheid that led him to participate in civic organizing:

At a very young age—I think I was about four years [old]—the Group Areas Act got hold of us; we moved . . . to the area that we are presently occupying, from a big house to a four-roomed house. The houses were so badly constructed that it couldn't escape my mind: why did we move from this big house? It was very comfortable, with a very big garden, with fruit trees; it was very near to town. . . . So we moved to these areas. Then we asked these questions, and our parents kept on ducking and diving around these issues. . . . As I grew up, I always had these unanswered questions in mind. (Goniwe, interview, August 8, 1997)

Many found the civic to be the only place where they could participate in finding solutions to their daily problems.

Conscientizing Communities around a Discourse of Rights

Civic leaders with backgrounds ranging from black consciousness to union organizing to ANC politics all stressed the connection between local struggles and apartheid. Though these three bases of organizing differed in many important respects, each contributed to forging critical linkages between basic material needs and broader political demands. Civic leaders influenced by BC thinking, such as the early leaders of the SCA and PEBCO, employed material struggles to empower black communities to actively resist the apartheid system. Unions by definition focused on improving material conditions, but union organizers learned through their experiences the limitations of addressing only immediate wage or other workplace-based concerns in a society that systematically discriminated against all black people. For this reason, union organizers such as Thomazile Botha in Port Elizabeth and Moses Mayekiso in Alexandra, outside Johannesburg, worked to organize civic associations in their communities and to press for political change beginning at the local level. Finally, the ANC encouraged these actions through its repeated statements that material concerns would never be addressed in the absence of full liberation.[1] This was demonstrated in the Freedom Charter drafted in 1955 by ANC leaders and aligned groups. This charter included demands for a democratic state in which all people have equal representation regardless of race as well as pledges to share the country's wealth and its land. It held out the promise of a future state in which both immediate material needs and broader demands for equality would be addressed, promising "houses, security and comfort" as well as "equal rights, opportunities and status of all" (Congress of the People 1955). BC, union, and ANC influences worked together to build a broad approach to community organizing.

The connection between material necessities and broader political processes, however, was seldom immediate. Civics tended to begin by addressing local needs first and building from there. One local civic organizer commented on her and her organization's learning process: "Initially it was the local conditions, but as we started developing, it became obvious that those local conditions are informed by something, and there is something or somebody that can address those local conditions and wasn't doing that, and . . . we felt that you cannot go and engage [or] confront government if you do not have the support of the people, if the people do not understand where you are taking them" (Ntingani, interview, June 25, 1997). Activists referred to this process as "political education" or "conscientizing" people around "bread and butter issues," linking their material problems to the broader political structure and their lack of representation and voice. A civic veteran, Ntsokolo Daniel Sandi, underlined the importance of this process, defining the civic as "a community school where residents learn about their rights as residents/rate payers and how to unite against their daily constraints and frustrations" (Sandi, interview, August 5, 1997). He argued that residents would come to a civic with their problems, and through the discussion of their concerns, they would begin to engage in a discourse of rights and the gross denial of their basic rights by the apartheid regime. A civic leader from the East Rand further stressed the importance of "schooling" concerning the concept of rights in a society where formal education was both poor and designed to perpetuate white power. He argued that the "civic was to educate people about their rights [in a context in which] most people were illiterate" (Maluleka, interview, August 31, 1997). The centrality of rights-based demands was often highlighted in fliers and images such as the drawing (see opposite page) that appeared in a Federation of Cape Civic Associations newsletter, urging residents to fight for "more than bread crumbs."

The civics established during this era focused on local conditions but also became part of a wider political movement for democracy. Even as they expanded their demands, local concerns continued to be the centerpiece of their actions. This focus on material issues helped attract great numbers to civic meetings, but it would also challenge the civics in subsequent periods when they proved to be only minimally effective in solving immediate material problems. Local government leaders repeatedly argued that residents would

Federation of Cape Civic Associations newsletter, no. 1.11 (1980): 3

not long support the civics because they were unable to deliver houses and improve services. David Thebahali, the Soweto council chairman, argued at the time of the formation of the SCA: "The newly formed SCA will not do anything without the approval of my council. . . . [They] cannot build a house, allocate trading, school and church sites for residents. They are an organization that can never do a single job in Soweto" (*Post*, September 27, 1979, 2). While clearly concerned about the formation of the SCA, Thebahali was also reassured by what he considered their limited focus on material concerns. This focus thereby also provided some cover for organizations as their leaders worked to carefully broaden civic goals.

Popular Campaigns to Undermine
the Apartheid State

Campaigns to address local issues worked to strengthen the civics by increasing resident participation and, ideally, ownership of civic programs. In seeking to challenge increasing rental and service fees, for example, civic leaders went door to door to collect money for legal help to fight the increases and research alternative plans. This collection of money was also a strategy to bring people into the struggle. Mbulelo Goniwe explained the Craddock civic's approach: "[The money] was intended to pay the legal costs. . . . It was also a mobilization strategy, because we could have gotten lawyers, human rights lawyers, etc. to help us, but we felt that in order to be effective, we had to make the people *own* the campaign, let it be theirs, that they don't just see a lawyer coming paid by international donation" (Goniwe, interview, August 8, 1997). Civic members frequently emphasized the importance of the civic as a forum for political expression: "I realized that there was an organization where you can say something and that voice can be heard somewhere; that is why I joined, because we had problems but we couldn't talk to anybody, but through the civic [our] voice could be heard somewhere" (anonymous member of SANCO Evaton, interview, August 1997).

One of the most successful civic campaigns was the rent boycott, because it built on residents' ongoing struggles to pay, along with their frustration with poor services. The rent boycott, more than any other action organized by the civics, sped the transition process at the level of local government and effectively linked local material to broader governance demands. Demands grew to include not only the setting of affordable rentals, exemption of pensioners from rental fees, collection of refuse and regular repair of sewerage pipes, and the erection of street lights, but also the resignation of all councilors and the removal of all soldiers from the townships (SCA 1986). The boycotts that began in Bophelong, Sebokeng, Sharpeville, and Zamdela (all in the Vaal Triangle) in September 1984 spread to at least fifty-four townships, including the Eastern Cape, East Rand, Alexandra, and Soweto by September 1986. Already in the first half of 1985, the *Financial Mail* (April 12, 1985) claimed tens of thousands of households were withholding rent and service payments, thereby bringing local authorities to a state of collapse (SAIRR 1985, 536). By August 1988 the accumulated debt as a result of the rent boycott was roughly R475 million (almost $200 million) (SAIRR 1988–89, 209).[2]

A primary reason for the sharp increases in rents was the simple fact that the financial structure of the townships was unfeasible. National government leaders argued that black townships should become financially self-sufficient,

Material Inequality and Political Rights

but residents were actually subsidizing the white suburbs. They were paying significantly more per unit of electricity than their suburban neighbors and, due to a legally mandated absence of most stores in the townships, shopping in stores that paid taxes to white areas (Swilling, Cobbett, and Hunter 1991). Self-sufficiency was impossible given the lack of a financial base in the townships. This fact undermined any state attempts to patch or suppress the problem and added credence to a key civic demand for a single tax base that included prosperous white cities along with poor African townships within one larger municipality.

A survey of residents in the Vaal and a report commissioned by the Soweto People's Delegation (established by the SCA) demonstrated popular support for the boycott. The Vaal survey, conducted in Sebokeng, Sharpeville, Bophelong, Boipatong, and Evander townships, found that by the middle of the 1980s, over 97 percent of residents did not pay rent, and less than 10 percent attributed their nonpayment of rent to intimidation by local organizations (Frankel et al. 1987, 83–84). In Soweto, analysts came to a similar conclusion: "Intimidation played a minimal role in the organization of the rent boycott. It is well organized and continues to be widely supported" (Planact 1989, 3). General support for the VCA was high. Over half the residents surveyed either supported or strongly supported the VCA; less than 18 percent opposed or strongly opposed it. Most residents viewed the VCA as a "representative body" and explained their support for the organization because it helped residents address local concerns and opposed apartheid (Frankel et al. 1987, 43–48, 90). The civics had successfully brought residents together to discuss their anger over the rent increases and channeled this discontent over high services into a concerted program of action. To end the boycotts, civics across the country demanded not only a reduction in rent and service charges but also the resignation of town councilors and the release of their leaders from detention. They explicitly linked material demands with demands for basic civil and political rights.

As the boycotts continued to spread, local authorities responded with carrots and sticks. In some areas, residents were offered an indefinite postponement of increases in rates as well as the possibility of owning their own homes. Local authorities also threatened to cut services in response to boycotts, and many staged evictions.[3] Despite uneven state attempts to stop the boycotts, support for them generally strengthened over time. This was true even as intense repression in some areas caused a short-term increase in payments after the enactment of the state of emergency in 1985. Overall, unlike other forms of civic action, rent boycotts were not affected by the detention of leaders. Once they were effectively begun, they continued even when state forces were able to undermine or completely stop the functioning of local civic structures. Basic material conditions, which for many residents included a lack of money to pay rent, reinforced the political objectives and therefore the success of the boycott.

Another key method of civic protest, the consumer boycott, became popular shortly after the rise of the rent boycotts. In contrast to the rent boycotts, which reduced residents' financial burdens, consumer boycotts potentially increased them by causing township residents to travel farther or pay higher prices for basic goods. For consumer boycotts to succeed, residents had to shift priorities from their immediate material concerns to support of a greater political objective. The boycotts therefore required greater levels of organization and more-determined community support. Like the rent boycotts that preceded them, the consumer boycotts were most effective when local socioeconomic demands formed the basis for the boycott action and were then linked to national political issues. Demands initially included the improvement of local township infrastructure and housing, but as the state clamped down on township community organization after 1985, they also included the release of community leaders, the lifting of the state of emergency, and the withdrawal of troops from the townships. Leaders played a central role not just in organizing the boycotts but also in working with local merchants to keep their prices low to reduce the economic impact of the boycott on township residents. Because of the greater challenge in organizing effective consumer boycotts, when successful they were an even more significant accomplishment for civic participation and the conscientizing efforts of local leaders.

While the epicenter of the emerging rent boycott was in the Transvaal region around Johannesburg, the consumer boycott was centered in the Eastern Cape and was most successful in Port Elizabeth. The boycotts began in earnest in the Eastern Cape in mid-1985 and soon encompassed Port Alfred, Cradock, Grahamstown, Port Elizabeth, and Uitenhage before spreading to other parts of the country, including Alexandra and Soweto (Helliker, Roux, and White 1989, 34–35; SAIRR 1985, 555–56). From the rise of this method of resistance in early 1985 to its demise in late 1986, consumer boycotts had a significant impact on African township organization, unity, and resistance. In areas where the boycott strategy was well organized, it comprised a cross-class alliance as potential consumers refused to patronize white and often Indian and coloured shops when their owners did not express contempt for the tricameral parliament. In communities across the Eastern Cape, civic leaders worked with student, youth, women's and labor organizations to coordinate boycott actions. Where organization was weak, boycotts did, at times, lead to violence as youths forced older consumers who had violated the boycott to eat raw chicken, rice, detergent, or cooking oil. When this occurred, it undermined support for the boycott (Seekings 2000, 164) and provided an opportunity for the state to argue that township resistance was merely a product of organized coercion.

In Port Elizabeth, negotiations to end the boycotts led to greater successes than in most other areas, but overall, negotiations with white businesses to end boycotts achieved few immediate victories. Leaders of township communities and businesses generally were unable to bridge the large divide between them. One Eastern Cape civic leader commented: "When [negotiations to end consumer boycotts] took place, they tended to be more sensational than a real talking relationship" (Kobese, interview, August 6, 1997). The boycotts did, however, underline the concerns of a growing number of business leaders that a nationally negotiated settlement of some kind would be necessary for the economy of South Africa to return to growth and for businesses to reap profits.

In an attempt to weaken the civics and to avoid any step toward substantial negotiations, authorities in Port Elizabeth distributed pamphlets that referred to the boycott leaders simply as "intimidators." They also attempted to use the centrality of material concerns to their benefit by pointing to community leaders' inability to address material demands. The pamphlets asked residents how many houses their leaders had built and how many hungry people they had fed. It went on to argue that these "intimidators" were actually curtailing residents' freedom of choice (Roux and Helliker 1986, 57). Apartheid had so decimated any notion of freedom that this effort to place the blame on local community leaders provoked little response except in those areas where the boycott had been enforced with violence. Overall, the state's response to consumer boycotts, like that to the rent boycotts, was not a quick, organized national assault but rather a more sporadic approach. This approach allowed the boycotts to continue until 1986, when they finally collapsed with increased state repression under a full state of emergency.

The state of emergency severely undermined civic organizations as leaders and ordinary members were imprisoned and organizations went underground or stopped operating. Nonetheless, civic resistance played a central role in bringing about the end of the apartheid regime. By the time the civics were driven underground, their means of action had been popularized in the townships, and though the consumer boycotts ended, rent boycotts continued. These boycotts caused the collapse of one local council after another. More importantly, the demands made by the supporters of civic organizations had grown from material demands that could be addressed with local improvements and local patronage to the far broader demands for equal political representation and rights, demands that required regime change. The apartheid state could no longer effectively govern most black townships. Internal resistance led by the civics as part of the UDF, as well as the organized resistance of labor unions in the late 1980s, strengthened the hand of the ANC. At the same time, the apartheid government was losing support among its own constituents. In 1989, South Africa's president and staunch defender of apartheid, P. W. Botha (referred to as *Die Groot Krokodil,* Afrikaans for "The Big Crocodile"), relinquished the party leadership after a stroke and was replaced by F. W. de Klerk. Emboldened by the collapse of communism and his mistaken belief that he might initiate reforms to keep his party in power, President de Klerk began a process of negotiations that would end apartheid, establish nonracial democracy, and bring the ANC to government.

Postapartheid Poverty and Inequality

It is difficult to overstate the incredible challenges faced by South Africans in the aftermath of apartheid. The measured language of the United Nations Development Programme (UNDP) report on South Africa stresses the severity of the economic and social crisis: "The first democratically elected government in South Africa inherited apartheid policies and institutions that had resulted in a stagnant economy, an exceptional level of poverty, inequalities in income and wealth and extremely skewed access to basic services, natural resources and employment" (2003, 12).

Although per capita growth improved from negative growth in the 1980s, annual rates of growth remained low, averaging less than 1 percent from 1994 to 2003. Growth rates improved in the following years to average 3.7 percent from 2004 to 2007 before declining again (RSA, Presidency 2009, 6). Despite this growth, the distribution of income has remained incredibly skewed against the poor. South Africa's Gini coefficient has actually risen since the end of apartheid and remains among the highest in the world.[4] When we consider former apartheid racial classifications, the overwhelming majority of whites remain in the highest expenditure quintile (83 percent), while less than 8 percent of black Africans belong to this wealthy group (Statistics South Africa 2008, 8). Labor and capital shares of the economic pie have also changed over time to the disadvantage of workers. The UNDP found a clear shift in the distribution of income from 1995, when wages and salaries made up 50 percent and profit 27 percent of gross national income; in 2002, wages and salaries were down to 45 percent and profit up to 30 percent (UNDP 2003, 12). Therefore while per capita growth did improve, a larger percentage of this growth went to capital at labor's expense, and the gap between the wealthy and the poor increased.

Unemployment has also risen in the postapartheid period. Under the expanded definition, which includes frustrated job seekers among the unemployed, unemployment rose from 29.3 percent in 1995 to 42.1 percent in 2003 (UNDP 2003, 20) and remained over 35 percent in 2010 (*Economist*, August 28, 2010). Under the narrower definition, which includes only those who actively looked for work in the four weeks prior to the survey, South Africa's unemployment rate in mid-2010 was 25.3 percent (SSA 2010, xii), still considerably higher than unemployment at the end of apartheid and just over the 24.9 percent reached in the United States at the height of the Great Depression in 1933. Unemployment in South Africa is therefore comparable to the highest rates recorded in the United States, a time remembered as one of incredible hardship for the majority of Americans. In the early 1980s, during the United States' greatest postwar unemployment crisis, unemployment never reached 11 percent; in 2009, amid great concern over job losses, American unemployment was just over 10 percent (U.S. Bureau of Labor Statistics, http://www.bls.gov).

A quick look at mean incomes across population groups shows the profound and continuing impact of apartheid. Although South African incomes have grown since 1995, they have grown at a faster rate for whites than for Africans. From 1995 to 2008, white mean per capita income grew over 80 percent while African income grew by less than 40 percent (RSA, Presidency 2009).

Poverty remains overwhelmingly black, almost exclusively so among the poorest. In the poorest quintile of households, 95 percent are Africans. Members of this segment of the population struggle to feed their families, allocating more than half of their total expenditure just to food. At the other end of the scale, almost 50 percent of the wealthiest twenty percent of households are white (J. H. Martins 2007, 217–18). White South Africans continue to dominate the wealthiest quintile even though they make up less than 10 percent of the total population. A comparison of human development index (HDI) scores compiled from three indices—life expectancy, educational attainment, and gross domestic product—underscores the impact of these inequalities on human well-being. Between 1980 and 2000, Africans made the greatest gains in HDI scores but still had the lowest scores of the four groups (African, coloured, Asian, and white) and continued to lag considerably behind whites (UNDP 2003, 45).[5] The continuing racial profile of inequality in South Africa led Thabo Mbeki to describe the country as composed of two nations: a white relatively prosperous nation and a larger black poor nation (Mbeki 1998). This understanding offers a partial picture of inequality corroborated by the data, but what Mbeki's presentation fails to acknowledge is a growing black elite that has joined the wealthiest quintile. Although whites still dominate the wealthiest

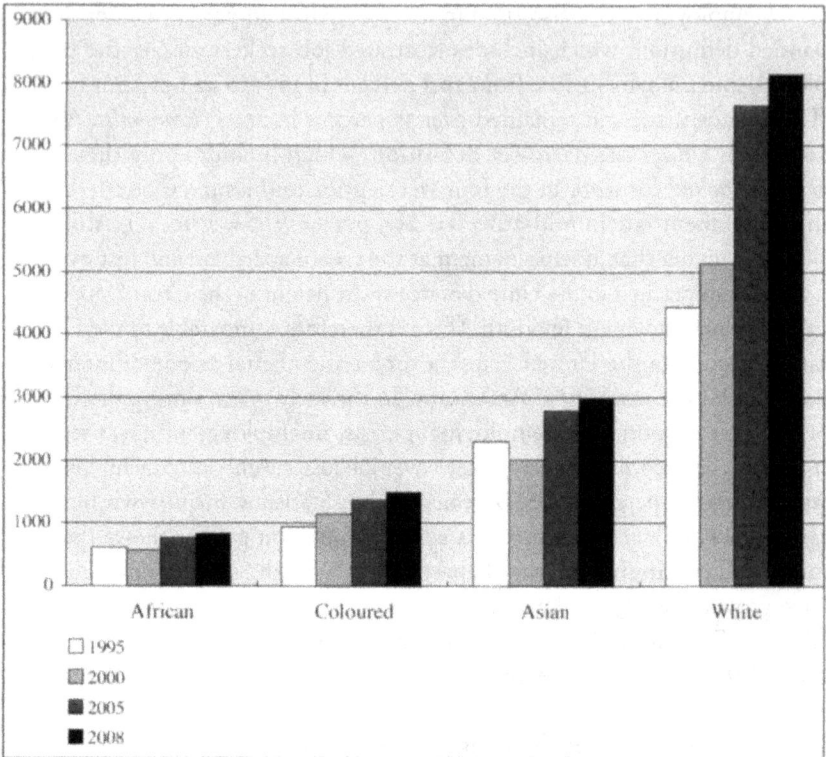

Mean annual per capita income by population group, 1995–2008 (2008 constant Rand) (data from RSA, Presidency 2009, 23; table by Sumedha Senanayake)

group, Africans made up over 37 percent of the wealthiest quintile in 2004 (J. H. Martins 2007, 217). Sampie Terreblanche argues: "More resources and opportunities were, in all probability, transferred from white people to the top 20 percent of the black population over the past 14 years through BEE [Black Economic Empowerment] and affirmative action than were transferred to the poor segment of the population through social spending and poverty alleviation" (2008, 108). Inequality is therefore a great concern both across population groups and within them.

The Consistency of Material and Political Demands

The connection between material demands and political rights was established by civic and other organizations during the struggle against

Material Inequality and Political Rights

apartheid. During this time, the ANC was for most South Africans the people's representative in their demands for the extension of a wide range of rights. After the ANC came to power in 1994 and apartheid was legally abolished, the linkages between material demands and political rights retained their significance. When citizens were driven to protest, they now immediately connected material demands to broader notions of representation and consultation as well as more-specific rights enshrined in the new constitution. Protest (aside from union actions) was dramatically lower in the first few years after 1994 in comparison to the previous decade. But the ANC's honeymoon was short lived. By the late 1990s, protests driven by material concerns increased significantly. The ten-year anniversary of democracy in 2004 was marked by widespread actions; for the 2004/5 financial year, the government reported 5,085 legal and 881 illegal protests (Atkinson 2007, 58). In 2009, protest actions once again reached new heights with the proliferation of so-called service delivery protests.

During the postapartheid period, protests have become more confrontational. In the mid-1990s, civic protesters tended to remind the ANC-led government of continuing material difficulties and to press for the full recognition of rights of representation and participation. The late 1990s, in contrast, were marked by more powerful and confrontational demands along with claims that the party of liberation was failing to uphold constitutional rights. By 2009, protesters in numerous townships across the country were demanding the resignation of their local government representatives. Many of these protests were marked by the destruction of public property. Some also entailed violent confrontations between protesters and the police.

Service provision has remained one of the most pressing issues addressed by local organizations, and residents' complaints regarding high rates for poor services continue to echo civic protests from the early 1980s. Though residents now elect their local government leaders, civics still argue that local government is not responding to residents' needs in service provision. Local government is now largely organized under the one-city principle, which created a single tax base to include rich and poor communities. Though this addressed a key demand made by the civics during the rent boycotts, it still does not provide sufficient funding to carry the poor townships. In most areas, services have been slow to improve, and their upgrading depends in part on the income that the municipality derives from residents' payments. Local civic structures have generally encouraged residents to pay for services, but they also continue to call for the improvement of those services.[6] A regional civic leader in the Vaal articulated the early postapartheid approach of most local civics: "We are no more a home of boycotters. We encourage people to pay for their services, but we also say to [the] government that they should be sympathetic because people are unemployed" (Mazibuko, interview, May 27, 1999).

Following apartheid, rates of payment remained low largely due to poverty, as well as poor administration, which led to incorrect statements.[7] Civic leaders worked to make what little inroads they could in their local areas to improve both services and payments for services. In Alexandra, for example, local civic leaders repeatedly called the authorities to report new problems in service provision while continuing to call for improvements. A local civic organizer noted the successes and failures of service delivery in much of Alexandra: "There hasn't been much improvement on a lot of things, most especially, part of the deal was that all the services would be put to working order; that there are no leaks, no drips. We still have those things. The only difference is that whenever you report it, they do come out, but that is not how we would like to see it. They always got people in the locations; they should go about maintaining these services" (Mbalukwana, interview, June 27, 1997).

Service rates provided one of the greatest challenges to friendly but critical relations between local civics and the newly elected ANC local government representatives. Even in townships where few other areas of conflict existed between the ANC and the civics, questions regarding services divided them. Differing perceptions of the government's Masakhane ("let us build together") campaign, which was meant to improve service delivery, offer an insight into the contrasting positions. A civic leader in the Eastern Cape explained the division this way: "People on the ground do not see any change. . . . [The ANC] government thinks that Masakhane means people should pay, while the civic thinks that it means there must be some delivery for the people on the ground" (Mqobe, interview, August 6, 1997). Local civics most often tried to tread a delicate line between their supporters and the ANC-dominated local government. They urged people to pay while still promising to push the government on delivery, but as rates continued to rise at a steady pace and services did not improve significantly, tensions grew.[8]

In Soweto, when the new councilors came to office in 1995, service rates were increased. The Soweto civic supported this, but approximately six months later more increases were levied without the local civic's input. The Soweto civic promised to encourage its supporters to continue paying old rates and threatened a march on the council if it tried to impose the new rates (increases of 20 percent in water and 40 percent in sewerage). The ensuing civic campaign against the councilors was the first such campaign against the new, postapartheid councilors. The civic held demonstrations outside the Western Metropolitan Sub-Structure offices and led a large march to the civic center in Jabulani, Soweto, to present a memorandum to the mayor of the Greater Johannesburg Metropolitan Council, Isaac Mogase (ironically the honorary president and former leader of the civic) (*Citizen*, July 4, 1996, 8; *New Nation*, July 5, 1996, 6; *Sowetan*, July 19, 1996, 3).

Material Inequality and Political Rights

In Port Elizabeth, similar concerns regarding rate hikes caused the local civic to plan a march on city hall in protest. Once again the civic complained that it had not been consulted regarding the increases. The ANC countered by asking its members not to participate in the march (*Eastern Province Herald*, July 19, 1995, 2), but about one thousand civic supporters still turned out to chastise the council chairman, who became quite emotional as he spoke.[9] The chairman, Nceba Faku, argued: "You voted this government into power. This means that you've a responsibility to pay your services to keep it [the government] going" (*Eastern Province Herald*, July 21, 1995, 1). While government representatives stressed citizens' responsibilities to the state, the protesters demanded greater respect from government for their newly won rights.

These two protests signaled the demands of ordinary South Africans for representation and consultation in the process of addressing continuing material hardships. Residents' demands were based on their expectations from apartheid-era struggles and the discourse of rights and participation popularized during this period rather than any current conscientizing action on the part of leaders. At this stage, most civic leaders, who were in a loose alliance with the new government, were actually seeking to mediate, at times even minimize, residents' demands.

In late August 1997 the Johannesburg Inner-City civic organized a protest in downtown Johannesburg. This protest provides an example of the expectations by many civics that their relationship with the government would help to address residents' needs even as protesters increasingly drew upon their constitutional rights. The marchers made demands for "reasonable rentals" and a minimum standard for services such as "working lights and maintenance," which landlords would have to supply to renters. They presented their memorandum addressed to Dan Mofokeng, MEC (member of Executive Council) for Housing and Land Affairs, calling for a moratorium on all evictions and a comprehensive review of public housing. Emboldened by the promises of the new South African Constitution, protesters repeatedly noted their rights to speak, to march, and to congregate and called on the ANC to support them in their struggles. What was clearly apparent at this protest was both the protesters' frustration that the new constitutional dispensation had not helped to address their concerns and an expectation that their connection to the ANC as part of the broader liberation struggle would help them to find ways to improve their situation. This was underlined by the fact that the MEC to which the protesters addressed their memorandum was also a member of the national civic organization to which the protesters belonged.

Another set of protests that same month suggested the beginning of a less friendly relationship between civic protesters and government officials and a growing need on the part of protesters to invoke explicit constitutional provisions. In response to slow payment rates in Gauteng (the province including Johannesburg, Pretoria, and surrounding areas) and a debt of R3 billion (over $600 million), the provincial government began a campaign of cutting services in early August 1997. At this time only 45 percent of households and businesses in the province had paid for their services (up from 23 percent in June 1996) (*Star*, August 1, 1997, 1).[10] In KwaThema, East Rand, on the first day of dramatic cuts, the electricity supply to more than 1,200 homes was disconnected as council task teams, guarded by heavily armed traffic police, dug up and cut cables to prevent reconnection. Cuts also affected the local police station, traffic lights, and many local shops. On the second day of cuts, violence erupted as some residents stoned cars and set a Telkom (the public telephone company) truck on fire. Overall, there were at least twelve incidents of violence related to the cuts in the township during the week, including the stoning of one councilor's home (*Business Day*, August 6, 1997; *Star*, August 6, 1997, 2; August 7, 1997, 1; August 11, 1997, 2). While authorities reported a tremendous increase in payments, the civic demanded an immediate moratorium on the power cutoffs and sought a legal interdict to stop the provincial government's actions.[11]

The local civic chairman, Isaac Makgubutlane, argued that though the decision to cut power was made by provincial government, local ANC councilors were clearly culpable. The provincial MEC for Local Government had asked local councils to compile data to separate the poor and pensioners from those not paying who did have the resources to pay. This request came to the council in February, but lacking an effective mechanism for compiling the data, the council never completed a report to provincial government. The civic chairman argued that he supported the principle of payment for services but not the approach that had been taken to compel such payment. He added that the civic was willing to go to extremes to stop the cable-cutting actions:

We are not fighting the principle, but we believe that we must be consulted. We also believe that these electricity cables that they are cutting [do] not belong to the council; [they] belong to us [the people]. So they must get what we are actually fighting for. . . . If you want to cut my cable, discuss [it] with me first. That is what we are fighting for. We paid electricity long ago to pay for the cable. . . . This is why we were involved last week. You saw us on TV and we stopped them. We are capable of doing that, because of [a] lack of consultation. . . . And if they want to push us too far we will go to such an extent of now putting stones and barricades so that those trucks cannot even move, but we still believe in negotiations. (Makgubutlane, interview, August 25, 1997)

In township after township across South Africa, civics were upset not just because of the general increases in rates since 1994 but also because of the lack

Material Inequality and Political Rights

of consultation between local government authorities, particularly ANC leaders, and the civics. Civic leaders repeatedly expressed their concern that the government was attempting to act too independently, and they often referred to their informal alliance with the ANC to argue that local ANC leaders had an obligation to the local civic structures to come to them for consultations on new projects and policies. A local civic leader in the Vaal commented: "When these councilors were elected, especially the ANC councilors, they were told that they must work hand in glove with the alliance structures. He must come and report to the structures what is already taking place in the council, what are the changes. This one is not reporting to anybody" (anonymous Vaal civic leader, interview, August 1997). Many civic members became increasingly frustrated.

In 1997, one year after the government had formally moved from the redistributive Reconstruction and Development Programme (RDP) to the neoliberal Growth, Employment and Redistribution (GEAR) plan, the effects of the policy of cost-recovery were beginning to be felt in many poor communities. Although the apartheid government's ideal of self-sufficient townships had been crushed by civic activism and replaced with racially unified cities and tax bases, the postapartheid cost-recovery model followed a similar logic to apartheid policies by expecting consumers in poor townships to pay most of the costs associated with service provision to their areas. By failing to address the dramatic inequality in resources created by apartheid, the refusal to offer greater subsidies to the poor promised to further entrench unequal access to basic services. The cost-recovery model led to government actions such as the removal of electricity cables in KwaThema to stop consumers from using electricity without paying and served as a tipping point for some residents. They began to challenge the government's actions, arguing that leaders were ignoring their promises of cooperation with community-based organizations and also increasingly arguing that their rights enshrined in the constitution were being violated. This opened the door to a more confrontational politics concerning service delivery.

The electricity crisis encouraged ever-greater resistance and defiance of government and the electricity utility, ESKOM. By 2000 the SECC was formed. At this time, most Sowetans simply could not pay their electricity bills, and the ANC had not delivered on its promise to give all consumers a free base amount of electricity. An estimated 89 percent of households were behind in their payments. The supplier, ESKOM, was increasingly addressing this state of affairs by cutting electricity supply to individual homes or even entire areas of the township. By 2001 these cutoffs affected an estimated twenty thousand households a month (Pape and McDonald 2002, 6). The SECC campaigned for a monthly flat rate for electricity in Soweto (R50, roughly $6.50), but local government councilors failed to address the SECC's demands, and residents continued to complain of grossly inaccurate bills, disconnections, and corruption. The SECC then responded with actions that have attracted not only national but also international attention. Operation Khanyisa—"switch on"— offered free illegal reconnection for residents whose service had been cut. Within six months, the SECC claimed to have reconnected three thousand households (Egan and Wafer 2006, 47) under the slogan "Electricity is a right, not a privilege" and later expanded its program to launch a campaign against water cutoffs and the eviction of homeowners for defaulting on bond and rent payments.

The SECC's actions offered a significant challenge to the authority and with it the legitimacy of the ANC government. As a result, the SECC's most vocal critics, largely members of the ANC government, described the movement as dangerously radical and "ultraleft." Trevor Ngwane, the most public face of the SECC, was referred to by his detractors as the "dreadlocked demagogue." Ngwane, a former ANC councilor in Soweto, was expelled from the ANC for his public criticism of the government's neoliberal Igoli 2002 program for Johannesburg. As a result, his interactions with ANC members have often been quite charged. Ngwane emphasizes, however, that the SECC's mass action is not just to pressure government but also to empower residents. He argues that mass action involves not only putting people back into their homes after they have been evicted or simply stopping the cutting of electricity cables but also showing "other people in the same situation that (1) it is wrong (2) you can fight against it and win (3) it is happening because we ordinary people do not have the power even though we might have the vote, but we don't have the power over the important decisions which affect our life, our destiny" (Ngwane, interview, July 19, 2002).

Despite the rhetoric branding the SECC as ultraleft, it, like the civics of the 1980s, works to connect material demands to a discourse of democratic rights. The SECC's acts of civil disobedience have been greeted with significant support in poorer areas of Soweto such as Phiri and Chiawelo (Egan and Wafer 2006), but the movement also employs other actions such as protest marches to draw wider attention to its demands. During the 2004 national and provincial elections, the SECC encouraged supporters to engage in legal protest actions on election day. In 2006 it joined the local government elections as the Operation Khanyisa Movement, rallying supporters with the slogan "Fight for your rights!" The demands made by the SECC built on a history of activism calling for greater political as well as economic rights. The committee's demands echoed the promises of both the Freedom Charter of 1955 and the South African Constitution of 1996.

OPERATION KHANYISA MOVEMENT

Say no to the rich getting richer and the poor getting poorer

SEKUNJALO! turn up the pressure on Mbeki!

VOTE FOR FREE SERVICES, EDUCATION AND HOUSING and living wage for everyone

Let's get organised!

FIGHT FOR YOUR RIGHTS!

Operation Khanyisa Movement poster (2006)

Township residents who supported the SECC were drawn to the organization by the dire electricity crisis and their own inability to pay rising charges and frequently inaccurate bills. The SECC sought to hold the ANC to its pledge to offer a base amount of electricity for free but argued that what the government offered was both poorly implemented and of too small a quantity to significantly help poor households. Although the SECC's discourse of rights and democratic accountability remains popular with many township residents, this does not necessarily mean that SECC supporters fully endorse all the goals of the leadership. Leaders of the SECC such as Trevor Ngwane often make broader claims, including demands for a socialist state and the end of capitalism. Most residents, in contrast, seek to more narrowly address their material needs and to press for representative leadership. They are not necessarily ready to endorse more revolutionary goals (Buhlungu 2006). This demonstrates the limits of the conscientizing process that leaders work to implement. Movement supporters endorse claims up to the point at which those claims appear to be too risky or detrimental to their interests. For the SECC this was most dramatically demonstrated in the 2006 local elections, when many voters continued to vote for ANC candidates (and not for Operation Khanyisa) despite their support of the SECC's material demands. Operation Khanyisa won only a single council seat in the local elections. Even with the ANC government's shortcomings, the majority still believed that the ANC was best placed to realize their aspirations for material and political transformation. Even the "service delivery" protesters in 2009 who demanded the resignations of local ANC councilors largely did not reject the ANC as the governing party. This position was both a strategic action in response to the national dominance of the ANC and a product of the continuing association of the ANC with the struggle for liberation.

Indivisible Rights

South Africa's civics and many of the movements that formed after the formal demise of apartheid were initially launched to address the pressing material needs of the communities in which they worked. They began with a discussion of grievances and increasingly framed their demands in the language of rights. In this way, a rights-based framework of claims developed through collective action and debate (Tarrow 1989, 128, 136). South Africa's social movements are not unique in this respect. Local organizations that played significant roles in their countries' democratization processes—from the Solidarity trade union movement in Poland to the popular organizations (lo Popular) in Chile's shantytowns—all began with material concerns. Perhaps the best-known case of this process is the Zapatista movement in Mexico. Rooted in a struggle for land and survival, the demands of the Zapatistas were framed not only in terms of material necessities and autonomy but also as a call for political rights (Harvey 1998). These comparative examples and the lessons they offer are addressed in greater detail in later chapters.

In the South African case, material demands have clearly served as the basis for broader rights-based citizenship claims. The quest for greater formal civil and political rights, while long and hard, was eventually won with the end of apartheid in 1994. The South African experience, however, should not be read as suggesting that wide-scale social mobilization will necessarily lead to an expansion of rights. Far too often analyses of social movements imply this conclusion by focusing only on successful cases of rights extension. Joe Foweraker and Todd Landman offer an important correction by demonstrating through their analysis of Brazil, Chile, Mexico, and Spain that social movement mobilization and the practice of civil and political rights is in general reciprocal but not immediate or necessary. In other words, broad-based demands for greater rights do not necessarily produce regimes in which such rights are upheld. The authors demonstrate that Mexico actually experienced a decline in "rights-in-practice" during the 1970s and 1980s despite significant movement organizing during that period (1997, 117). A similar decline in rights occurred in South Africa in the late 1980s as civic activism and the actions of the UDF led to successive states of emergency during which the state detained and killed innumerable activists and ordinary black South Africans. Earlier peaks in mobilization in South Africa had produced similar clampdowns: the 1960 protest and police massacre in Sharpeville led to the banning of the leading antiapartheid movements (the ANC and PAC), and the 1976 student march and police shooting of school children in Soweto led to the banning of black consciousness movement organizations as well as outside gatherings deemed to be political.

In all the cases that Foweraker and Landman investigated as well as South Africa, demand making under authoritarian regimes became increasingly focused on rights-based claims as protest grew. But while Foweraker and Landman note the importance of material demands in motivating many protesters, they disqualify socioeconomic rights from their study, arguing that "they do not qualify as integral to the discourse of rights" (1997, 14). This focus on civil and political rights to the exclusion of socioeconomic rights contradicts the basis of much of the movement activism that they explore. By focusing on civil and political rights while defining material concerns as external to the definition of a democratic regime, the authors follow the dominant approach to studies of democratization (Arat 1999). They argue that demands shift "away from material and economic demands to political and civil demands" in the course of movement mobilization (Foweraker and Landman 1997, 163). It is certainly true that as social movement actors identify their lack of progress in attaining socioeconomic goals with an overall lack of democracy, they increase demands for political and civil rights. This does not mean, however, that other demands have been forgotten or become less important to local actors.

Civil and political rights are important not just as a significant set of rights, but they can also be employed as a strategic vehicle to achieving socioeconomic demands. Considering the Mexican case, Sergio Tamayo (cited in Cadena-Roa 2009, 116) demonstrates the increased focus placed by social movements on civil and political rights from the 1970s to 1994 even though this period saw the introduction of neoliberal economic reforms and increasing material hardship for many. Takeshi Wada (2006), investigating the period up to 2000, supports Tamayo's findings with quantitative evidence that demonstrates this increased focus on political rights. He concludes, contrary to Foweraker and Landman, that a focus on civil and political rights does not imply a decreased emphasis on socioeconomic demands. Wada argues: "The real importance of political rights lies in the fact that protesters are more likely to make political claims *strategically* even when their main goal is civil rights, social rights, or other issues." He adds: "This finding advances our understanding of democratization: durable and powerful democratic movements like the one in Mexico will emerge when they are closely—i.e., strategically— tied to people's everyday economic and material concerns" (2006, 96, emphasis in original). During any process of political democratization, which is by definition focused on the expansion of civil and political rights, these rights assume national prominence. This does not, however, imply that social movements are now no longer concerned with socioeconomic rights or that they do not employ civil and political rights as a means to securing greater socioeconomic rights.

As we have seen in this chapter, demands for political and civil rights did not replace material demands in the eyes of the protesters in South Africa. They simply expanded them. Movements pressing material demands continued to do so after the formal democratization process. They worked to demonstrate the indivisibility of political, civil, and socioeconomic rights, arguing that the promises of citizenship will be undermined in the absence of basic economic rights. In South Africa since the late 1990s (Ballard et al. 2005) as well as in many states across Latin America since the early 1990s (Almeida 2007; Stahler-Sholk, Vanden, and Kuecker 2007), material concerns have served as the basis for new mobilization under formal democracies. Examples of powerful present-day movements demonstrating the weakness of political rights in the absence of economic rights abound. In Brazil and Mexico, such movements include the broad-based Landless Rural Workers Movement (Movimento dos Trabalhadores Rurais Sem Terra, MST) and the teachers' strike and Popular Assembly of the Peoples of Oaxaca (Asamblea Popular de los Pueblos de Oaxaca).

Material concerns have remained central to the demands of the majority of South Africa's citizens whether or not they define themselves as "the poors." As the example at the beginning of this chapter suggests, even when claims are decidedly material, the debate is not merely over the particular demands that protesters make but also concerns who has a right to make those demands and what in fact he or she should reasonably expect. The capacity to aspire, so fundamentally repressed by the apartheid state, was encouraged by a wide range of movement actors and was not only fundamental to anti-apartheid resistance but also left a powerful legacy in present-day South Africa.[12] It is this capacity that encourages building on the discourse of rights to expand democracy. The very process of mobilizing and conscientizing provides a framework for the further pursuit and even expansion of rights.

3

Power to the People!

Social movements do not necessarily promote democracy.
They constitute a challenge. This challenge may be to
an established authority such as a state or regime, to commonly accepted ideas
and beliefs, to powerful nonstate actors such as international organizations or
corporations, or to other social movements. They draw on, redefine, and also
create collective identities to bring about some form of change or to resist the
changes sought by others. They are mobilizers seeking to raise their concerns
outside the sphere of institutionalized and bureaucratic politics, employing
tactics ranging from petitions and sit-ins to mass marches and targeted attacks.
Their aims and actions vary. As a result, their individual impact on democracy
is variable as well. Although the socially beneficial effects of movement organizing are often assumed, they are far from certain. This begs the question of
if and when movements and the actors and organizations that comprise
them might expand the proposals for democracy as they seek to challenge
authority.

There are innumerable reasons why they may not. First, popular organizations must not necessarily be emancipatory (Mamdani 1996; Ndegwa 1996).
They may seek to limit or reverse any expansion of rights. Second, movement
actors are often involved in the same conflicts along class, ethnic, religious, or
political lines that affect society as a whole (Fatton 1995). Such cleavages can
create zero-sum politics whereby one group's gain is immediately perceived
as another's loss. Third, popular organizations and movements working for
democracy may simply be crushed by the state. The repression of nonviolent
movements from Burma to Zimbabwe starkly illustrates the harsh methods
that states may employ. Finally, even social movements seeking to promote
democracy may bring about change that leads away from more-democratic
governance as fears of instability and violence lead powerful state and nonstate
actors to support greater restrictions on a broad range of citizens' rights.

Social movement mobilization may therefore lead to greater exclusion, conflict, state repression, or instability. Democratic outcomes, locally or nationally, cannot be assumed. Where they do occur, they require explanation. This chapter offers a pragmatic assessment of how and why social movement organizations operating in authoritarian contexts might employ democratic means and pursue democratic ends. We consider the key factors that influence the development and success of such strategies by investigating the South African civics. In order to tease out the comparative lessons of the South African case, the chapter concludes with a brief look at leading movement organizations in very different contexts. The Zapatistas in Mexico and the Movement for the Survival of the Ogoni People in Nigeria offer two examples of mobilization that garnered great international attention in the early 1990s. Like the civics, they began with material demands and, in the process of organizing, expanded their goals to press for broader political rights. Each, however, made different decisions concerning the participatory nature and goals of their organizations. This played a significant role in their development and achievements.

Movements as Promoters of Democracy

Too often movement success is measured by the swift enactment of policy changes, and in the case of democratization, the rapid expansion of formal rights. The expansion of legal protections and the institutional changes required to bring them into effect are clearly significant, but they are most often only part of longer struggles. To understand the deeper processes that bring about regime change, we must focus on shifts in societal actions, actors, and aspirations that may result from social movement mobilization and organization. There are three central avenues whereby social movements may work to bring about and expand democracy: by broadening the scope of demands, by including greater numbers of actors making claims, and by creating new, more participatory processes for organization.

First, as we have seen, movements often work to expand the scope of demands. For many people, participation in community-level organizations is motivated by daily material concerns and, at times, responses to sudden disasters. In instances such as the bus crash in Soweto and the more widely devastating 1985 Mexico City earthquake, disasters became the basis for increased community organizing to meet pressing needs. The Diepkloof Civic in Soweto and the Asamblea de Barrios (Assembly of Neighborhoods) in Mexico City (Hellman 1994; Ramírez-Saiz 1990) grew out of these human tragedies. These community organizations, when frustrated by a nonresponsive state, encouraged broader mobilization for greater rights buoyed by the hope that democracy might offer the best chance to address persistent poverty through the development of infrastructure, public services, and even health and welfare benefits. In this way, immediate material concerns were expanded to include demands for greater rights as movements helped to construct the space for present and future aspirations.

Second, successful social movements may expand the range of actors making demands. They work to increase popular participation to enhance their own power and influence. In South Africa, civics informally expanded the scope of citizenship and pressed the regime to formally acknowledge this larger group of actors, to consult with them, or at least to respond to them. People are often drawn to participate by the appeal of inclusion and voice both within the movement and through the movement. Movements that work to capitalize on these ideals may be rewarded with greater strength in numbers. Popular participation can thereby offer a grassroots-based mechanism for more-democratic governance. As leaders engage in a process of conscientizing, encouraging rights-based discourses and demands, ordinary people seek to make their demands heard and their actions count. This process underscores the influence of position. Ordinary people are not necessarily more democratically inclined than those who assume leadership positions, but they are more likely to support organizations when they believe their participation matters. This is demonstrated by the successful mobilization of South Africa's civic organizations under apartheid as well as their later dramatic decline.

Third, movement organizations may expand the participatory democratic experiences of ordinary people. These experiences may, in turn, encourage demands for a regime that incorporates some of the more successful democratic practices of local organizations. Although this process is by no means immediate or necessary, it can produce long-term institutional effects by providing a basis for the construction of democratic processes. As stressed earlier, not all social movement organizations will attempt to create democratic processes. Within movement organizations, a lack of stable structures and well-defined democratic procedures may lead to significant inequality in decision making. But when local organizations are able, despite the conditions under which they are forced to operate, to create participatory democratic processes, these experiments provide a stark contrast to authoritarian government practices. They offer the potential to create and reinforce mechanisms of accountability, including the need for leaders to engage in discussions of ideas in order to receive a popular mandate, to maintain processes of consultation, and to report back when they represent members in other forums. Participatory structures also serve as a training ground for future leaders as well as engaged citizens. They work to frame demands to help bring about regime transformation and to encourage aspirations for the continued development of a democratic regime.

The Twin Goals of Liberation and Democracy

South Africa's civic organizations pursued two potentially competing ideals: liberation through revolutionary means and democracy through participatory organization building. This leads to a number of central questions concerning the interaction of revolutionary and democratic goals. First, why did local community groups call for democracy? Why not simply demand liberation by whatever means necessary? On one hand, groups might endorse democracy to demand the basic rights they had long been denied, such as the political freedom to organize and raise demands, the right to participate in governance, and the right to hold leaders accountable for their actions. Alternatively, such appeals for democracy might simply be rhetoric designed to energize domestic crowds and please potential foreign supporters. This raises a second set of questions. How committed were the civics to democratic models? Did the focus on participatory organization-building constrain their revolutionary potential? To address these questions, we must now investigate the actions of civic leaders and supporters as well as the meanings they attributed to their actions. These various meanings can be deduced both from statements given at the time, recorded in court proceedings and newsletters, and from more recent, retrospective interviews.

Analysts discussing the civics in South Africa have all too often understood them as either local organizations engaged in a project of democratization (Swilling 1992a, 1992b) or part of a revolutionary struggle for hegemony (Shubane 1992; Friedman 1992). The tendency for most commentators to sit in one camp or the other has obscured the important interaction of the contrasting currents of democracy and hegemony that exist within single organizations. At the ANC's National Consultative Conference held in Zambia in 1985, both of these approaches toward civic organizing were discussed. In the first discourse, civics were described as embodiments of direct and popular forms of democracy. Within the second discourse, they were presented as actors pursuing liberation by working to make the townships ungovernable (Steinberg 2000, 186). The dual goals of liberation and democracy were matched by two complementary projects: a tearing down of old structures to support liberation and a building up of new structures to develop democracy. Participants in the struggle often found the first goal of challenging the oppressive institutions of the past less difficult than laying the groundwork for new institutions. Tearing down the old involved largely spontaneous acts of uprising, violence, and destruction, while building up required the creation of viable mass-participatory institutions.

Leaders at various levels of the civic structures have argued that grassroots civics were the key to both the development of democracy and the revolutionary liberation process. The ANC, in contrast, while recognizing the importance of the civics as a link between national-level organizations and grassroots participants, tended to emphasize the importance of liberation over democratic practices. Although the ANC in exile sought to strengthen and encourage the civics, it also attempted to direct them. An internal commission report of the ANC's 1985 conference argued that the civics' "main characteristic is that they operate at the primary grassroots levels. As such, they are of strategic importance in reaching and mobilizing the masses. Because they deal with bread and butter issues, they have an immense potential for galvanizing a whole community. At the same time many of these civic bodies have a tendency towards confining their activity to the narrow limits of specific issues, and their leaders tend to inhibit their members from participating within the context of the political struggle. Their mass base, however, offers a tremendous potential for converting them into militant organizations" (ANC 1985, 14).

This ANC critique directly challenged the organizing strategies of most civics. ANC leaders were frustrated by the focus on local material issues first and assumed that this would diminish the civics' role in the broader struggle. In this way, ANC leaders often misunderstood and indirectly undermined a central strength of the civics. This quotation also reinforces the argument made by civic leader and ANC member Patrick Lephunya that the civics were not "an ANC child." From the perspective of many ANC leaders in exile, the civics were often undisciplined, even misguided. The ANC repeatedly argued that the immediate pursuit of liberation, rather than the establishment of local democratic practices, must be the primary emphasis of local organizing. It championed a "people's war" led by the ANC's military wing, MK, which was increasing its attacks on targets inside South Africa in the 1980s (Seekings 2000, 162).

Within the civics, ideals of democracy and revolution existed side by side. A discourse of democracy emphasized the building of grassroots mass-participatory organizations to allow communities to act on their own behalf, while a revolutionary discourse stressed the need for unity within these organizations to bring about a process of dramatic change. Civic leaders and supporters most often described the key elements of this democracy as accountability of leaders, consultation, inclusion of the greatest number possible in decision-making processes, and freedom of expression (Cherry 2000; UDF

1987 [March], 26–28). This goal was both ideologically driven and pragmatic since the democratic aspect of the structures attracted township residents, and the empowerment of these residents benefited local civics. First, the civics' power was directly tied to the level of community participation in their activities; more community participation meant more civic power. Second, residents welcomed the opportunity to help determine which issues should be addressed in their communities and how they should be addressed. A former Sowetan civic leader explained: "What people appreciated [most] was that whatever happened within the [civic] was [a result of] issues or matters that they themselves had raised and participated in the decision-making process and that gave them a sense of confidence and a sense of belonging. For the first time, people in our country could dictate their own lives" (Buthelezi, interview, July 22, 1997). Although the representative nature of local civic structures varied from area to area, overall they offered an important departure from the clearly unrepresentative apartheid local councils.

Civic activism led to the increased politicization of communities, the rise of the rent boycott as a strategy, and the popularization of consumer boycotts. These were all components of what was commonly called "people's power." As the struggle intensified in the mid-1980s, the participatory structures of the civics were increasingly employed to demonstrate the power of township organizations and to produce hegemonic discourses (Carter 1991, 192). Democratic practices were uneven but continued to form a key part of the domestic movement. By late 1986, however, the state of emergency had pushed most forms of community activism underground and dampened much of the optimism of the early 1980s. The state banned organizational meetings for almost all groups, and the South African Defense Force patrolled the townships, which were transformed from a state of virtual civil war to one of state-imposed martial law. Still, the precedents and accomplishments of the early 1980s were not forgotten. The organizing and mobilizing actions of the civics would have powerful long-term implications for community- and national-level politics. It is therefore crucial to understand what people's power entailed.

People's Power

In early 1984, as civic organizations across the country sought to find the best means to incorporate the largest number of township residents into their activities, activists in Cradock led by a former school teacher, Matthew Goniwe, pioneered a new organizational model that was to revolutionize civic action. The street-committee structure was developed to link township residents in a tiered representative system. Yard associations would elect representatives to attend block meetings, which would then elect representatives to attend street meetings, which would then elect representatives to township-level civic meetings. The plan was based on an adaptation of the M-plan devised by Nelson Mandela for the ANC in the early 1950s. Although Mandela's M-Plan was never widely implemented, Goniwe seized on the ANC leader's idea. While Mandela's plan had been designed for the underground ANC to create a structure through which leaders could secretly communicate with ANC members, Goniwe used the tiered system as a means to incorporate greater numbers into participatory structures.[1] Instead of a largely top-down clandestine organization, the tiered civic structure would ideally encourage communication from the grassroots and would allow for smaller meetings, which were less likely to attract the attention of the authorities. Mbulelo Goniwe, Matthew Goniwe's nephew, argued: "We felt that we needed to adopt it [the M-plan] to the conditions that we were in then. . . . We were operating legally" (Goniwe, interview, August 8, 1997). In Lingelihle, the African township outside white Cradock, local organizers were assigned to visit each house and tell residents about the need for street committees and the purpose they would serve (Mene, interview, August 8, 1997). Residents were invited to attend meetings, and a project was initiated to train leaders "to be exemplary in every respect" (Lodge 1991, 74).

At the time that the Cradock Residents' Association (CRADORA) began organizing street committees, legal organization was possible, but it was difficult. During 1984, approximately one hundred detentions occurred nationally each month, primarily in the area around Johannesburg but also in the Eastern Cape and elsewhere (Coleman and Webster 1986, 113–15). The numbers represented sharp increases from the previous year. Under increased pressure, the government continued to crack down on activists using the 1982 Internal Security Act to justify "indefinite preventative detention." Police also used numerous other methods to intimidate activists and members of a wide range of community organizations. "Call-in" cards would be left at individuals' homes, requiring them to report to a local police station for an interrogation, which might lead to indefinite detention. Offices of township organizations were raided, documents were confiscated, telephones tapped, and individuals followed. The apartheid state also used intimidation tactics to keep organizations such as the SCA from finding venues for their meetings; if a venue was found, meetings were often banned.[2] Activists received death threats, their cars and homes were vandalized, and even their pets were not safe (Coleman and Webster 1986, 119–21). All outdoor meetings remained banned, and indoor meetings were also increasingly banned. Under these conditions, the development of more-localized forms of organization became imperative.

Power to the People!

Street committees became the key to civic strength in the mid-1980s. Through their structures, they became a tool for "obtaining legitimate consensus" within an area (Lodge 1991, 82; Pashe, interview, July 3, 1997). Derek Swartz, a member of the UDF executive committee, described the street committees as an attempt to involve ordinary township residents "in democratic organizations and structures and decision-making processes." People were told, "In the streets where you live you must decide what issues affect your lives and bring up issues you want your [local civic] organization to take up. We [the UDF leadership] are not in a position to remove debris, remove the [night-soil] buckets, clean the streets and so on. But the [local civic] organization must deal with these matters through the street committees" (quoted in Riordan 1992, appendix, 9). Civic activists repeatedly stressed the importance of material concerns. Swatz's statement demonstrates the connection between these material necessities and the democratic participatory nature of the civics. People were encouraged to engage in local structures to determine how best to address urgent needs. The very first sentence of SCA's self description in its newsletter also underlined the connection: "SCA is a democratic civic organization primarily concerned with the bread and butter problems of Soweto residents. It is an organization of the people, stressing the need for people to unite and take an active part in solving their problems" (SCA 1984, 13). This notion of civics as participatory bread-and-butter organizations was repeated across the country.

People's power was also repeatedly described as an attempt to bring democratic practices to the grassroots by creating a "democratic sub-stratum or sub-culture" within a climate of repression (Saloojee 1987, 17). In a 1984 survey of township residents, respondents indicated that their primary reason for supporting the UDF and its affiliated organizations such as the civics was the fact that they "fight for democracy" (Swilling 1988).[3] UDF and SCA statements as well as popular surveys demonstrate at least rhetorical support for democracy. This begs several questions: Why was democracy such an important aspect of local organization in South Africa? What form would the idealized practice of this democracy take, and what was the experience of this democracy on the ground? Each of these questions will be addressed in turn.

First, the emphasis on democratic practice within local civic organizations was certainly pragmatic. This was true for a number of reasons at a range of levels from the local to the global. At the global level, the demand for democracy worked to rally support for the "just fight" against apartheid institutions. Although outside support for any self-proclaimed democratic organization was far from assured, local organizations that could claim they were working to build democracy often benefited from various forms of assistance from nongovernmental organizations in the West as well as a few progressive states, particularly the Scandinavian countries. At the national level, actors such as the UDF encouraged democratic organizations as a direct contrast to the non-democratic nature of the apartheid state. Democracy, understood as majority rule and popular participation, was also a winning proposition for opposition organizations that claimed to have the support of a large portion of the country's disenfranchised population, and therefore a majority of the potential electorate in a nonracial democracy.

At the local level, democratic organization also made practical sense. Writing of American experiments in participatory democracy, Francesca Polletta makes an argument that is just as relevant to South Africa's civics as it was to American civil rights organizations: "Talking through issues and options enabled people to connect local injustices to national policies, exposed them to diverse rationales for participation, and helped them negotiate short- and long-term goals" (2002, 204). Tiered democratic structures such as the street committees encouraged greater community participation and established a clear network for communication. It was crucial for organizers to incorporate residents into civic organizations so that they felt that they "owned" the structures and would work to keep them functioning despite state repression. The UDF journal, *Isizwe*, argued that it was "necessary to deepen and democratize the organization, so that the struggle would survive the loss of leadership" (UDF 1986 [March], 10). If hundreds or even thousands of residents were integrated into various tiers of the structure of a local civic, simply jailing a few leaders or banning mass meetings would not wipe the organization off the map. Well-organized community associations could instead meet in smaller groups and pass their concerns and resolutions on to other levels of the civic structures via the tiered network of communication.

Popular support for local leaders also acted as a form of insurance for the leaders and their families. A local civic leader argued: "If I am elected today as the chairperson of the street, then I got arrested tomorrow, that means the whole street is responsible for my family, to see to it that my family eats [while I am detained]" (Mbata, interview, July 17, 1997). Democratic street committees also encouraged leaders to pursue actions local residents would support. Popular programs were simply more likely to succeed than those that leaders sought to press upon unwilling residents. Through its tactics of repression and exclusion, the nondemocratic state had actually created an environment within which a democratic response was often the most effective vehicle for its opposition.

The form of democracy that civic leaders and supporters most often mention does not follow the liberal, elite model (Schumpeter 1947; Dahl 1971) that

Westerners and many civil society theorists (Putnam 1993, 2000) most often associate with the term "democracy." Civic leaders instead preached a form of participatory democracy (Bachrach 1967; Pateman 1970; Polletta 2002) that was in practice a mix of participatory and representative democracy. The idea of simply electing leaders once every few years (as in established Western democracies) and having little interaction with those leaders between elections was commonly criticized as elitist and far too restricted. Leaders consistently stressed the need to create a system that would empower all members of society, particularly the poor and oppressed. An article titled "Democracy" in the March 1987 issue of *Isizwe* argued: "We are struggling to build a future SA in which the broad working masses of our country have a real control over their lives. This means control over *all* aspects of their lives—from national policy to housing, schooling and working conditions. This, for us, is the essence of democracy" (UDF 1987 [March], 21, emphasis in original). This ideal participatory system also included a strong critique of capitalism and was repeatedly distinguished from various versions of liberal democracy. Models from other revolutionary struggles such as those in Nicaragua and the Philippines were offered as examples of "daily democracy."

The liberal democratic model was often slighted for emphasizing debate and pluralism above all else. Though leaders of civic organizations and the UDF often stressed the need for debate, they also placed limits on it. Criticism had to be constructive, and debate had its time and place and could not endlessly continue. Clearly these criteria were subjective. The underlying fear was that too much debate and a lack of explicitly defined goals would undermine the project of liberation by weakening the prospect for united action. The need for unity was consistently stressed whether at the level of the local community or in the country as a whole or even beyond the country's borders. This is made clear in civic documents and statements, such as the description of yard committees in an Alexandra Action Committee (AAC) flier: "The yard committee remains the mouthpiece of the people to represent their views in the running of their township. It also has the task of building democratic values, discipline and a sense of responsibility to maintain unity and common objective in the people" (AAC 1986, 3).

Ideally, the civics represented a unified community of residents asserting ownership of local areas and wresting control from the apartheid state. But the struggle was not just against the apartheid state but also among rival political interests within the opposition. By the mid-1980s, most civics had affiliated with the UDF and had become relatively open supporters of the ANC. Members of other political movements were less enthusiastically welcomed into civic structures, and those who challenged popular civic programs were often accused of supporting alternative movements or parties. Hostel residents living in the townships, largely men who were forced to leave their families behind in the so-called homelands while they worked in urban centers, often formed their own hostel residents' associations, which would later form a national structure in opposition to the civics. Concerned residents' associations also formed in many townships. Some allied themselves with civics; others stood as alternative associations. This diversity of associational groups does not minimize the importance of the civics, for they were the largest network of local groups across the country. It does, however, underscore the fact that the civics did not represent all township residents, and their claims to unify all residents had the potential to lead to coercive actions.

Creating Consensus

The civics generally operated on consensus, for their campaigns' success depended on widespread community support. Civic structures employed the tiered street-committee structures and mass meetings, where possible, to devise and implement programs. Within street-committee structures, the degree of democratic practice was strongly affected by the selection of leaders in that street. Some local leaders did attempt to rule via patronage and coercion (Lucas 2000), but the use of patronage by civic leaders was starkly limited. The most attractive patronage resources, such as housing, jobs, and business licenses, were all controlled by those in the pay of the apartheid state, particularly town councilors. Those with access to such resources were therefore the same people who were commonly labeled "collaborators," ostracized, and, at times, forcibly driven out of the townships.[4] Given the support that most residents offered to leaders who helped them organize to address their daily needs, most leaders found it much more effective to emphasize participatory democracy rather than the relatively minimal benefits of any patron-client relationships they might be able to establish.

Coercion certainly did exist but was also limited in important respects. First, it is important to separate the actions of township residents in general from those of the civic leaders and supporters in particular. Oft-repeated moments such as Winnie Mandela's address to a crowd in Munsieville (West Rand), when she stated, "Together, hand in hand, with our boxes of matches and our 'necklaces,' we shall liberate this country" (SAIRR 1986, 515), have supported the impression that much township activity against the apartheid state was based on violence.[5] Mandela's alleged statement referred to the gruesome practice of forcing a tire filled with gasoline over a presumed collaborator and setting it on fire. Between September 1984 and February 1987, an estimated "660 people were burned to death, over 300 through necklacing" (Lodge 1991, 142). There was clearly significant violence in the townships perpetuated by both state and nonstate actors, but it is crucial to note that most civic leaders across the country argued for nonviolent protest. Evidence regarding the actions of civic leaders such as the extensive documentation and testimony in support of the defense in the Delmas treason trial as well as the trial of the Alexandra Five (Abel 1995) demonstrated that civic leaders worked to discourage violence. They followed a pragmatic policy of nonviolence whenever possible since they knew that while violence might draw attention to their demands, state responses to such violence could devastate local organization and action. A former civic organizer commented: "There were incidents, but it was not the norm. There were incidents where one or two people would buy [during the consumer boycott] and maybe their groceries were spilt. One or two persons would send their children out to school during the [schools] boycott; the youths would go to that house and demand that those children come back and join the boycott, or one or two houses would be burned. But we were consistently, consistently condemning such acts, because we felt we did not have the capacity to meet violence with violence, so we took nonviolence as our strategy" (Goniwe, interview, August 8, 1997).

Surveys of township residents in the Eastern Cape and elsewhere have demonstrated that the level of coercion to support civic actions was generally low, and certainly much lower than state actors quoted in the press or at treason trials claimed. When violence was used, it was most often on the part of youths acting without the consent of civic leaders or broader civic structures (Cherry 2000; Helliker, Roux, and White 1989; Roux and Helliker 1986; Frankel et al. 1987; Planact 1989).[6] The increase in violence in many townships after the removal of civic and student leaders during the state of emergency supports this point and underlines the complicity of state actors in many violent episodes. Janet Cherry's findings in Kwazakele, outside Port Elizabeth, also demonstrate the strong support that residents who worked within the civics voiced for "their" structures. Those inside civic structures overwhelmingly described them as representative and highlighted the democratic aspect of the structures as a key reason for participating. Those outside the civic structures, in contrast, generally defined them as nondemocratic and exclusive (Cherry 2000). Given the rather starkly drawn lines (by the mid-1980s) delineating those who supported civic and UDF structures from those who did not, these opposing viewpoints are not surprising.

Still, the structure of both street committees and mass meetings offered a limited experience of democracy. When residents met either in local committee meetings or mass meetings (while they were still possible), everyone ideally had a chance to make his or her voice heard, but election procedures were compromised by a lack of anonymity. Most areas used a show of hands to vote, which meant that supporters and dissenters could be easily identified. Given the heightened fear of informers in the townships as the decade progressed, it was at times difficult to disagree with popular measures. Once a majority had decided on a specific action, all members were then expected to support the action. Many township residents, however, seemed to feel this practice was just, arguing that it was similar to the actions of a democratic state, which would enforce compliance with its laws once legislation was approved (Helliker, Roux, and White 1989, 43). Numerous civic leaders also remarked that their proposals were, at times, quashed in mass meetings or street meetings when a resident with a dissenting view was able to attract greater support for his or her alternative plan. Such alternative plans were often more radical or confrontational than the ones civic leaders had suggested.

Women in the civics were starkly underrepresented within leadership. While women were most often the early organizers around the material issues that led to the formation of the civics and comprised many of the rank-and-file members at the yard and block level, they were generally sidelined as organizations grew. In the case of the Zwide Residents' Association, for example, local residents were alarmed by a sharp increase in water service charges. The original group of residents that registered a complaint with the area manager was mainly composed of women. The manager told the women that not they but their husbands would be able to meet with the chief director of the administration board. A group of men was then selected to attend the meeting as the Zwide Residents' Association (Riordan 1992, 9). In this case, it was an official's pronouncement that effectively transformed a group originally dominated by women into one that would be run by men. While the reason for this particular shift may have been unusual, almost all townshipwide civics across the country were run by men. At meetings, men's voices dominated discussion. In group interviews conducted by the author after 1994, this pattern continued to repeat itself. The muted voice of approximately half of the defined community underscores significant weaknesses in the democratic representivity of the civic structures as well as the fact that local civics were far from immune to the power hierarchies operating within the communities in which they formed.

Violence under People's Power

As township activism grew, so did state-based violence. In May 1985 three PEBCO executive officers, including the president Qaqawuli

Godolozi, disappeared on their way to the Port Elizabeth airport.[7] In June four Cradock area organizers, including Matthew Goniwe, the leader of CRADORA, disappeared on their way back from a UDF meeting in Port Elizabeth.[8] All were later found dead. Massive gatherings were planned for the Cradock Four's funeral on July 21, 1985, but just after midnight on the twenty-first, a state of emergency was declared across much of the country. Within four days almost 1,000 priests, lawyers, students, community activists, and labor leaders were detained (Murray 1987, 242); within three months over 5,000 people were detained. Leaders and members of PEBCO and the SCA, among many others, were taken into custody. Many were tortured, and deaths related to political violence rose significantly. Prior to the state of emergency, an average of 1.5 people died per day over a ten-month period; after the enactment of the state of emergency, 3.5 people died per day (Coleman and Webster 1986, 126).

Under the state of emergency, another form of people's power began to grow: people's courts. Similar to other aspects of people's power, people's courts flourished where the best-organized community structures already existed: primarily in the Eastern Cape and the Transvaal, which included the greater Johannesburg area. In contrast to the so-called kangaroo courts, nonstate courts that were often run by local apartheid functionaries, particularly councilors, or by small bands of youths or gangs, the people's courts were intended to emphasize discussion and education (SCA 1987, 3). They ideally relied on peer pressure to discipline those found guilty of offenses ranging from fighting to theft and some criminal violence. More-serious criminal cases such as murder were left to state officials and state courts. These new structures created by civic organizations and run by street committees, when successful, worked to replace the violent kangaroo courts with forms of consensual, nonviolent justice. The state responded by demonizing them. It portrayed the courts as brutal, violent forums for mob justice (Buthelezi, interview, July 22, 1997; Kobese, interview, August 6, 1997). Despite its efforts, the state was able to produce almost no conclusive evidence of the involvement of people's courts in murders or necklacings (Seekings 1989, 128).

Civic and UDF leaders set up general criteria for the operation of people's courts, stressing the need for popular support and nonviolent methods of action. The March 1986 issue of *Isizwe* discussed people's courts as an important aspect of the development of people's power but repeatedly stressed that such courts could be organized only where they received broad community support and were run by "democratically elected persons" (UDF 1986 [March], 8). In Alexandra, civic leaders established numerous courts, and their experiences serve as an example of both the greatest successes and the challenges surrounding the establishment of such structures. In 1986, civic leaders, through the newly formed AAC, established street committees and local courts and encouraged residents to report their problems to the civic structures (Mayekiso 1996b). These community networks were employed not only to resolve disputes but also to patrol the streets at night. This led to a widely reported decrease in crime and late-night bar brawls as well as a reported 60 percent decrease in complaints filed with the police (Lodge 1991, 136–38). In Alexandra a local newsletter proclaimed in May 1986: "Residents are no longer reporting cases to the police. Cases are being handled by the People's Courts" (*Speak*, 1).

Transcripts of court proceedings entered into evidence in the 1987 trial of five Alexandra civic leaders demonstrate the court's workings.[9] One case involved a sixty-four-year-old man who accused a much younger man of theft and initially argued that the young man required a good beating (*sjamboking*). During the proceedings, the two were encouraged to talk to each other, and interpreters were provided to facilitate the discussion. Once the accused agreed to give up drinking, the judge convinced the relatives of the accused to let him live with them, arguing: "You cannot hope to rehabilitate a renegade, a vagabond who does not even have a place to stay." It was agreed that the faithful execution of the agreement would be monitored by the civic (Abel 1995, 322–23). Well-organized civic structures offered training to community court leaders in addressing situations such as disputes between neighboring families, conflicts within households, and accusations of witchcraft and other practical problems (Lephunya, interview, July 24, 1997). Parties involved in disputes were encouraged to come to some form of agreement, and community pressure was intended to reinforce these agreements. In the words of a civic leader from the Eastern Cape: "If you are unruly in the area, the community will reject you; . . . it was an effective means of governing" (Mali, interview, August 5, 1997).

After the declaration of the complete state of emergency in 1986, the courts fell into disarray, and the sense of order and discipline that civic leaders had worked to create was dramatically undermined. In townships such as Alexandra, the leaders who had overseen the court operations were detained, and in some cases unaffiliated youths took over the courts. These youths were often not part of established organizations since both the civic and the youth structures had been decimated by the jailing of leaders and the banning of organizations and meetings. This was the exact situation that the writers of the *Isizwe* article quoted earlier had hoped to avoid. As a result, the courts became violent (Mhlongo, interview, July 1, 1997). In communities such as Alexandra, reports of crime increased significantly, and the actions of the courts worked to discredit the idea of popular justice. It was not until the end of the decade and the end of the state of emergency that civic leaders were able to regain control of the courts. In Alexandra, with the help of the Community Dispute

Resolution Trust, civic leaders established the Alex Justice Center, where community members were trained in paralegal skills to advise residents and act as mediators (Stavrou 1992; Van der Merwe 1994).[10]

People's power created many other precedents for the postapartheid period. These included the development of alternative curricula for teachers, the creation of people's clinics, the occupation of land or vacant housing, the reinstatement of residents in their homes after evictions, the organization of neighborhood clean-up programs, the reconnection of electricity cut off by local authorities, the creation of soup kitchens, and the development of people's parks by clearing rubbish from vacant lots.[11] The purpose of each of these actions was at least twofold. First, they all aimed to meet pressing needs such as housing and clean park spaces for children. Second, each of these actions was designed to encourage community organization to present an alternative to authoritarian apartheid structures. Richard Mdakane stressed the need for continued organizing in his announcement of an Alexandra clean-up campaign in the late 1980s: "The main objective is to eliminate fears instilled into our community since the declaration of the State of Emergency and to re-mobilize our people into their organization" (AAC 1989, 1).

In some areas, self-defense units, popularly referred to as SDUs, were also formed. They were largely created in response to the rising levels of state-sponsored violence from the mid-1980s to early 1990s. In Alexandra, for example, SDUs were formed in the aftermath of a well-orchestrated attack against several local activists. In April 1986, on the same day that the local apartheid council finally collapsed, the homes of numerous activists were burned and stoned, and a number of people were assaulted; some were killed. These "vigilante" actions were similar to those that occurred in other townships in the Vaal, Soweto, and the Eastern Cape. At a mass rally held at the Alexandra stadium, residents agreed to form self-defense units, which the local civic, the AAC, played a key role in establishing. In Soweto the SCA worked with the ANC to establish SDUs after a sequence of police killings. In both cases, the stated purpose of the SDUs was to protect residents, but as violent attacks increased dramatically in the next few years, SDUs were drawn into pitched battles against state authorities and their allies. A Sowetan civic leader involved in the local SDU argued, "[We were focused on] arm[ing] ourselves and defend[ing] ourselves against these marauding policemen" (anonymous Sowetan civic leader, interview, July 1997). By the time SDUs were formed, government actions had reduced many communities to a state of extreme fear, at which point the concern for self-defense overwhelmed almost all other priorities. Under these extreme circumstances, democratic practice became secondary. Mass meetings were banned; therefore one of the best opportunities for resident participation and decision making was no longer available. By late 1986, with the important exception of Soweto, very few civic structures in South Africa were still functioning.

People's Power Revisited

Although the South African state was able to temporarily incapacitate the vast majority of civic associations and many other UDF affiliates after 1986, it also suffered as a result of the clampdown. Civic organizations and their allies in the UDF had pressed the ruling NP into a corner. The crackdown on opposition in the latter half of the 1980s drained the state's financial resources, fractured the NP's already ailing support base, and led to greater international sanctions against the apartheid regime. This economic and political weakening of the state made it more susceptible to a range of popular and elite pressures (Wood 2000), which together led to what Timothy Sisk has called a "mutually hurting stalemate" (1995, 14) between government and extraparliamentary opposition forces. Despite its control of the institutions of the state, the government realized it could not unilaterally establish the peace and stability necessary to address the country's political and economic problems. The ANC, on the other hand, had the support of the majority of the population but lacked the military and economic resources to take control of the state.

In early 1990, President F. W. de Klerk announced to parliament the unbanning of thirty-three resistance organizations including the ANC, the UDF, and several leading civics, including CRADORA, PEBCO, the SCA, and the VCA. He opened the doors for negotiations, and a new phase in the struggle. In response the civics worked to intensify their past campaigns while also negotiating with local authorities. Early 1990 saw a significant rise in the number of protest actions led by civics as well as the continuing spread of the rent boycott. Consumer boycotts also increased, particularly in towns governed by the Conservative Party (CP) such as Brakpan and Alberton, whose businesses were boycotted by residents of the nearby townships of Thokoza, Katlehong, and Vosloorus (*Star*, June 2, 1990, 1; October 30, 1990, 12). Just two days after de Klerk's groundbreaking speech, the Alexandra Civic Organization (ACO) organized a march of fifty thousand residents to demand the resignation of the township council; the council agreed to "consider" their demands (TCLSAC 1990 [May], 15). In March the SCA called for all Soweto residents to march in support of similar demands including the creation of nonracial democratic cities with a single tax base and affordable service charges

Soweto March

All Soweto residence are invited to join the march on the 24th March 1990.

We demand that all councillors must resign immediately and join the people's organisation.

We demand that Soweto and Johannesburg should be combined to be one non-racial democratic city.

We also demand transfering of houses to the people and affordable service charges, which we can only get if Johannesburg and Soweto share a single tax base.

Date : 24-March-1990
Place of depature : Elkah stadium
Destination : UBC
Time : 9 00 am

Long live Soweto Civic Assosiation

Issued by SCA, SOYCO, SOSCO, FEDTRAW and COSATU local

Soweto march flier (1990)

(SCA 1990). Around the country, civic supporters took to the streets in record numbers.

The number of participants in the rent boycott increased significantly. By July 1990, the majority of the Transvaal's eighty-two townships were withholding rent with some townships such as Tokoza boasting a 100 percent boycott (*Star*, May 1, 1990, 5). This increase in the number of boycotters brought about a rapid rise in the amount of arrears owed to the Black Local Authorities (BLAs) (SAIRR 1991/92, 355). The Transvaal Provincial Authority (TPA), for example, spent its entire annual budget trying to keep the councils afloat for just six months (Swilling, Cobbett, and Hunter 1991, 189). By August, provincial authorities suspended emergency bridging finance to the BLAs. This lack of resources pushed many local councils to the breaking point, forcing the resignation of town councilors and threatening communities with service cutoffs.[12] By the end of 1990, 40 percent of the BLAs in South Africa had collapsed (Shubane 1991, 72). At this time, the ANC was still quite weak at the local level, so civics were seen as the only organizations that could attempt to represent local community interests vis-à-vis the apartheid state. By the end of 1990, civic leaders in approximately ninety townships in South Africa (Swilling 1992a, 97) and fifty in the Transvaal alone were involved in wide-ranging local-level negotiations (Planact 1990a, 2).[13] The government was pressed to act and to acknowledge the fiscal need for nonracial government and a common tax base, but by acting quickly it hoped to pave the way for discussions that it could control (Swilling and Shubane 1990).

The first of these negotiations—one of the most successful examples for the civics—occurred in Soweto. By 1989 the city of Soweto was faced with a combined debt of over R700 million ($270 million), at least R200 million ($77 million) of which was a result of the withholding of rent and service charges (Planact 1989, 4). The city council was bankrupt and desperate to find a way to end the boycott before bridging finance from the TPA was cut off (Molzen and Mabin 1990). Prior government campaigns ranging from intimidation and violence to promises of infrastructural improvements had not brought about any improvement in payment levels.

In place of the SCA, which had been restricted under emergency regulations since 1987, a new body, the Soweto People's Delegation (SPD), was formed to open negotiations with the government. In March 1989 it presented five demands: the writing off of arrears, the transfer of houses to the people, the upgrading of services, the introduction of an affordable service charge, and the creation of a single tax base for Johannesburg and Soweto (Lodge 1991, 271). By August 1990 the SPD had reached a tentative agreement with the TPA and the local city councils that satisfied these five demands. After holding

Power to the People!

street-committee and mass meetings to inform Soweto residents of the agreement and seek their approval, the SPD signed the Soweto Accord on September 24, 1990, on behalf of the people of Soweto.[14] The final agreement provided for the write-off of R516 million (roughly $200 million), the entire amount of arrears owed by the residents to their local city councils, and an affordable interim service charge for municipal services and electricity. It also mandated the creation of a metropolitan chamber that would implement the SPD's demands and establish a nonracial, democratic local government system for the entire Central Witwatersrand region as well as the Greater Soweto People's Fund, to be used solely for development projects in Soweto (*Star*, August 31, 1990, 1). The agreement thus, at least officially, ended the Soweto rent boycott that had begun townshipwide more than four years earlier.

Despite the positive precedent set by the Soweto Accord, civic leaders in other areas attained widely varying degrees of success; most achieved significantly less than their comrades in Soweto (Shubane 1989, 37–40). In the words of one civic organizer: "The government had changed its attitude from one of trying to crush local organizations to trying to co-opt them" (Mzwanele Mayekiso, interview, May 27, 1997). Civics found that local authorities often "negotiated in bad faith" and were not willing or able to fulfill their obligations as detailed in the agreements. Civic leaders who signed agreements on behalf of entire township populations also found it difficult to encourage residents to pay (Planact 1990a, 1990b, 1991b). Participation in the rent boycott had become a means of signaling dissatisfaction with local government services. Residents understood payment as part of a social contract that required a certain level of services as well as respect for rate payers. They therefore resisted paying before seeing significant improvement in the townships. The participatory nature of the civics undermined leaders' attempts to convince residents to pay. It also demonstrated that leaders had little leverage to force communities to accept agreements that were contradicted by the basic material facts on the ground.

By mid-1991, despite the flurry of negotiations, rent boycotts continued in twenty-two townships in the Transvaal, seven of which were in areas where the local civic had negotiated an end to the boycott (Seekings, Shubane, and Simon 1993, 88). Even in highly successful negotiating experiences such as Soweto, civic leaders were often unable to implement the agreements. In many areas, state negotiators now began to doubt the power of the civics, an assumption they had formerly taken for granted. This decline in the perceived power of many civics led, in turn, to a decline in the role that many state and nonstate actors were willing to apportion them in the formal negotiation process to define new local government authorities and the democratic regime as a whole. Critics of the civics used the lack of civic control over the rent boycott as the key example of their ephemeral position in township communities.

For many of the reasons that the rent boycott proved to be so effective in the 1980s, it was extremely difficult to end in the 1990s. As civic negotiators met with local authorities to iron out deals for the future of their communities, they made promises to resume payments so that township conditions might be improved. This line of reasoning, however, directly contradicted the earlier position of the civics that services and housing must be improved *before* residents should be required to pay for them. Although most residents offered greater support to transitional authorities than to the old apartheid regime, they were still clearly concerned with local material conditions. These conditions did not improve during the transition process. Instead, many townships became even worse places to live as state funds to keep services operating ran out and state-sponsored violence reached new heights.

In Soweto the signing of the Accord brought about considerable but short-lived enthusiasm that change was indeed occurring in the township. Newspaper headlines read: "Soweto Payments 'Pick-Up'" and "Sowetans Queue to Pay Rent." Shortly after the signing of the agreement, town councils across greater Soweto reported increases in payments ranging from a mere 15 percent to 917 percent (*Star*, October 8, 1990, 3). Although payment levels definitely increased, they did not increase as much as the negotiators (on both sides of the table) had expected, nor did they stabilize at a high level of payment. On one side, the state argued that it needed residents to pay and be patient since improvements could not occur overnight. On the other side, residents had grown weary of government promises and had little faith in the state's willingness to uphold its end of the bargain. State actors proved to be incredibly slow, in some cases inactive, in implementing projects such as the transfer of housing and the upgrading of facilities and tended to prioritize the payment of staff when funds became available through community payments. Given the communities' long-standing adversarial relationships with local councilors, such funding priorities worked to further discourage payments.

By early 1991 the Soweto rent boycott was back in effect in response to popular frustration. State authorities reacted by threatening electricity and water cuts (*Star*, August 16, 1991, 13).[15] Civic leaders, following their communities, complained that although three months had passed, the councilors had not yet resigned, and township conditions and services had not yet improved. One civic organizer commented that the civics needed to "act drastically" to bring about real change: "The only way to act drastically is to make sure that they don't get the finance to run their activities so hence we are now just only

Power to the People!

saying we are not paying and if you can get rid of the councilors and all the officials there, we will start paying, and if you create a nonracial democratic chamber . . . we will start paying because we will be having confidence in those people" (Mbata, interview, July 17, 1997).

The difficulties experienced by civic leaders both in convincing their communities to uphold their end of the negotiated bargain and in pushing government actors to fulfill their promises prompted several analysts to point to the weaknesses of the civic structures and their reactive approach. Another frequent criticism of the civics concerned the question of their true support within the communities they claimed to represent. Steven Friedman argued: "While it would be folly to deny that civic associations are influential, their representativeness is not demonstrated. . . . The sole test of support to which civic associations have been subjected is the ability of those in the Transvaal to secure residents' compliance with rent boycott settlements and few, if any, have succeeded" (1992, 94). This statement, however, rests on a false understanding of what civics were in fact organized to do and what was possible in South African townships at this time.

Although civic leaders may have wished that they could control community interests and actions, the civics were established to give expression to community grievances and link local to national campaigns. The civics, at their finest, were participatory democratic organizations.[16] This model helped to create programs that appealed to large numbers of residents who felt a sense of shared ownership in their success. It helped to foster community solidarity in the struggle against apartheid and gave people a sense that they had control over their lives. The committee structures of the civics allowed large numbers of residents a voice in their organization and enabled the rapid sharing of information. Although the state often accused civics of forcing compliance with their campaigns through intimidation and other violent means, civic leaders were generally not capable of imposing their will on entire communities. Most civics were loose structures that included residents with varied interests. If the majority of the residents did not support a particular appeal, it would generally die a quiet death. The success of civic programs, such as the rent boycott, was due to its ability to connect the material struggles of residents to the larger political goal of ending apartheid. The lack of civic leaders' abilities to bring about a quick end to the boycott was due not to a weakness of the civic structures but rather to their participatory basis. Residents were simply not convinced that change was really on the way when local conditions were deteriorating. Although they were generally willing to support negotiations, the majority were not willing to increase payments until they saw change on the ground.

Social Movements as Promoters of Democracy—Lessons from Mexico and Nigeria

South Africa's civics effectively expanded democratic participation under a nondemocratic regime by broadening the scope of demands made by residents, including larger numbers of actors making claims, and creating spaces of democratic organization. While the democratic practices of civics varied across time and space, many local organizations encouraged residents to become engaged citizens who demanded accountable and responsive leadership. Local civic organizations overwhelmingly supported the ANC, but they also made decisions that were contrary to the wishes of the party and even of civic leaders. These experiments with democratic practices were dramatically weakened by the repressive context within which the civics were forced to operate. As state authorities arrested, detained, and tortured civic leaders and ordinary members, participatory structures proved difficult, at times impossible, to maintain. The fear of informants and the threats that supporters faced considerably decreased trust and tolerance of difference within many organizations. Although civic leaders claimed to welcome everyone in the context of the struggle against apartheid, by the mid-1980s the overwhelming majority of civic supporters were also ANC supporters. This is understandable given the fact that the overwhelming majority of black South Africans voted for the ANC in 1994, but the pressure for unity often made the inclusion of supporters of other antiapartheid parties such as PAC and AZAPO difficult. Overall, the civics played a leading role in bringing township residents into organizations that supported the struggle against apartheid. They could not, however, undo the fear and trauma that the brutal system of apartheid created. As a result, while they encouraged support for principles of participation and accountability, they did not create broader support for notions of political equality and tolerance for those outside the struggle as they defined it. It is hard to imagine how they could have accomplished this in the context of apartheid.

South Africa's civics serve as an example of both the strategic benefits of participatory democratic organizing as well as the limitations to such organizing under a repressive regime. A brief investigation of two quite different cases further underlines the strengths and limitations of social movement organizations as promoters of democracy. First, the Mexican case offers an excellent example of another regime that, similar to South Africa, saw decades of social movement mobilization before any significant move toward more-democratic governance. In Mexico a long and complex transition to democracy reached an important milestone with the 2000 defeat of the Partido Revolucionario

Institucional (PRI), which had dominated the political system for over seventy years. Second, the case of Nigeria offers an example of the stark repression of movement actors. Although mobilization in Nigeria in the early 1990s generated significant hope, it was unable to help bring about a change in regime. As one would expect, domestic and international contexts are crucial in explaining the different outcomes, but the mechanisms whereby organizations generate popular support are also significant.

Writing in the early 1990s, Judith Hellman, a leading analyst of Mexican politics, observed: "The democratizing influence of the popular movements on the Mexican political system has turned out to be very modest indeed" (127). She argued that this was largely due to the widespread clientelism and co-optation practiced by the long-ruling PRI, which left popular organizations with a difficult set of alternatives. On one hand, they could work with the state to receive material benefits for their supporters, an appealing option since most organizations were formed to address material demands. On the other hand, organizations might seek to define themselves as independent and take a critical stance toward government actions, but by doing so, they would forgo any material benefits (Hellman 1994, 133). Overall, Hellman's conclusions regarding the democratizing potential of Mexico's movements were discouraging at best. While she importantly pointed to the continuing role of clientelism in Mexican politics (Holzner 2006), she did not expect that a movement would successfully connect material needs to demands for greater political rights in order to break out of the Mexican state's politics of co-optation. In 1994, the Zapatistas (Ejército Zapatista de Liberación Nacional, the Zapatista Army of National Liberation, EZLN), who draw their name from Mexican revolutionary Emiliano Zapata, sought to do just that.

The movement has focused on the material demands of the indigenous community in Chiapas (Harvey 1998) but has also played an important role in the democratization of the Mexican state. Rooted in a struggle for land and survival, the Zapatistas have worked to change perceptions of indigenous people and draw attention to the ways in which the state has excluded and disenfranchised them. In this way, they have expanded the scope of political claim making and the population empowered to make such claims. The demands of the Zapatistas are framed in terms of material needs and autonomy as well as a call for "authentic" democracy and the enforcement of universal rights (Marcos 1995). Only five years after Hellmann's pessimistic conclusion concerning Mexican social movements and democracy promotion, Chris Gilbreth and Gerardo Otero offered a very different argument: "The social movement set in motion by the Zapatista uprising has been a driving force in Mexico's democratization" (2001, 7).

The Zapatistas have played a significant role in expanding national-level democracy in Mexico.[17] By exposing "inequality, oppression and exploitation," they effectively demonstrated the lack of representation in the party system and the weaknesses of an electoral system that had repeatedly returned a corrupt political elite to power (Cadena-Roa 2009, 123). Their actions and demands have worked to encourage a broader discourse of rights and opened space for other actors critical of the government (Lopez 2005). In doing so, they have "deepened the democratic debate" (Gilbreth and Otero 2001, 7). The Zapatistas have successfully expanded participation through an inclusive framing of their movement; the language and symbols they employ are designed to appeal to a broad audience and to create a sense of unity in a common struggle. This approach has worked to draw support from many organizations across Mexico and the world (Bob 2005; Esteva 2001; Harvey 1998).

The Zapatistas have also, importantly, created an organizational structure with a considerable degree of internal democracy (Barmeyer 2003). They have done so by drawing on local traditions to claim democratic practices as their own and have, like the civics, distinguished their understanding of democracy from a representative system of liberal democracy. The Zapatistas' redefinition focuses on democracy as a process based on discussion and listening, the education of citizens, and an ideal of leadership as "rule by obeying" (Swords 2008, 295). They have also stressed the centrality of women's rights as part of their demands and have given prominent voice to women leaders within the movement. A communiqué issued by the Indigenous Clandestine Revolutionary Committee in 1994 illustrates their reclaiming of democracy: "He who leads obeys if he is true, and he who follows leads through the common heart of true men and women. Another word came from afar so that this government was named and this work gave the name of 'democracy' to our way that was from before words traveled" (quoted in Nash 1997, 264). The Zapatistas have worked to put these ideals into practice through the formal creation in 2003 of the *caracoles*, five autonomous local government units, which are designed to combine participatory democracy with electoral democracy (Casanova 2005, 87). The governing councils include two representatives from each autonomous municipality who rotate frequently to allow maximum participation and accountability. While this may raise concerns regarding the continuity of this form of local self-government, it also works to deepen the role of participants in their own governance by including more community representatives and by curtailing the role of the EZLN political-military apparatus (Stahler-Sholk 2008).

It is important to note, however, that although the Zapatistas have effectively brought a greater diversity of demands and perspectives into the public sphere and in so doing have strengthened pressures for democracy at the national level and institutionalized participatory practices at the local level, they have experienced limited success in changing the stark material inequalities that helped to mobilize their actions. The government has offered some limited funding for poverty alleviation in Chiapas, but the Zapatistas have expected communities to refuse government aid (Swords 2008, 301). This policy has led to a substantial loss of indigenous Zapatista supporters. A former EZLN women's representative who felt pressed to leave the movement explained that the EZLN was unable to deliver basic necessities to the community. She argued that while the government did not offer much, "at least they [gave] something" (quoted in Barmeyer 2008, 517). The continuing militarization and violence in Chiapas underlines the great hardship and repression under which many still live.

In both Mexico and South Africa, social movements played a central role in bringing about a transition to formal democracy. Political rights were expanded in Mexico and increased even more dramatically in South Africa. But in both cases, socioeconomic rights lagged despite the work of social movement organizations. This situation resulted from each governments' responses to international economic pressures and the movements' lack of success in destabilizing a broader economic regime even as they successfully weakened local political regimes. In the case of Mexico, the North American Free Trade Agreement (NAFTA) was completed prior to the Zapatista uprising and determined the date of its launch. Although there was no shortage of public criticism of NAFTA, government leaders in both the United States and Mexico have defended the agreement and the broader framework of economic liberalization (Morris and Passe-Smith 2001). In South Africa, key ANC leaders were convinced, prior to their election to government, that greater economic liberalization was necessary to bring about economic growth (Habib and Padayachee 2000). The leadership of both countries therefore pursued both political and economic liberalization. South Africa and Mexico are not exceptions in this regard but rather followed a clear trend in the last three decades for newly democratizing states. This course was not the desired outcome for either the civics or the Zapatistas. The implications of this twofold process of liberalization will be explored later in this book.

While the civics and the Zapatistas did attain important successes, the experiences of Nigeria's social movements in the early 1990s offer a sobering reminder of the great risks involved in mobilizing against authoritarian regimes. In Nigeria in the 1990s, as in Mexico and South Africa in the 1980s, pressure for the expansion of political rights led to their further contraction. Although the Nigerian government did hold elections in 1999 after the sudden death of the country's military leader, these elections were neither free nor fair. Plagued by electoral manipulation and corruption, the Nigerian regime still fails to uphold many basic rights more than a decade after the end of military rule. Despite this fact, several movement actors have attained important, though small, victories. The Movement for the Survival of the Ogoni People (MOSOP), the closest Nigerian parallel to Mexico's Zapatista movement in its international appeal, offers the most dramatic example of these hard-won victories. Although it failed to attain most of its defined goals and suffered incredible repression, MOSOP has contributed to pressure for democracy in Nigeria.

MOSOP was one of the first local organizations formed in the Niger Delta region to engage and challenge the state. Its actions marked an important departure from earlier associations led by traditional leaders and community-development associations, which focused on obtaining basic social amenities from oil companies operating in the area (Ikelegbe 2001, 441). MOSOP was formed in response to the incredible material hardships faced by those living in Ogoni areas and the lack of basic human rights and democracy in the country as a whole. Ogoni communities lived, and continue to live, in stark poverty in a landscape devastated by oil drilling, flaring, and spilling. In 1990, under the regime of Major-General Ibrahim Babangida, MOSOP organizers drafted the Ogoni Bill of Rights, which listed material demands for a significant proportion of oil revenue as well as political demands for greater representation within a framework of self-determination (MOSOP [1990] 1992). While MOSOP initially presented its struggle as one of minority rights, its leaders realized that they would gain greater international attention by defining their actions within a context of environmental justice and, as repression increased, basic human rights. They were right; by shifting their framing, they gained the support of a number of leading international NGOs including Amnesty International, Human Rights Watch, the Sierra Club, and Friends of the Earth (Bob 2005). This external support and publicity helped to stimulate local mobilization. In January 1993, MOSOP organized the largest recorded protest in the Ogoni areas up to that time, including by their estimate three hundred thousand people (Welch 1995, 642).[18]

In June 1993, MOSOP offered a stark challenge to the government by calling for a boycott of the presidential elections, which it argued had been stage managed by the military dictatorship (Ikelegbe 2001, 458). The election proceeded, but once it became clear that the wrong candidate (from the perspective of the sitting government) would win, the results were annulled. This action led to waves of protest and corresponding repression. M. K. O. Abiola, the actual winner of the election with an estimated 59 percent of the vote (Lewis 1999, 144), fled the country after receiving death threats. Mounting public pressure forced Babangida to resign, but after a brief period of interim government, a military coup brought the brutal regime of Sani Abacha to power. Even then, there was still hope that a regime transition might occur. Abiola returned to Nigeria in June 1994 to claim his electoral victory but was accused of treason and imprisoned for what would prove to be the rest of his life. Once again protests and strikes were called, and the government responded with more arrests and violence. This series of events demonstrated that the changing governments were not immune to popular pressure but also that each was willing to use significant force to repress dissent. This was most acutely the case under Sani Abacha.

In Nigeria, successive national governments have exploited the potential for both inter- and intracommunal conflict to undermine challengers. As MOSOP engaged in ever-bolder challenges to the state, conservative Ogoni leaders withdrew their support (Bob 2005; Osaghae 2005). This split in MOSOP fueled factionalism among the Ogoni elite "and strengthened the determination of the state and oil multinationals to neutralize the Saro-Wiwa faction" (Obi 2000, 64–65). So-called ethnic violence by neighboring communities targeted the Ogoni, but movement leaders, many observers, and the head of a government-appointed committee investigating the violence argued that the 1993 violence that left over one thousand Ogoni dead was politically motivated (Osaghae 2005, 337–38; Obi 2000, 65). The following months saw similar so-called ethnic clashes and further attacks against Ogoni villages. The government also increased military maneuvers in Ogoni areas, leading to the destruction of many villages, great human rights violations, and numerous deaths (Bob 2005, 92; Human Rights Watch 1995).

In May 1994 the government of Sani Abacha accused Ken Saro-Wiwa and other MOSOP members of complicity in the killing of four conservative Ogoni leaders. Although there was no evidence that Saro-Wiwa or the others accused encouraged the killings, the state sought to depict the dead as loyal citizens and targets of a radical and violent movement. A quick military trial led to the execution of the accused in late 1995. MOSOP's international supporters were powerless to influence politics on the ground. Pleas by respected leaders such as Nelson Mandela were not enough to stop the hanging of the Ogoni nine. Although the United States and United Kingdom stopped exporting arms to Nigeria, and the country was suspended from the Commonwealth, as expected South Africa's call for a full embargo on Nigerian oil sales never materialized (Welch 1995).

The brutal outcome of MOSOP's quest for regional autonomy and greater control over oil resources may seem overdetermined given the great stakes for a notoriously violent regime, but MOSOP offers another lesson aside from its clear relevance to Nigeria's domestic context. In seeking to attract international support, MOSOP shifted its framework of demands to entice global NGOs and expanded its actions in a way that was targeted more toward building international attention than toward shoring up its national support within and beyond Ogoni-speaking communities. MOSOP did effectively expand the scope of the demands made by the Ogoni people and dramatically increased Ogoni participation in these rights-based claims, but it was less successful in enlarging its domestic support base.[19] It failed to address a central challenge in Nigerian politics—to overcome state strategies of exploiting divisions drawn along ethnic lines—and lost support among some leading members of the Ogoni-speaking community (Cayford 1996). MOSOP arguably put too much faith in international support, and its experience suggests the dangers of relying too heavily on outside actors. The success of South Africa's civics as well as that of the Zapatistas lay first and foremost in their local support base. International support in each case complemented, but could not take the place of, a broad range of domestic supporters.

MOSOP did, however, succeed on several fronts. Although it was not allied with the broader democracy movement in 1993, it did consistently call for nonviolent protest in an effort to peacefully extend the rights it deemed most crucial. It employed petitions, statements of rights, legal appeals, and international support to make its claims. There is little evidence of MOSOP's creation of internally democratic structures, but its activism and the state's response have encouraged the formation of a range of Nigerian associations including explicitly panethnic organizations and those focused on environmental and civil rights. It has also drawn the attention of both national and international organizations concerned with civil and political rights to the Niger Delta (Ikelegbe 2001). In this way, it has promoted a culture of rights-based demands. Although the oil-rich state was able to crush popular protest, MOSOP's central corporate target, Shell, was much more sensitive to the responses of consumers in the West and worked to improve its public image. Shell's missteps and pleas of innocence worked to further increase international attention, and in 2009 it agreed to pay $15.5 million to settle a suit alleging its participation in significant human rights abuses in the region (*New York Times*, June 9, 2009).[20]

Increased international awareness of the stark challenge faced by communities in the Niger Delta region continue to provide opportunities for other organizations to work to improve material conditions through environmental and human rights networks. This remains true even as more radical groups, such as the Movement for the Emancipation of the Niger Delta, have gained far greater press attention (Ukiwo 2007; Schmidle 2009). MOSOP paved the way for a broader discourse of rights: for autonomy on the model of the Ogoni Bill of Rights as well as for environmental and human rights. Its experiences also suggest the benefits of defining demands that will be relevant beyond a narrow ethnic constituency. In this way, like the Zapatistas, MOSOP has drawn attention to great domestic inequalities and encouraged further debate about how they might be addressed.

Each of these cases demonstrates that social movements do not necessarily or quickly bring about democracy, but the contentious processes in which they engage do offer the prospect for expanding demands, participation, and ultimately democracy itself. They offer this possibility not via the linear process that T. H. Marshall assumed, in which rights naturally unfold, but rather by the active challenge and contentious politics of social movement organizations. Although the tragic outcome of MOSOP's mobilization and the great shortcomings of democracy in Nigeria demonstrate that movement success cannot be assumed, the long struggles in South Africa and Mexico also show that movements can build on and expand even the small successes of past attempts to effect change. Both South Africa and Mexico became more democratic as their national governments formalized some of the rights that movements demanded. But neither of these movement organizations was able to achieve the dramatic material change that its organizers initially demanded. The next chapter demonstrates how formal regime change and the reduction of political inequality can actually work to mitigate pressure on governments to address material inequality.

4

Disciplining Dissent

We were used in order to further the interests of the private sector [and]
the government. We would be invited to go to give credibility to meetings throughout the country, and I am still bitter about the fact that
SANCO [the South African National Civic Organization] is being used.

Ntsokolo Daniel Sandi, interview, August 5, 1997

The frustration expressed by a civic leader in the Eastern
Cape three years into South Africa's new democratic
dispensation was often repeated by supporters of local civics and ordinary
citizens: their new democracy was not sufficiently accountable or responsive.
People were asked to attend meetings, but their inputs seemed to be ignored.
Democracy was not offering citizens the participatory and inclusive system of
governance for which they had fought. These shortcomings provide an important contrast to the often idealized image of South Africa's victorious struggle.
Because of the great sacrifices so many had made, expectations were high for
what democracy would mean in practice. Under apartheid, the opportunity
for real voice brought many to civic meetings and encouraged their participation in civic campaigns. The domestic antiapartheid movement extolled basic
principles of empowerment through participatory democracy. This ideal was
not forgotten with the ANC's election to government. Citizens who played a
role, raised their voices, and contributed to change in their country expected
to be empowered by their new regime.

South Africa is hardly unique in the central role that social movements
played in bringing about regime change or in its failure to fully realize popular
ideals of democracy. Popular mobilization was crucial to regime change in
countries in Latin America (Brazil, Chile, Peru, Uruguay), Eastern Europe

(Bulgaria, Czech Republic, Hungary, Poland), and other parts of the African continent (Benin, Malawi, Mali, Zambia). Each of these countries faces challenges in creating effective and accessible democratic institutions. In the decades since the beginning of the so-called third wave of democratization, several regimes that were initially considered democratic have been relabeled by analysts as limited, partial, incomplete, or simply false democracies. South Africa's democracy, in contrast, is frequently praised for a number of its key strengths: a progressive constitution detailing a wide range of rights, an independent high court (the constitutional court), an impartial electoral commission, a critical media, and a range of well-established political parties (Alence 2004; Friedman 2009a). Despite these facts, the expansion of political rights coincided with complaints of citizen disempowerment and a broader demobilization of representation.

This demobilization of representation was in part a product of the decline of social movements, which is in and of itself not surprising. South Africa's decrease in wide-ranging popular mobilization echoed similar movement downturns in countries as different as Brazil, Chile, Uruguay, Hungary, Poland, Hong Kong, and Spain (Canel 1992; Hipsher 1996; Pickvance 1999). In each of these cases, liberalizing authoritarian regimes had encouraged the expansion of social movements as a product of the opening of political space in a context of weakened political parties (O'Donnell and Schmitter 1986). The presence of large numbers of movement actors prior to a successful regime change was understood as part of a "cycle of protest" (Tarrow 1994) that would be expected to decline over time regardless of the success of the movements in bringing about change. But this decline in cases of regime transition is often much more dramatic than that which occurs in regimes that have been largely democratic throughout the cycle. In democratizing regimes, this decline is a product of momentous changes occurring both within the movements themselves as well as their environment. While new democratic regimes are expected to provide greater space for the representation of a wide range of interests (McAdam, Tarrow, and Tilly 2001), they also seek to strengthen their own institutions. Through a process of institutional disciplining, regimes work to rein in the multiplicity of actors that had taken advantage of a weakening old regime, and often the state itself, to make their claims to power. This entails the routinization of claim making through the institutions of the state and the discouragement of protest actions outside of these institutions or government-sanctioned events. Institutional disciplining is central to the consolidation of any new system. In the case of democratization, it also contradicts the broader expectations of democracy as opening spaces for dissent, protest, and debate.

The process of institutional disciplining helps to explain a second aspect of the demobilization of representation: as the state works to shore up its institutions in the aftermath of regime change, individual organizations seek to redefine themselves to more effectively compete in the new context. This process of organizational transformation as a product of both internal and external pressures has not been adequately explored. Social movement theorists have established the important influence of changes in political opportunity, institutional structures, and corresponding formal and informal power relations on movements' character, methods, and aims (Tilly 1978; McAdam 1982; Tarrow 1996). In response to broad changes in political opportunities, movements formed during one period of the political cycle will often be qualitatively different from those formed during a later period (Zdravomyslova 1996). But it is far less clear what happens to the actors that make up these movements in the crucial period (which may last a few years or a few decades) between their first exposure to significant external change and the institutionalization, co-optation, death, or reconfiguration of their organizations.[1]

The implications of downturns in popular organizing for representation and claim making in new democracies have also not been broadly analyzed. In the South African case, the struggle of actors such as the civics, as they sought to address the opportunities and challenges offered by the new democratic regime, has often been presented as a short-term "crisis of adjustment" (Cherry, Jones, and Seekings 2000, 891). Although many of the difficulties the civics faced in postapartheid South Africa were a product of their own shortcomings, this approach fails to address the larger context within which they were attempting to operate. The decline of the civics was a result not just of their own failures but also, importantly, of a dramatically shifting political and economic environment that has implications for democracy and governance reaching far beyond the demise or decay of any single movement organization.

The significance of the decline of social movements in new democracies therefore rests on a crucial question: Is this decline a product of individual organizations' inability to redefine themselves to fit the new context, or is it due to broader constraints significantly limiting *how* they might redefine themselves? Both external pressures on movement organizations by state and party institutions as well as internal understandings of what the new context requires can lead to the disciplining of organizations. First, state-based pressures stem from a quest for broader oversight and control (Foucault 1995; Chatterjee 2004). In the post–cold war world, the "good governance" agenda promoted by the World Bank (1989) and endorsed by leading bilateral donors such as the United States, the United Kingdom, and France (Abrahamsen 2001, 30–31) calls for a more efficient and competent state to devise technocratic solutions to promote neoliberal economic development. This technocratic model requires experts to devise policy. Educational and professional criteria work as a buffer to mitigate the influence of popular organizations (Teichman 2009; Paley 2001). Second, party-based pressures of institutional disciplining stem from a desire to reduce competition from popular organizations within a newly democratic setting in which political parties are often still working to strengthen their own structures. Finally, many leaders of popular organizations also feel broader pressure to conform to what they see as a more conventional hierarchical organizational model that will lead them away from the inefficiencies of participatory practices to systems of decision making meant to offer them greater influence in regional and national debates (Polletta 2002).

This chapter focuses on the South African civics' experiences of institutional disciplining during the 1990s. After considering the challenges presented by the creation of a new democratic system, we will consider the logic behind the reorganization and centralization of civic structures, the relationship of competition and cooptation between the civics and the governing party, and the broader shift in processes of participation in politics. Chile and Benin, two quite different cases in which movement organizations also played a significant role in their respective transitions to formal democracy, offer startlingly similar processes of institutional disciplining that help to tease out the lessons offered by the South African experience.

The Challenges of Democracy

In 1990, with the beginning of South Africa's formal transition process, the civics stood at a crucial turning point in their history. After working to tear down the old regime, they were now arguably well positioned to participate in a grassroots process of building up a new state and society. At this time, they still perceived the state as a powerful and dangerous adversary. As one civic leader commented: "We had another perception that maybe we still need to strengthen the fight against the enemy . . . because we wouldn't say we were free, only Mandela was free by 1990; the Black Local Authorities were still intact" (Tseleii, interview, July 11, 1997). Civics across the country took advantage of the greater space now available for activity and organization.[2] Community leaders worked to revitalize civic structures that had been forced into dormancy due to state repression and established new civics in areas such as Alexandra and Vosloorus.[3] This brought the civics' own estimates of their local structures to two thousand nationwide.[4] They were now able to convene meetings openly, and in response to the perceived lowered risk of participating in civic actions, their supporters turned out in record numbers. An activist in Vosloorus commented: "The only people that did not support us now, I would say, it was the people that were working for the then government, mainly the councilors . . . and the police" (Sibisi, interview, July 31, 1997).

Civic leaders in many areas obtained crucial technical and financial support from a number of nonprofit agencies and with this assistance began a concerted effort to increase local organizational capacity, improve national- and regional-level coordination, and train civic leaders and organizers. This support was, however, short lived. The hope pinned on civic organizations in 1990 and the subsequent disillusionment is best illustrated by the changing stance of Kagiso Trust toward the civics. Kagiso was at the time commonly referred to as the best-connected and therefore most knowledgeable funding organization in South Africa in terms of local community groups. In early 1990, Kagiso Trust decided to play a larger role in South Africa's poor communities. The support of civic organizations became a key, if not the central, pillar of its new strategy. Other nonprofit institutions such as Planact, described as "the largest and most influential of the technical service organizations" (Seekings, Shubane, and Simon 1993, 32), also emphasized the wealth of experience of the civics and their key role in local communities (Planact 1991a, 25). Both organizations argued that the civics were important local-level institutions that could have a major impact on the creation of a new democratic state and society. One Planact policy document even went so far as to present a ten-year plan for community-based development that included civics with equipped offices; full-time, well-trained staff; stabilized organizational procedures; and reliable forms of finance (1991b, 28).

The support given to many civics in the form of technical, financial, training, and consulting resources was designed to encourage the further development of local structures. Planact helped design a training course for Johannesburg-area civic leaders. Kagiso Trust offered considerable financial support for civic advice-center operations and training courses for local leaders, and another nonprofit, the Urban Foundation, offered strategic planning workshops that addressed issues surrounding community-based development (Seekings, Shubane, and Simon 1993, 66–67).[5] Although such outside assistance went a long way in helping many civics, the overall performance of the civics did not meet the expectations of their funders.[6] In a report published in late 1993, Kagiso Trust evaluated the programs and the performance of the civics that it had funded. By late 1994, financial support for civics from all external funding sources suffered a steep decline. While the new post-election environment in South Africa would have called for changes in funding strategies in

Disciplining Dissent

any case, the Kagiso report spelled out key civic shortcomings including poor administrative capacity and a disconnected leadership and suggested an increasingly critical approach toward them (Zuern 2001). The writers of the Kagiso report concluded: "The overall impression is one of a civic movement which has not taken full advantage of the liberalized political climate to strengthen its organizations" (Seekings, Shubane, and Simon 1993, 88). The following discussion explores the factors contributing to civic failures and the constraints of the "liberalized political climate" within which they worked.

Coping with Violence

In a number of township communities around Johannesburg, the year 1990 signaled less the beginning of a peaceful transition than the beginning of a civil war. A resident of the Meadowlands in Soweto described the situation in his neighborhood: "It seemed like someone had put a light to the fuse in a powderkeg; in our zone, 1990, that's when the war started. It reached on until . . . late 1993. It wasn't just a fight, it was a war with guns and bombs and machine guns, you name it" (Shegoak, interview, July 16, 1997). In the Vaal, civic leaders referred to their attackers who acted with police support as the "Vaal monster" (Schabala, interview, August 28, 1997). From the unbanning of the ANC in early 1990 to the first nonracial democratic elections in April 1994, an estimated fifteen thousand people died in fighting between rival political organizations and state agents in the townships (Klopp and Zuern 2007).[7]

ANC leaders and ordinary township residents, and, with time, most South Africans, began to speak of a "third force" as the source of much of this violence (Ellis 1998). Though it would be incorrect to argue that the third force existed as a single, centrally organized conspiracy against the ANC and its supporters such as the civics, it is quite clear that the security forces played an important role in fomenting violence and received support from high-level actors within the government (Guleke 2000). Security force actions included support for a staunch adversary to the ANC, Inkatha, which became the Inkatha Freedom Party (IFP) in 1990. In 1986, 200 Inkatha hit men were trained in Namibia by the South African Defense Force Department of Military Intelligence. These paramilitary personnel were deployed in the Johannesburg and Durban areas in the early 1990s in hit squads that attacked ANC-dominated communities. Eugene de Kock, who was eventually convicted on 89 of 121 charges of murder, kidnapping, arms smuggling, fraud, and theft and sentenced to 212 years, led the infamous Vlakpaas unit that organized such massacres. The unit funneled arms, funds, and other support to Inkatha in areas such as the volatile East Rand, which later turned into war zones between ANC and IFP militants. Though these security forces were cut off from formal oversight, they received thinly veiled support from key political leaders such as Adriaan Vlok, the minister of law and order, who was caught on tape in 1990 endorsing political assassinations (Taylor and Shaw 1998, 21). Subsequent investigations ranging from those of the Goldstone Commission, the Steyn Report, and the Truth and Reconciliation Commission as well as the testimony of key security force agents including Dirk Coetzee and Eugene de Kock have repeatedly confirmed the role of security units in the violence.[8]

Civics often attempted to organize or at least participate in negotiations to end violence, but such talks were ineffective without the intervention of neutral, outside authorities to confiscate arms, arrest combatants, and patrol "hotspots." In Katlehong, Thokoza, and Vosloorus (collectively referred to as Katorus) the civics were dramatically undermined by the violence: "[The civics in] Katorus could mobilize people to support [the] ANC, peace and justice, and reconstruction, but violence was destroying everything that the civic was trying to do" (Nxumalo, interview, July 28, 1997). In these areas, in particular, civic members often became actively involved in the violence and civic leaders became targets. This was most extreme in Tokoza, where the civic leadership was literally wiped out. In 1991 the civic executive committee had eight members, and by June 1993 only one remained in Tokoza; he described himself as a "walking corpse" (*Weekly Mail*, June 11, 1993, 12). Six civic leaders were assassinated, including Sam Ntuli, the chairman, who was ambushed in his car in September 1991. One leader fled the township. The local parish priest, Father Peter Hortop, explained that residents accepted that "the enemy," meaning the IFP, had killed the civic leaders (Hortop, interview, July 22, 1997).

State support for the IFP ranged from training, arming, and transporting IFP combatants to refusing to arrest (or even confiscate arms from) those affiliated with the IFP. In Katlehong, civic leaders were suspicious that IFP and state authorities would take information from peace talks and use it to continue the war against civic and ANC supporters (Raisa, interview, July 30, 1997). In the Vaal, one civic leader commented: "Some of those meetings we would just get there and fight and not come up with any solutions. . . . I don't think that the [meetings ended violence]. . . . After the death of most people who we know as warlords in the Vaal the violence seriously subsided" (Mazibuko, interview, August 24, 1997).

Civic organizations in particularly violence-prone areas often became involved in self-defense. In Tokoza and Katlehong, street committees set up night watches and used a whistle or other method to wake residents when there was trouble. In Naledi, which was close to the hostels and one center of violence in Soweto, the civic set up road blocks and collected funds to purchase illegal weapons. Civic leaders argued that since the ANC was unable to protect the community, the civic had to do it (Mbata, interview, July 17, 1997). In one area of Soweto, a civic leader made single-use guns with a pipe, a carburetor spring, and some ammunition (Sowetan civic leader, interview, July 1997). While the initial waves of violence beginning in 1990 caught many communities off guard and unarmed, forcing them to use only stones and knives to protect themselves, by 1993 many communities were well armed and organized. While they were initially unsure who was attacking them, over time they learned to distinguish between friend and foe.[9] One local organizer boasted toward the end of the transition period: "We could take whatever came to us. Even the security forces couldn't just play around" (Mbata, interview, July 17, 1997). While this war readiness often benefited those who were armed, the divisions that were drawn in township communities and the massive influx of arms would have severe repercussions for years to come.

Civic participation in community self-defense most often occurred at the street or area level rather than at the local level. Local level structures, which were often involved with negotiations with local authorities while violence raged in their communities, did not explicitly endorse such actions but also did not condemn them. In Alexandra, for example, only a few area committees, such as that for the Beirut area, actually formed SDUs; locations where violence was less problematic could survive with less aggressive approaches. A civic member explained the way things worked:

One area would decide we are going to arm ourselves this way or that way, but . . . because it was not part of our constitution, then it was not something that we could sit down as ACO as a whole branch and discuss how it will work. . . . We would discuss that wherever you are, you must try and organize people against what is happening, but you may not specifically state this is how you must do it. And wherever arms were used, ACO as a branch would not dictate this is what you are supposed to do. . . . ACO would warn its members against using any criminal means, because ACO was involved in negotiations so it wouldn't allow anything out of hand, for its members to be found doing anything criminal (Mbalukwana, interview, June 27, 1997)

Civic leaders did not consider the arming of self-defense units to be a criminal action. Many township residents felt that they were in the middle of a civil war. Under such conditions, self-defense was simply necessary. One civic leader who returned to study at a local university after the 1994 elections commented that even the United Nations, arguably an institution primarily concerned with the promotion of peace, made provisions for its members to defend themselves; he asked why local communities should not also have this right (Tseleii, interview, July 11, 1997).

Centralization of Authority

As violence raged in a number of areas outside Johannesburg and Durban, civic leaders began the process to form a national civic body. In early 1991, UDF activists Pat Lephunya and Zohra Ebrahim were called on to help create a new structure under the guise of the National Interim Civics Committee (NICC). Despite discussions surrounding the establishment of this new overarching structure, no national-level civic was launched until March 1992, and the national body did not include the vast majority of local civic organizations until after the 1994 national government elections. Even after 1994, the new South African National Civic Organization (SANCO) remained a weak and divided body.

The reasons for the lack of quick and effective coordination were ironically a product of past civic successes. First, local civic structures had gained great popularity by becoming a forum for local residents and many were therefore hesitant to sacrifice their much-championed local autonomy. The second key factor was rooted in the civics' alliance with the ANC. Members of the newly legalized party raised concerns that a national civic body might generate unproductive competition. By late 1990, divisions between the ANC's exiled leadership, which was accustomed to making decisions without significant consultation, and those who had remained within the country and supported the mass participatory culture of the UDF had become apparent. When leading UDF activists and civic leaders met in Bloemfontein in May 1991 to discuss the formation of a national civic, rumors spread that the creation of this civic structure would draw supporters away from the ANC. This occurred despite the clearly articulated assurances of the NICC coordinators that the civic should in no way be considered a rival to the ANC, that it sought to be a non-partisan organization, and that its formation had nothing to do with any existing tensions within the ANC (*Star*, May 11, 1991, 1; May 18, 1991, 6, 12).

Nonetheless, a considerable number of ANC supporters felt that all energies at this early stage of the transition period should go toward strengthening the ANC nationally and locally. One ANC activist argued: "There will be a stage when this [the creation of a national civic structure] will be necessary, but now the ANC is not in power and the important issue is to strengthen ANC branches" (quoted in Daniels 1991, 13). The strength of many local civic branches across the country also caused concern within the ANC, leading some ANC leaders to work to undermine the civic structures at both the local and later the national level. As a result of these tensions as well as coordination problems, the formation of the national civic initially slated for the middle of 1991 was delayed for almost a year.

SANCO was intended to coordinate local actions to give the civics a stronger voice in national and regional politics, but the question remained as to how it might best do this. At its launch in March 1992, a number of local civics challenged the organization's proposed structure. SANCO's constitution defined a unitary structure that was underlined in its name (The South African National Civic Organization), which used the term "Civic" in the singular, instead of "Civics" in the plural as several earlier regional associations had done. Many local civic leaders preferred a federal structure such as that of the UDF. Despite these concerns, the argument for the unitary structure won the day as national leaders argued that a federal structure would allow opponents to divide the civics. The argument for a unitary constitution was also based on the idea that the civics should follow the model of the anticipated postapartheid state as well as the ANC rather than defining an alternative structure that drew on past, apartheid-era organizing strategies. A unitary structure, it was argued, would be more efficient and therefore promote a stronger voice. The question remained: for whom?

The Civic as Watchdog

As national-level negotiations between the ANC and the apartheid government slowly moved forward, civics across the country were pressed to define their role in the new and changing environment. In 1991, Pat Lephunya described three options. First, local civics could either fold to leave greater room for the organization of ANC branches or simply become ANC branches or ANC residents' associations.[10] Second, local civics could take over the administration of the communities in which they worked, effectively replacing the defunct town councils. Third, the civic movement could become an autonomous, nonparty political movement (Collinge 1991, 8). In some local areas, the role of civics as nonparty actors seemed so clear to civic organizers that the issue never came to much debate. In other areas, however, there was considerable disagreement and confusion particularly between those who argued that the civic should fold into the ANC and those who opposed this move. A regional civic leader explained: "Some individuals saw the civics as a threat to the ANC, saying that the civics would in the future contest elections" (Mali, interview, August 5, 1997). In time, however, the general consensus became that the civics would play a "watchdog" role over local and national government. This meant that the civics would continue to address the material, or bread-and-butter, issues regardless of which party was in government.[11]

The problem was the ANC's lack of interest in being watched by a "watchdog." In an ANC political education discussion paper, the official ANC view toward the civics was outlined: "We believe that civics have their own specific character and identity which is different to that of the ANC. Their independence must be jealously protected" (1991, 6). The same document, however, betrays a resistance on the part of the ANC toward too critical a role for the civics. "It is the task of the ANC to aid the civics in drawing these links between bread and butter issues and national political issues. Through ideological debate, the actions of its members, joint strategizing and campaigning, the ANC must win its leadership role in relationship to the civics. . . . There is no conflict of interests between the ANC and civic organization, but a community of interests. . . . It is the duty of the ANC to re-enforce the hand of civics" (1991, 5, 10). The ANC argument for civic independence was compromised by the party's desire to ensure that civics would work to pursue the same goals as the ANC.[12] The ANC was clearly hesitant to relinquish what it saw as its role as the leader of the liberation movement.

The civics, on the other hand, made much stronger statements about their independence from the ANC and their nonpartisan stance. The new "watchdog" role that the civics championed was offered as the best insurance for the future of democracy and a stable state in South Africa as well as the best plan for the preservation of the civic structures. Instinctively, members of the civics tried to protect the continued existence of organizations that they had long worked to strengthen. The civics would, however, prove unable to uphold their agreement to become and remain nonpartisan.

Cooperation and Co-optation

In South Africa since 1994, the separation of antiapartheid social movements from the leading party of liberation, the ANC, has been a contradictory and halting process. Both the ANC and its former allies, primarily the civics and the unions, have resisted a stark separation, but for different reasons. The ANC, realizing that its own local structures have been weak, sought to maintain its linkages to the grassroots through local associations. A local ANC councilor and former civic leader explained: "We need SANCO more than yesterday, today. It provides us with an opportunity at government level of realizing our intentions of building partnerships with communities, and partnerships cannot be loose. There is no way that you can interact with that community if that community is not organized. Therefore organs of civil society provide that type of organized formation that will serve as a good link between the community and the government, hence practicalizing the partnerships that we want to build" (Buthelezi, interview, July 22, 1997).

Civic leaders, on the other hand, hoped that a continued close relationship with the ANC would give the national civic structure a privileged position to voice its concerns directly to the government. From its inception in 1992, SANCO was engaged in an informal alliance with the ANC.[13] This informal arrangement was to be on a case-by-case basis, and SANCO repeatedly pledged that it would not work with the ANC if and when "its policies go against the interests of the community" (Moses Mayekiso, interview, August 19, 1997). Both the ANC and SANCO wrapped their program ideas in the rhetoric of working for the best interests of "the community." But their views differed on who constituted "the community" and what "the community" for whom they claimed to speak actually wanted. SANCO largely drew its support from poor South Africans, while the ANC increasingly developed policies that it felt would appeal to a greater cross-section of South Africa voters, importantly including, if not favoring, the wealthy (M. McDonald 2006).[14]

These strains tended to be relatively muted at the national level, and national-level SANCO leaders continued to closely support the ANC, deriding any antigovernment or so-called revolutionary rhetoric. The third president of SANCO, Mlungisi Hlongwane, argued in 1996: "If you want to be an instant revolutionary these days and be involved in boycotts, SANCO is no longer a home for you." He added: "Although SANCO was an organization that mastered the art of boycotts, it has made a complete break with the past. SANCO will never be the same again" (quoted in *Saturday Star*, December 28, 1996, 8). In postapartheid South Africa, the national structure of SANCO now urged members to support the government's Masakhane plan, which called on residents to pay for services. At the same time, SANCO leaders put limits on their disagreement with the ANC, arguing that too much discord would only feed into the hands of their adversaries. "If we don't disagree, it is unhealthy. We must disagree. But the moment where we disagree to the point where we actually fight publicly, it doesn't help our cause. . . . Whenever we disagree such that there is lack of movement, it works in the hands of conservatives. . . . There will come points where as SANCO we don't necessarily completely agree with this policy, but we will go on with you, we will continue the debate with you" (Williams, interview, May 10, 1999).

In 1995, following its support for the ANC in the 1994 national and provincial elections, SANCO endorsed the ANC for the local government elections. Local SANCO branches were instructed to work for the ANC's campaign (Mothibe, interview, June 19, 1997). In return for its support, the ANC placed SANCO leaders on its election lists, ensuring many a position in local government. As a result, SANCO stood to lose up to 80 percent of its local, regional, and national leaders. If all SANCO leaders were forced to re- sign their positions as they entered government, SANCO structures in Mpu- malanga, Gauteng, and the Eastern Cape would not have enough elected rep- resentatives remaining to form a quorum (defined in the constitution as half the committee members plus one [SANCO 1997a, 13.1]) to call a meeting to elect new leaders (*New Nation*, November 3, 1995, 12). SANCO had already grappled with the problems that the departure of key leaders from its ranks would have. Its first president, Moses Mayekiso, left SANCO in 1994 to be- come a member of parliament; in January 1995 its second president, Lechesa Tsenoli, joined parliament to fill a vacancy.

At this time, SANCO policy stipulated that any leader joining govern- ment would have to resign SANCO leadership. But since SANCO had al- ready lost two presidents within the first year of the democratic regime, many felt the need for at least a slight change in policy. SANCO's National Execu- tive Committee therefore agreed to allow both Mayekiso and Tsenoli to attend executive meetings but not to vote. The idea was that these leaders could con- tinue to share their experience with SANCO without determining its policies. In practice this policy failed to define clear roles but allowed SANCO leaders to simultaneously hold SANCO and government offices. When over half of SANCO's leaders did enter government through local elections, many re- tained their SANCO positions. A regional SANCO leader commented: "How will a SANCO leader, who also holds the position of councilor, conduct him- self if he is called on to lead a march of residents against the local authority? Who will he lead the march against—himself?" (*New Nation*, February 28, 1997, 33). Another regional leader argued: "As a former leader of SANCO, now an ANC leader in government, you don't account to SANCO. You ac- count to ANC and report to SANCO. You report to SANCO what is happen- ing but cannot be held responsible for actions by SANCO" (Sandi, interview, August 5, 1997). The conflict became one between pragmatism (SANCO simply could not afford to lose so many of its leaders) and principle (SANCO leaders had consistently argued that SANCO was an independent "watchdog" of government). Principle lost out to pragmatism.[15]

By 1996 most local civics that would eventually join SANCO had joined, and though some civics left SANCO because of its support for the ANC in the national, provincial, and local elections, the majority remained. By this time, the level of activity of local civics across the country had reached a new low.

As individual civic leaders and at times entire civic structures worked to help the ANC in national and local election campaigns, little energy was spent on independent civic programs. Volunteerism within the civics had also decreased markedly as those who could find new positions in government and business understandably did so. A regional civic leader explained: "I suppose that in any situation in any country, when people fought for something that they finally thought they have achieved, the activism declines. It is only those leaders who will still feel the need for continuing to fight to redress the problems that will continue . . . but there is that decline, but not because people are not members of SANCO, but the activism there, the commitment sort of declines" (Ntingani, interview, June 25, 1997). SANCO's support for the ANC in the elections only worked to sharpen the decline in popular participation in civic affairs. A local civic leader in Alexandra commented: "It was after the elections that things became worse because we lost most of the leaders [to political office], and most of the people didn't understand how we may deign to be something else and not ANC when we were voting ANC during the elections" (Mbalukwana, interview, June 27, 1997).[16]

From Resistance to Development

A seasoned civic activist, Mzwanele Mayekiso, summarized the central problems facing civics by the mid-1990s:

Then, our common enemy was apartheid; today we face confusion about who to struggle against. Then, the political economic vision shared by most activists was socialism; now we lack clarity about our long-term goal (socialism, social democracy, or a successful form of neo-liberalism?).

Then, we saw the role of civil society as revolutionary; today, civil society is sometimes posed as a pliant partner to shrink-the-state, or merely as a watchdog for social democracy, and more rarely, as a stepping stone to socialism via community-based-struggle.

Then, the progressive hegemonic line was UDF non-racialism through mass politics; today, we suffer from top-down politics based increasingly on the politics of "corporatism" (pacts between elites).

Then the dominant bottom-up sentiment was ungovernability and militancy; today, we find popular anger about the gravy train, alienation due to non-delivery, and activists now sometimes degenerating into "on-the-make" activities, not progressive organizing. (Mayekiso 1996a, 7)

The civics were experiencing a deep crisis of identity. Despite these difficulties, local civic structures in most areas continued to operate, even though they were struggling. The challenge was to clearly define the tasks of the civic. While the national structure had rallied for a shift to development, "development" proved to be an incredibly broad, almost all-inclusive mandate.[17] It was up to local structures to determine what they felt their role in "development" should be and how they should interact with the government on the issues they chose to address. In 1995 the Soweto civic defined a shift in its focus "from resistance to development." It promised to direct greater attention to addressing concerns such as voter registration, the payment of services, and the development of the civic organization itself (*Star*, May 9, 1995, 2). In Port Elizabeth, a ten-point plan was released that included training for civic leaders and members, promoting peace and justice through community policing forums and engaging in local development debates with the state and other actors (*Eastern Province Herald*, July 22, 1994, 7). Across the country, four broad themes of civic activity attracted the greatest attention: service provision, crime prevention, advice centers, and participation in community-development projects. The first three were broadly consistent with the activities of civic associations in the 1980s and early 1990s; the last was a new addition and proved to be the most problematic for the continued existence of the local civics as grassroots, mass-participatory organizations.

Most often local civic organizations simply did not have the necessary skills to actively participate in devising technical plans for community development. In some cases, they became involved as "community partners" for privately funded development projects. The possible civic benefits of involvement in such projects were great, since they would bring in much-needed resources. In Evaton, for example, the civic helped a private developer in the marketing of his project to build new houses by encouraging residents to apply for the houses. The civic charged the developer R65 ($15) per house completed. Such projects allowed civic branches to pay for basic organizational needs such as telephone lines and administrative work (Mazibuko, interview, May 27, 1999). In other cases, such as in Soweto, a civic-sponsored program to clean railway stations offered the civic the opportunity to select the workers for the project.[18] In cases where development projects were organized with civic involvement, unemployed residents came to the civic hoping to benefit. The overwhelming majority of local civic branches were never involved in serious allegations of accepting bribes or stealing funds from projects, but a common complaint by township residents as well as NGOs was that local civics attempted to act as local gatekeepers on development projects. In some cases, competition between the local ANC branch and civics also delayed development projects as each sought credit for the results (*New Nation*, April 19, 1996, 8; *Sowetan*, March 17, 1998, 10).[19]

At times the conflicts between the ANC and the local civics were simply the result of power struggles. Such struggles were most intense just before and during local government election campaigns and declined sharply thereafter. Less overt conflicts, however, did continue when local civics attempted to assert an independent role. When civics criticized the work of local government in general or ANC councilors in particular, local ANC leaders responded defensively and often aggressively. A February 1997 summit between SANCO and the ANC noted the "widespread tensions between structures of the ANC and SANCO, especially at a local level" and the negative impact this had on the "delivery and development" of infrastructural and economic upliftment projects (SANCO 1997c, annexure C, 16). Concerns in many townships about the level of support that civics gave to the ANC also led to tensions. One civic leader frankly noted: "Our problem with our alliance with the ANC is that we cannot be seen with people who are against the ANC" (Makgubutlane, interview, August 25, 1997). Some local civic leaders also claimed that they were discriminated against within the ANC structures. A popular complaint among civic leaders in numerous townships was that they felt that they did a good deal of local work for which the ANC would later take credit.

Many local civic leaders began to question the decision by SANCO's national leadership to align with the ANC, arguing it would have been better to remain independent. A Sowetan explained: "Even though I am a card-carrying member of the ANC, I believe, we should . . . not have aligned with the ANC. We should have gone it solo" (anonymous Sowetan civic leader 2, interview, July 1997). Another civic leader explained that since the ANC had promised SANCO that some civic leaders would get into government, there was no great initial conflict within SANCO concerning its backing of the ANC. After several civic leaders moved into positions in government, they effectively left SANCO for the ANC. "SANCO is complaining now that it seconded councilors to government and now they are no more answerable to SANCO. . . . A number of branch executive members, some people, use that as a stepping stone towards their personal gains" (Modise, interview, July 18, 1997).

Competing for Resources

In response to the difficulties experienced by the local structures of SANCO and national leaders' estimation of the challenges and opportunities that lay ahead, the national office worked to create a number of programs designed to strengthen the civics while still maintaining a close relationship with the ANC. Each of these programs worked to institutionalize the top-down approach of SANCO that its unitary constitution had outlined. As SANCO's self-professed commitment to participatory democracy was brought into considerable doubt, the response from local civics ranged from disinterest to anger and rebellion.

In 1995, SANCO announced that it would launch an independent investment arm, SANCO Investment Holdings (SIH), under the umbrella of SANCO Development Trust. This move was intended to support SANCO's mission of "people-centered and people-driven development" (SANCO 1997a, 1.1, 4).[20] The company promised to search for socially responsible joint ventures, "guided by the aspirations of our communities," and pledged to use 74 percent of the profits from the new enterprise to fund development projects and black empowerment schemes in poor communities (Moses Mayekiso, interview, August 19, 1997). By March 1997, SANCO's own unaudited accounting indicated that the civic group was almost R1.4 million ($300,000) in debt (SANCO 1997c, annexure A, 3). Tension had grown between SANCO and SIH as SANCO was barely able to operate while SIH seemed to be reasonably financially secure (SANCO 1997c, 27).[21]

When SIH announced its participation in a water-privatization program in Nelspruit that would raise water tariffs for local communities, grassroots activists were alarmed and demanded that SIH withdraw from the project. SANCO leaders argued that such clear contradictions between SIH's actions and SANCO's self-professed role as protector of the poor were part of a learning process in establishing new structures, but SIH's actions demonstrated that it was driven by a quest for profit that would at times contradict the populist aspirations of SANCO. SIH confirmed this in its own overview of its work: "SANCO Investment Holdings' main objective is to make a profit, not to directly fund SANCO's socially responsible projects" (SANCO and SIH 1997, 4). Another problem that SANCO leaders and critics of SIH soon discovered was the lack of any clear directive on the disbursement of funds. The funds that SIH shared with SANCO were received by SANCO largely at SIH's discretion, creating an enormously unequal power relationship. SANCO depended on SIH for its continued operation.

Many local and regional branches of SANCO became strongly disillusioned with SIH not only because of questions concerning its investment choices but also because of the dearth of resources that it shared with SANCO.[22] A former SANCO Gauteng executive member noted that after SIH's establishment, other SANCO provincial offices would call the Gauteng office asking if Gauteng had received any money from SIH:

When the investment arm was established, the [branches] were of the view that they were going to get financial support from the organization, but as time went by it became clear that this type of assistance was not going to be forthcoming. . . . At times even the national office would be in trouble. They would find themselves unable to pay for running costs, phones, and other things for some time. Sometimes the staff would go without salaries for a few months and so on. It became clear to us that the investment arm was not making as much money as was expected. (Tleane, interview, June 3, 1999)

A few local SANCO branches did, however, benefit from this turn to business. By the end of the decade, community economic development centers (CEDCs) had been established in Alexandra, Vanderbiljpark (the Vaal), the Eastern Cape, and Johannesburg. Each of these centers was established by SANCO Ilima Community Development under the umbrella of SANCO Development Trust.[23] The centers were intended to participate in local development projects as community partners with private corporations or public agencies. In the Vaal, for example, the local CEDC worked with the Emerald Group on a casino project. The Emerald Group benefited from SANCO's involvement because it needed to demonstrate a mechanism for community development in order to acquire a casino license. The local CEDC benefited from the funding it received as well as the opportunities it was able to provide to local residents (Mazibuko, interview, May 27, 1999; Mothung, interview, May 27, 1999). In Alexandra the local CEDC hoped to offer training for skills ranging from bread baking to waste management but had difficulty in securing the necessary funds to launch these programs (Machitela, interview, June 10, 1997); in mid-1999 the office's electricity was turned off due to lack of payment.

Two key issues of contention arose surrounding the local CEDCs. The first question concerned who controlled the centers. SANCO's constitution stipulated that ultimate authority lay with the national structures of SANCO rather than with local organizations or community members.[24] The principle objectives of all SANCO structures included the aim "to establish, and participate in, trusts, investment companies . . . economic and community development centers . . . as decided from time to time by the National Executive Committee" (SANCO 1997a, 5.1.9). In Alexandra the launch of the CEDC was met with considerable controversy because of its control by national-level structures. Local residents questioned whether the CEDC would actually be "their" organization and represent "their" interests (Mzwanele Mayekiso, interview, May 27, 1997). Second, local CEDCs in partnership with private companies or other funders were given a much-needed opportunity to offer skills and even employment to unemployed community members. Such opportunities often brought allegations of favoritism. Representatives of the Vaal CEDC admitted that they carefully chose whom to inform of job opportunities and that some people were "never told." One CEDC member explained: "You don't necessarily have to be a SANCO member for you to participate in the CEDC in the economic affairs; you must, however, belong to the broad MDM [mass democratic movement]. We then become very selective as to who belongs to that family for historical reasons" (Lephoto, interview, May 27, 1999).

Most residents seemed unaware of the presence of these CEDCs, which were ostensibly established to serve the entire community.[25] Those who were aware of the centers became increasingly critical of them as wide-scale empowerment projects failed to materialize. A branch-level civic leader in Alexandra argued:

Since they introduced this SANCO investment thing, they seem to have changed focus. Now they no longer care about the needs of the poorest; they are only concentrating on business of which we don't know who benefits out of that business. The projects they create are projects for individuals. So now people are not happy about that because you cannot create jobs for everyone, whereas when you introduce these projects you create the impression that everyone will be covered only to find that there only may be five people who will run those projects and it is only those people and their families who will benefit out of those projects, and you will never know where are the profits. (Mzonke Mayekiso, interview, May 25, 1999)

In December 1996, as part of the national leadership's effort to make the civic a financially viable organization, it also launched a new membership drive. Prior to this time, membership fees and programs were determined by local-level structures (SANCO 1992, 7). The new program and the 1997 constitution of SANCO moved the responsibility of membership to the national level and also mandated that funds collected be paid to the national rather than the local offices (SANCO 1997a, 6.2). The idea was to offer a product, at a cheap price, as part of the membership deal to encourage millions to join. In order to do this, SANCO entered into a joint venture with the American International Group (AIG) to offer South Africans burial insurance. SANCO promised AIG that it could enroll approximately two million members into the scheme, which offered a one-time payment of R1,500 ($330) in the case of death (SANCO 1997c, 7). Residents who signed up for SANCO membership were also to receive a coupon booklet for large discounts at local retailers. AIG received the largest portion of the R30 (roughly $6.50) membership fee, followed by the national structure of SANCO. Only R2 was to be given back to the local civics.[26] This was a high-cost membership in comparison to the fees generally charged by local civics, which tended to run about R5 per year. It also offered a particularly low return to the local civics, which were expected to do much of the work in encouraging new members to join. In the majority of local civics, even the executive members did not become formal members

SANCO

STOP CRIME!
STOP RAPE - STOP ABUSE
BUILD HOUSES - DEMAND YOUR RIGHTS

The South African National Civic Organisation (**SANCO**) is a mass-driven, community based organisation who will fight for your rights and our newborn Democracy. With over 3000 branches country-wide, **SANCO** can ensure that the pressing issues of housing, services, land and environment are not forgotten, and that they will be delivered.

WHY Should your electricity and water be cut off?

WHY Should you pay rates and taxes for poor or non-existent services?

WHY should you pay high rentals?

JOIN **SANCO** NOW

Join **SANCO** now and you will have an organisation with mass strength and the muscle to take up these issues on your behalf and ensure fairness for all!

SIGN UP NOW! Complete the form on the back of the leaflet today!

SANCO membership flyer (1997)

of SANCO. At the SANCO national conference in April, the president scolded the delegates: "It is because of this self-centeredness that four months after the launch of our membership drive the General Council still had to compel all Congress delegates to be paid up members of SANCO. . . . If a question may be asked, how many of the delegates here joined SANCO last week or yesterday?" (Hlongwane 1997, 12). Even with the forced recruitment leading up to the national conference, only five thousand people had joined nationwide by the end of April 1997 (SANCO 1997c, 7).

In areas where members had signed up, local civics still voiced numerous concerns.[27] First, the coupon scheme never materialized, which in the words of one civic leader was a case of "complete fraud" (Mzwanele Mayekiso, interview, May 27, 1997). Second, there were technical problems in producing the membership cards, leading to delays of four to six weeks before a new member received his or her card. Third, for unemployed residents, R30 was simply too large a sum to be paid all at once. At the national office, there were also problems with the new membership system that were largely the result of the leadership's lack of experience in business. When SANCO learned that AIG would not pay burial insurance for people over the age of sixty-five, it was forced to cover the costs itself. When middlemen in certain areas charged people extra to sign up when they were already on their deathbeds, SANCO and AIG were effectively defrauded. The end result was that even the local branches that had enrolled fairly significant numbers of new members received nothing. By late August 1997 the program was cancelled, and a new one was established offering a choice of a R14 membership or a R30 membership that included a funeral benefit. Once again, SANCO attempted to set up a coupon scheme that never materialized, and the membership program was pulled. A third program offering a R5 membership and a higher-priced membership with insurance was suspended on June 1, 1999, after SANCO realized there was no insurance coverage (Williams, interview, May 31, 1999). In the following years, SANCO offered a R10 membership with no extra benefits. It also continued to pursue various commercial deals (Mngomezulu, interview, January 14, 2004; Hlongwane, interview, June 9, 2004).

Institutional Disciplining

Most civics became less participatory and less democratic at the same time that the state became a formal democracy. This contradiction is explained by the process of institutional disciplining that was occurring at three levels: the state-based discourse of neoliberalism and good governance, party leaders' actions to reduce perceived sources of challenge, and a leadership-driven reorganization of the civic meant to increase efficiency and political influence.

Democratization is often described as a process of changing the rules of the game and institutionalizing uncertainty (Przeworski 1991). This refers to the drafting of a new constitution and accompanying national legislation as well as a certain degree of uncertainty about who will win elections. Political liberalization in South Africa offered the prospect of greater political uncertainty, but the accompanying economic liberalization dictated neoliberal policies that constrained economic policy choices, effectively reducing economic uncertainty. The civics experienced what might best be labeled a professionalization of participation in which discussions of policy became increasingly technical and specialized. This made civic participation in debates concerning tariff structures or the upgrading of communities increasingly difficult. Meetings with government representatives usually took place during regular working hours, making it difficult for civic representatives with daytime jobs to attend. The civics' role in development projects, therefore, increasingly became one of publicizing projects or recruiting workers rather than participating in planning. In this way, civics acted as gatekeepers that could include a chosen few but could not empower large numbers of citizens. The civics' understanding of the new rules of the game underlined the need for far greater financial resources in order to have a voice. The creation of an investment arm and a relatively expensive membership scheme were thus designed to increase the fiscal strength of the civic. This approach represented a clear shift from the civics' previous focus on broad popular participation and mobilization to a focus on building organizational power through financial and institutional resources. The pursuit of financial security occurred at the direct expense of participation, as decisions about how to raise and where to invest funds were made without community discussion or local input. These decisions were instead made by a small number of individuals working in office buildings located outside the poor townships in which the civics had long organized.

Second, ANC leaders at the local, regional, and national level sought to reduce challenges from the civics. This was true both of ANC leaders not affiliated with the civics as well as those who still nominally represented civic structures. The informal alliance between SANCO and the ANC had brought many civic leaders into positions of government. Interestingly, both civic leaders who remained outside government as well as many who had taken positions in government described this as co-optation. This process of co-optation further weakened the participatory promise of the civics since leaders who were in government were expected to enforce government policy rather than convey grassroots demands. The ANC employed its alliance with SANCO when it wanted to demonstrate support for its new policies. When SANCO failed to endorse ANC policies or programs, such as its initial response to the Masakhane program, the ANC simply excluded SANCO until it toed the line. In the case of Masakhane, this practice worked to undermine the civics since the well-funded and widely publicized program focused on a long-standing civic issue: the improvement of material conditions in townships. By the time SANCO formally endorsed the Masakhane program, the program had lost both its support in government and its popular appeal. Other attempts by SANCO to defy the ANC also ended in failure. When SANCO leader Moses Mayekiso threatened a national bond boycott in 1992 if banks did not offer better terms to township residents, the ANC made it clear to SANCO that such actions were not in the ANC's or SANCO's best interests (*Mail and Guardian*, August 6, 1993, 39).[28] SANCO withdrew its call for a bond boycott. When discussions within SANCO of the possibility of the civic fielding candidates against the ANC in the 2000 local government elections hit the press, SANCO was pressured to quickly retract such statements. It then went to great lengths to demonstrate its continued support for the ANC by offering a blanket endorsement of all ANC candidates for local elections.[29]

When SANCO leaders were offered sought-after seats in the National Assembly or provincial or local government by the ANC, their assumption of public office worked to benefit the ANC at SANCO's expense. The ANC benefited, because SANCO leaders often came with a built-in support base that could be mobilized to support ANC policies. Their experience within SANCO also offered them valuable training in leadership and other skills. The departure of large numbers of leaders from SANCO to government as ANC representatives led SANCO to formally endorse the "two-hats" policy. This allowed government representatives to maintain their leadership positions within SANCO but weakened SANCO in two ways. First, its leaders were no longer spending much time on civic activities. Second, ANC representatives also in SANCO leadership positions could work to influence civic policies to support the ANC, but SANCO leaders were generally unable to influence ANC policy to benefit SANCO. The ANC demanded party loyalty within its ranks. ANC leaders who challenged the party's policies or decisions risked losing their jobs. As a result, SANCO leaders could not support any SANCO policies that went against ANC decisions without fear of unemployment. Ali Tleane, the former mayor of Tembisa, lost his government post because of his support of a civic refusal to endorse rising rent and service fees in the township.

At the local level, ANC branches often worked to undermine civic actions as they competed with the civics for local influence and resources. Local ANC leaders often attempted to instruct SANCO branches regarding which actions they should and should not take. ANC leaders also worked to take control of some projects initiated by SANCO. When civic leaders complained of these actions in both local and national forums with the ANC, the ANC generally gave lip service to promises of greater consultation and cooperation but took no actions to bring about any changes on the ground. When local civics were critical of the actions of ANC leaders in government—for example, if they refused to endorse continuously rising service fees—civic leaders were criticized as opposing transformation or acting in support of rival political parties. These were powerful claims meant to undermine civic support in township communities that overwhelmingly voted for the ANC. After decades as an illegal opposition movement, the ANC was intent on establishing control at all levels of the state and pressing its influence at all levels of society. The party's great popularity in South Africa, as well as abroad, further strengthened its position vis-à-vis other actors.

Given these constraints, civic leaders made crucial and difficult choices. Since the ANC was the dominant power in national and most local and provincial governments, the civics attempted to create a new structure that their leaders felt would allow them to interact with key power holders. Unfortunately for the civics, their new structures and the co-optation of many leaders by the ANC brought about a sharp disconnection between the civic and its traditional power base in local communities. As part of the transformation to a formally democratic regime, civic leaders seized what they thought was an opportunity to assert greater influence. This organizational development undermined the democratic participatory nature of local civics across the country, which in turn further undermined the very strength of the civic voice at the national level. Local civic leaders and potential supporters were not interested in volunteering their time simply to follow the dictates of higher-level civic leaders to attain little to no local benefit for their actions. The declining influence of local civic structures, in turn, further undermined the national structure, which could no longer claim to represent the interests of millions of township dwellers across the country.

The creation of a unitary civic with such broad powers and control of resources at the top undermined the participatory ideal of the civics. The frustration voiced by local activists was both wide and deep. The general failure of the programs that SANCO championed in the late 1990s and the controversy surrounding its ventures into business increased the growing disconnection between SANCO branches and the national-level civic structure. The decisions to pursue these programs and to restructure the civics were all defended by national leaders as the best way for the civic to become a more effective, streamlined, and powerful organization in a new period of South Africa's history. Each decision was meant to professionalize the civic so that it might more effectively participate in formal development programs and work with government and private businesses. The civic set up structures to mimic government departments at the same time that it sought to provide the services of an NGO.

Local civic leaders generally did not agree with the logic offered by their national-level comrades. At the local level, those working within the civics were often hesitant to implement programs that they felt had been forced on them, and they feared that the multitiered civic structures were being transformed from pathways for communication to instruments of control. National-level SANCO officers eventually had to admit that whenever SANCO attempted to implement top-down programs, they were bound to fail, but this did not fundamentally change the logic of their actions. Instead, they sought to institute better procedures to guide local civics. National-level civic leaders made a critical error in assuming that they could "convince" branches to follow national instructions. In the words of one civic leader: "People have been wearing out their shoes walking to the SANCO offices to volunteer their time; the question is how much longer they will do it" (Tofile, interview, May 18, 1999).[30]

Local civics often felt that when SANCO leaders did communicate with them, it was in the form of an instruction or a correction rather than a conversation. A local civic leader in Soweto neatly summed up his experiences within the civic after the SCA became SANCO Soweto: "Nothing has changed. But of course we have lost our independence." He added: "Now, if we take a decision here, someone questions you at the other levels, saying, 'How can you give us a decision? This is not the policy of the organization.' So whatever we do now, we have to look over our shoulders and say, 'Are we doing the right thing?'" (Tseleii, interview, July 11, 1997). The unitary structure of SANCO fueled tensions between the various levels by effectively making each level of SANCO responsible to the next higher level rather than the one below. The constitution of SANCO gave regional-level officials the power to determine where a branch structure should be located. It did not create a mechanism for gauging community need or interest or develop a process whereby local residents could approach regional representatives (SANCO 1997a, 9.3.1). Although the unitary structure of SANCO was designed to acquire lucrative contracts with government and private businesses and play a significant role in policy debates, it worked to stifle participation and thereby weaken the civic structure as a whole, leading to the collapse of almost all of its programs.

The Demobilization of Popular Representation—Lessons from Chile and Benin

In Benin and Chile, like South Africa, civic coalitions played a central role in bringing about an end to authoritarian rule. Benin and Chile each serve as a key example of successful and largely peaceful civic mobilization for democratic change on their respective continents. Although protesters did risk violent state responses, neither country during its political transition saw the high levels of violence that occurred in South Africa. Aside from the broadly similar roles that a range of civic and popular organizations played in each case, the contexts of their transitions were starkly different. Since the end of colonial rule, South Africa had been a so-called settler democracy, which entailed authoritarian rule for the black majority. Although the country had avoided formal military rule, the majority had never been granted the most basic rights. Benin experienced short periods of formal democracy since its independence in 1960 but was wracked by instability and repeated coups. Chile established a comparatively stable democratic system in the 1930s. In the early 1970s the governments of both Benin and Chile fell in military coups. In the case of Chile, the United States–backed coup removed the democratically elected president. In the case of Benin, the coup removed a presidential council created after an election marred by violence. By the end of the millennium, Chile, Benin, and South Africa were all commonly cited as among the most successful cases of electoral democracy on their respective continents. Chile and South Africa are classified as upper-middle-income economies by the World Bank, while Benin is a low-income economy. The three countries thus offer broadly different conditions within which to investigate the impact of political transitions on key popular actors.

Bratton and Van de Walle begin their survey, *Democratic Experiments in Africa*, with a discussion of the dramatic case of Benin. They argue that Benin is important not just because it was one of the first countries on the continent to experience a transition but also because "the emblematic drama that unfolded in Cotonou's public arenas combined in one country's experience the core attributes of a landmark transition to democracy" (1997, 3). The president of neighboring Niger's National Assembly echoed the significance of Benin's transition, describing it as a "school ('le Bénin fait l'école') for democratic change elsewhere" (Gisselquist 2008, 792). Protests began in January 1989 over bread-and-butter concerns and developed into a stark challenge to the legitimacy of the regime (Decalo 1997, 51). University students demanded their overdue bursary payments, and civil servants and school teachers took to the streets to demand the payment of their salaries. Members of the Communist Party, workers, religious leaders, and intellectuals also joined the protests (Gazibo 2005, 74). Since the government was perilously close to bankruptcy, it was unable to address the economic demands of the protesters. The demonstrations continued to grow, and protesters expanded their demands to include political and civil rights. By late 1989 an estimated forty thousand people rallied in downtown Cotonou (Bratton and Van de Walle 1997, 2).

In response to the protests, as well as to direct pressure from France and slightly more indirect pressure from the World Bank, the government agreed to hold a broadly inclusive national conference in early 1990.[31] The delegates surprised the government by suspending the constitution, voting to create the position of prime minister, and initiating a process that led to multiparty presidential and legislative elections the following year (Heilbrunn 1993; Nwajiaku 1994). In 1991, Nicéphore Soglo, a former executive director for Africa at the World Bank, defeated incumbent Mathieu Kérékou to become the new president, and legislative elections accorded the largest number of seats to an alliance of pro-Soglo parties. Despite allegations of irregularities, subsequent elections in Benin have led to alternations of executive power in 1996 and 2006 as well as shifting legislative majorities.[32] The alternating power of Benin's parties offers a clear contrast to the dominant position of the ANC in South Africa. At the local level, however, the majority of Benin's electoral districts are noncompetitive (Wantchekon 2003, 406). Although electoral politics have often been described as heavily influenced by clientelism, Leonard Wantchekon demonstrates that clientelist appeals "are not universally accepted even among poor voters at low levels of economic development" (2003, 22).

Sally Scott's (2001) fieldwork with a development association (ADESS, l'Association pour le Développement de la Sous-Préfecture de Sakété) based in the district of Sakété offers several crucial parallels to the challenges faced by South African civics once democracy had been established. District development associations were found across Benin from the 1960s but were disbanded by the regime in the 1970s. In the late 1980s and early 1990s, well-educated professionals in many areas returned to their hometowns to relaunch these associations. Although Kérékou initially encouraged these actions, hoping they would shore up his faltering regime, most associations supported a return to democracy and defined themselves as independent of political parties. Development-association representatives comprised 70 of the 488 conference participants at the national conference that called for an end to the Marxist regime and demanded market reforms as well as multiparty elections (Gisselquist 2008, 796). In Sakété the development association and a competing district youth association (AJSS, l'Association de la Jeunesse de la Sous-Prefecture de Sakété) were relaunched shortly after the 1990 transition. When the Sakété organizations were drawn into election campaigning, their regular organizational activity ceased, and all energies were focused on the campaign. ADESS campaigned for its leader, and AJSS supported an important backer of the organization. The leader of ADESS became a member of parliament, but the politician supported by AJSS did not win elected office. Despite the success of the first campaign and the failure of the second, both organizations declined as a result of their focus on electoral politics.

While neither ADESS nor AJSS began with a membership base as strong as that of the civics, they were comprised of people supporting a range of parties. Because their organizations were not allied with any single party, they were seemingly better placed than the civics to operate outside the fray of party politics and maintain their organizations as independent actors. But, this desire to maintain their independence led them to suspend their organizational activities during the election period. In the case of ADESS, the congress meeting was postponed. This seems to have been the result of the leader's concerns that a meeting could provide an opportunity for others to question his leadership skills and thereby impact his election campaign for parliament. Other members of the association did not press for a congress because this "would have highlighted the tense intermingling of the development association and politics, after virtually everyone had advocated the separation of the two" (S. J. Scott, e-mail, July 3, 2009). In the case of AJSS, some members of the leadership team did not back the party of their benefactor, but with most members focused on supporting a single candidate, there was little room for other activities. In both cases, the divisions created by the campaigns fractured the organizations, which were heavily dependent on their leaders.

The experiences of Sakété's organizations were not unique. They formed part of a larger pattern in which many associations were declining as their leaders engaged in party politics (Seely 2009, 74). Although both ADESS and AJSS defined themselves as independent of party politics, their experiences illustrate the draw of electoral politics for nongovernmental actors. While civic leaders in any democracy may be drawn to elected office, the appeal of government office is often far stronger in new democracies. Authoritarian rule and its prohibitions on opposition parties by definition exclude many actors from politics and press political activity into formally nonparty political organizations. The end of authoritarian rule encourages movement back from community and nongovernmental organizations into national politics, leading to a brain drain of successful candidates. The attraction of electoral politics in a new democracy thereby works to reinforce a cycle of demobilization as leading actors shift their energies from community organizing to institutionalized party politics, whether they run for office themselves or support a favorite candidate. Community organizing then becomes a get-out-the-vote campaign. The focus of activity in both ADESS and AJSS was internally disciplined by their leaders' attraction to institutional politics and the various benefits it offered. The political parties themselves and the broader opportunities offered by the new regime acted as background conditions encouraging this shift.

Benin's return to democracy was also marked by a return to capitalism and a donor-supported economic recovery (Gazibo 2005). But the economic growth that other areas of the country experienced did not come to Sakété, where material conditions remained pressing for most residents. Given the continued difficult material circumstances, the decline of the district development association cannot be attributed to the organization's success at meeting the needs of the community that it claimed to represent. Like South Africa's civics, the development and the student organization participated in a general move toward more-institutionalized forms of collective action, seeking to establish permanent organizations and participate in party politics, supporting and even fielding candidates for elected office. Local organizations faced different challenges in the largely rural district of Sakété, where three-quarters of residents earned their living from farming (S. J. Scott 2003), and in the largely urban townships across South Africa, but in each case the rise of political party competition weakened local organizations. At a national level in Benin, additional conferences were held during Soglo's tenure, but despite their symbolic importance, participants were unable to effectively hold the state leadership to account (Heilbrunn 1999, 232). Under Soglo, Benin continued to implement its World Bank–driven economic reform program, which left little space for productive input from popular groups (Amuwo 2003, 168).

The experiences of Chilean urban popular movements during the return to democratic rule offers another example of the diminishing space for popular inputs in new democracies pursing neoliberal economic policies. In Chile, urban popular organizations, including community soup kitchens, self-defense organizations, and youth and religious groups, put increasing pressure on the authoritarian regime through their protest actions from 1983 to 1986. Their mobilization created an opportunity for opposition parties to once again challenge the government and the regime (Posner 2004, 64). Over fifteen parties and movements worked together to campaign for a no vote in a 1988 referendum on whether General Augusto Pinochet should receive another eight-year term in office (Paley 2001, 96). The campaign shocked Pinochet by winning over 55 percent of the vote and ushered in the end of the military dictatorship (Schneider 1995, 193).[33] Multiparty elections in the following year brought Christian Democrat Patricio Aylwin to the presidency as the head of a coalition of seventeen political parties, Concertación. In 1993 another Christian Democrat and leader of Concertación, Eduardo Frei Ruiz-Tagle, became president. In 2000, Socialist Ricardo Lagos won the presidential election. Like Benin and unlike South Africa, Chile does not have a single dominant party, though it was governed by parties belonging to the Concertación coalition for the first two decades after its return to democracy.[34] In the aftermath of authoritarian rule, Chile has also pursued a decentralization of power (Eaton 2004), while South Africa has centralized power to address the gross inequities of apartheid.[35]

Despite these significant differences, Chile's shantytown neighborhood organizations have followed a remarkably similar trajectory to that of South Africa's civics. Both developed in response to basic material needs and grew to make rights-based demands under authoritarian regimes. Both engaged in high levels of mobilization that played a key role in helping to bring about a transition, and both declined markedly with the advent of formal democratic rule. The simple explanation for this decline might at first glance seem to be that the goals of these organizations were achieved through the transition of power, but this would be to misunderstand both the purpose of these organizations as well as the experiences of the community residents who participated in their actions. The material conditions that had initially motivated community organization and mobilization failed to significantly improve in either case. Speaking of Chile, economist Rafael Agacino echoed Thabo Mbeki's words concerning South Africa's two nations: "It appears, we have become two countries divided by the abysmal inequalities between rich and poor" (2003, 48). In both countries, residents of poor urban communities often expressed disappointment at the lack of more-substantive change as a result of formal democratization (Olavarría 2003; Paley 2001; Teichman 2009). Despite the great differences between the countries' histories and their previous experiences of democracy and authoritarian rule, the reasons for the decline of these movements are strikingly similar. Local organizations in Chile, like the South African civics, experienced a process of institutional disciplining at three levels: within the organizations themselves, as a product of interactions between the organizations and political parties, and through the formal and informal rules of the new regime.

In Chile, shantytown organizations were central to the rising protest movement. Although they existed throughout the authoritarian period, they grew dramatically after the economic crisis of 1981 as they worked to meet the needs of poor residents. By 1986 an estimated 220,000 people participated in popular organizations (Oxhorn 1995, 81; Garretón 2003), the overwhelming majority of which were formed to address urgent material needs (Salman 1994). Like South Africa's civics, these organizations formed to address housing, services, and cost-of-living concerns. They also engaged in numerous self-help initiatives such as communal kitchens and education programs. Similar to the civics, the organizations engaged in consciousness raising and worked to develop ideals of participation and democracy: "[The residents of the *poblaciones*] sought not merely the absence of torture and disappearance and the holding of periodic electoral rituals but a political and social system that offered them meaningful opportunities to participate in shaping the direction of social transformation based on the values of solidarity and social justice that had underpinned Allende's Unidad Popular project" (Bresnahan 2003, 4). They also carved out their own democratic spaces, which contrasted sharply with the politics of the authoritarian regime. As shantytown dwellers organized and protested, the state responded with violence and attempted to discredit the opposition, but the government was weakened and under pressure eventually agreed to the 1988 referendum (Hipsher 1996, 280–85).

In 1986, even before the dramatic no vote, Chile's shantytown organizations began to demobilize as political parties reemerged as the leading political actors. Popular organizations threw their support behind the parties in an effort to offer the strongest challenge to the still-repressive military regime, and many parties sought to limit the demands made by popular organizations as they pursued a negotiated end to authoritarian rule. The leftist parties with strong connections to shantytown organizations (the Socialist Party faction, PS-Almeyda, and the Communist Party) tended to be slower in abandoning their support for popular resistance, but they too realized that their best chance for continued relevance lay in joining the broad coalition of parties seeking to discourage popular protest (PS-Almeyda) or they would be sidelined in the transition process (Communist Party) (Posner 2004, 65–66).[36] When political parties were legalized in 1987, popular organizations were pressed further into the background of the unfolding transition process.

The earlier and stronger marginalization of popular organizations in Chile than in South Africa (where a comparable demobilization took place only after democratic elections had been held and the new government had taken office) is explained by three key factors. First, leading opposition actors in Chile drew on what they understood to be the lessons of Pinochet's coup: too much mobilization and polarization could trigger a violent authoritarian backlash. Second, popular organizations were not as clearly allied to the leading political parties, nor were they as crucial to the parties' strategy for bringing about a transition. In South Africa, the ANC encouraged mass protest to press its demands at formal negotiations. It actively sought to further politicize and mobilize ordinary South Africans until the democratic elections had been held. Third, the Chilean parties that supported popular organizing among the *pobladores* risked their own political future by continuing to encourage resistance. As a result, citizen participation in Chile in the late 1980s was largely focused on electoral processes such as registering and voting in the plebiscite and the following election. Philip Oxhorn quotes a woman active in soup kitchens: "'Everything was for the elections, including the best leaders, which led to a decrease in' popular-sector organizational activity" (1995, 256).

Once in power, "the governing parties no longer needed grassroots activists" (Schneider 1995, 201). Party leaders pressed all actors to work through the institutions of the state as they sought to revive its institutions. In a statement that could have come from SANCO leaders in South Africa, Hugo Flores, the president of the Chilean national shantytown organization Solidarity, argued in 1991: "The protests are over now. We will not use land seizures anymore. . . . There has been a lot of debate in our organization about land seizures, and historically this is not the moment. We must support this democracy" (quoted in Hipsher 1996, 284–85). After helping to bring about a transition and campaigning in an election to bring the coalition government into power, many local organizers felt a need to continue to support their allies, now in government, by moderating their demands. Nonetheless, popular organizations struggled with disillusionment due to their formal exclusion from the broader political process, frustration with the slow rate of change and limited local level democratization, and the task of redefining themselves within the new context (Oxhorn 1995, 273–78). Each of these challenges parallels those faced by the civics in South Africa. By 2001 an estimated 1 percent or less of *pobladores* participated in neighborhood associations in Chile; during the military dictatorship roughly 15 to 20 percent participated (Posner 2004, 70). Speaking of one neighborhood, an activist argued that those seeking political office now used local organizations as a vehicle for their professional goals: "They [local activists] use the social work in the neighborhood associations to be a candidate in the municipal elections" (quoted in Olavarría 2003, 31).

Like their South African counterparts, Chilean popular organizations struggled to actively engage the complex policy-making process. Looking at the first decade after the return to democracy, Julia Paley's (2001) work in La Bandera, a highly politicized shantytown in Santiago, offers a sober assessment. Even this area experienced a marked demobilization of participation. Paley defines a broad process of institutional disciplining that she terms the "marketing of democracy." As part of this process, community organizations were encouraged to work to support the state and donate their labor at the same time that policy making was reserved for those with formal educational and professional credentials. This technocratization of policy making was not unique to La Bandera. It was a product of a broader neoliberal vision of development that limits policy discussions to elected political leaders and high-level bureaucrats, who are expected to make decisions free of the "irrational influences" of the general public (Teichman 2009, 68–69).[37] The removal of social problems from the scope of politics encouraged many organized *pobladores* to distance themselves from political parties (Olavarría 2003, 31). A neoliberal approach to development therefore came at the expense of participatory democracy.

In the surviving community organizations in La Bandera, Paley found continued resistance to the forms of participation encouraged by the state and a demand for the richer forms of community participation that were created during the 1980s. State officials promoted a politics of loyalty and pressed local organizations not to march or protest against the government. The state also encouraged individuals to work to support government programs, to vote, and to participate in surveys to generate data. In this context, challenging the government's policies was quickly labeled by elected representatives as undemocratic. The shantytown residents' organization, Llareta, pressed for a different understanding of participation. Its members sought to create a process in which they could engage and critique policy and not be limited to the elite form of democracy that the South African civics had also criticized. This struggle for a more participatory system demonstrates that despite the strong effects of institutional disciplining, this process was not absolute or by any means complete. Although the structural pressures of the transition process were strong, they did not singularly determine individuals' and organizations' actions. Though the members of Llareta were unable to change their formal democracy from one that might best be termed "low-fat" (Paley 2001, 3), they did resist its impact on their own ideals and understandings of what democracy should entail.

Centralizing Power under Democracy

In South Africa, Benin, and Chile, regime change created significant challenges for autonomous local organizations through a process of disciplining that was central to the institutionalization of the new democracy. In each case, popular organizations receded into the background of national politics as political parties assumed center stage. Local organizations were further weakened as they spent time and energy engaging in electoral politics, and they lost leaders to elected office. In order to establish a new system, individuals and organizations understandably needed to support that system. Demobilization was therefore encouraged by leaders of popular organizations in both Chile and South Africa when they believed it would improve the chance of creating and strengthening democracy. This created a paradoxical, at least short term, perceived trade-off: strong, independent local organizations or democracy.

More surprising than the pressures placed on organizations by political parties seeking to gain and then maintain office were the pressures that the political transition itself created. In both the organizations in Sákété, Benin, and South Africa's SANCO, the desire to compete in the new arena of democratic politics encouraged increasingly centralized structures that disconnected leaders from their intended constituencies. The structures of their organizations did help some leaders to attain elected office, but they discouraged greater participation and weakened the organizations overall. More broadly, discourses of democracy and development in both Chile and South Africa worked to generate consent but discouraged active participatory processes. Both Chile's shantytown residents and South Africa's township residents found it difficult to participate in policy discussions increasingly governed by technocratic processes that limited participation to government and educated specialists. SANCO's attempts to compete in the newly liberalized and marketized environment led it to take a further step by creating an investment arm and what was meant to be an income-generating membership program. Even if these programs had succeeded, and they clearly did not, they would have strengthened the centralizing tendency in the civic organization, giving even more power to those at the top and less opportunity for input to those below.

Regime change toward a more democratic system by definition brings new, formerly excluded actors into formal politics. It gives all citizens, with few exceptions, equal formal legal standing. It is also a process of institutionalization and thereby the centralization of power. Even in a system that decentralizes power through regional and local institutions, as Chile has done, a democratization process includes centralizing tendencies as actors previously outside the formal political system are brought inside it. Ideally, this aspect of centralizing power through formal political institutions makes political processes more transparent, open, efficient, and accessible to all citizens. But the very process of institutionalizing power, at its best, will exclude those who do not have full access to state institutions due to factors such as distance or a lack of information, education, material resources, or continuing discrimination.

Poor residents in both South Africa's and Chile's shantytowns complained of exactly such exclusion. Add to this the increasing technocratization of policy-making and the demand for policy-specific forms of knowledge in order to engage key issues, and some citizens may feel they have a lesser voice in the new political system than they did during the struggle to bring about the democratic regime.

The process of institutional disciplining produces several fundamental contradictions for a new democracy. First, it rests on the logic that it is necessary to limit mobilization and even organization in order to protect democracy. This directly contradicts pluralist arguments that democracy requires the active expression of a range of interests and demands. Second, the material needs that formed the original impetus for mobilization and organization are not addressed by the political transition. If the new democratic system does not provide avenues for addressing these concerns and the new government does not act, the original cause for mobilization remains largely unchanged. Third, for those organizations that developed internal democratic processes and an ideal of a responsive democratic system, the very argument that they should now reduce their participation contradicts their basic philosophy. Fourth, new democratic institutions of the state are not created overnight. Although the opportunity to vote in free national elections and the guarantee of rights formerly denied mark a dramatic shift for all citizens, local government, the sphere of government closest to the people, will often be slow to change and may not be organized to encourage critical participation. However, in both the Chilean organization Llareta and some of the local civics in South Africa, the participatory ideal remained alive. The next chapter turns to the challenges of addressing the contradictions of this ideal within the realities of a new democracy.

5

Contentious Democracy

What rights are you talking about, we do not have rights, none of us have rights. I mean if we did have rights, we would be treated with more respect. If ESKOM [electricity utility] thinks [it] can just come and cut us off do you see rights and democracy in that? I don't. This democracy of theirs ends with the vote [*democracy e ya bona efella ka go vota*].

Mr. Ntobong, quoted by Grace Khunou, in "'Massive Cutoffs':
Cost Recovery and Electricity Service in Diepkloof, Soweto"

Democracy in South Africa brought all adult citizens the right to vote, but at the same time that political and civil rights expanded, envisaged socioeconomic rights seemed to contract. A policy of cost recovery was introduced, reducing subsidies and requiring consumers, even in desperately poor communities, to pay close to the full cost of services such as electricity and water.[1] Banks and municipalities were able to quickly evict poor residents from their homes after relatively short periods of nonpayment and low arrears. At the same time, democracy reshaped expectations for claim making and for popular contention. All South Africans were now expected to play their formal role in the electoral process by turning out to vote. Their newly elected representatives would then chart a course for democracy and development. When citizens sought to challenge decisions, large or small, they were to employ legal processes, to work through formal institutions, and to be patient. More radical demands, it was argued, needed to be deferred in order for democracy to take hold. But the legacies of the past could not be undone overnight. As many grew increasingly desperate as a result of the government's economic policies and frustrated by feelings of political marginalization, South Africa saw a resurgence of social movement activity. The movements challenged government policies, but they also confronted structures of power that they defined as antidemocratic.

This leads to a number of fundamental questions for any new democracy. When some choose to protest, what impact will this have on the institutions of the new regime? Is there room for popular action, for contentious politics and the expansion of demands? Do demands need to be restrained to reduce threats to the potentially fragile regime? Just five years into South Africa's new democracy, a rising chorus of popular actors responded with a resounding no. Most government and business leaders begged to differ.

There are many potential challenges to the viability of any new democracy. Some of the most often cited include the continued authority of nonelected elites, threats of military coups, biased electoral processes, economic crises, the lack of institutionalized party systems, partial judiciaries, the role of patronage and corruption, and the existence of antisystem movements (Gunther, Diamandouros, and Puhle 1995; Linz and Stepan 1996; Mainwaring, O'Donnell, and Valenzuela 1992). The unfolding debate over the role of social movements in new democracies reflects two broad sets of concerns. On one hand, those working within newly democratized state institutions point to the threats that movements may pose and suggest the need to reduce political and economic instability by restraining protest. On the other hand, social movement activists argue that governments use the fear of instability as an excuse to repress valid claims and thereby undermine popular representation, critical debate, and democracy itself. These concerns tug at the roots of the struggle for democracy. What was the struggle actually for? Have these ends been achieved or thwarted? Should the struggle continue? These questions become all the more difficult when the new leaders of the democratic state are the same people who participated in and often led the struggle against authoritarian rule.

In the case of South Africa, ANC leaders had once encouraged wide-ranging protests and even ungovernability in the townships in order to bring down the apartheid state. Now in government, they raised concerns that protests might undermine their intended restructuring and reform of state institutions. Protest, they argued, could also cause instability in the markets and provoke capital flight. In seeking to address these fears, they worked to channel popular actors such as SANCO to support their policies and their power. Some NGOs also presented mass-mobilization as "out-dated" and "backward apartheid-era struggle tactics" that were not appropriate in the new era of political and economic liberalism (Mueller-Hirth 2009, 431). As local organizations became frustrated with these attempts to influence their actions, they considered when and how they might press their demands more forcefully to their former comrades, who now seemed too busy with the business of the state and private business ventures to receive the petitions of poor communities.

After a hard-fought struggle to achieve democracy, it makes sense to try to protect the new institutions of that democracy. Those who make this argument point to the dangers posed by a mobilized citizenry and draw lessons from breakdowns of democracy in Europe in the first half of the twentieth century and Latin America in the second half. From this perspective, antisystem movements triggered by populations frustrated with a lack of material improvement offer a clear threat (Schedler 1998, 96). The politics of necessity could, according to this logic, lead to the downfall of democracy. This suggests a danger for any democracy with significant economic inequality or a large number of poor citizens. Analysts looking specifically at South Africa and its high levels of inequality and poverty have pointed to the possible role of a "mobilized citizenry" as an "active agent in the breakdown of democracy" (Mattes and Thiel 1998, 95–96). But organizing to address poverty does not on its own signal antisystem tendencies.

Arguments emphasizing the dangers of antisystem movements tend to be a bit unclear about how such movements might be identified. Richard Gunther, P. Nikiforos Diamandouros, and Hans-Jürgen Puhle argue that "an antisystem party or movement must be unequivocally opposed to the existing regime," but they add that such actors may "often try to subvert existing institutions, even when elected to serve in them" (1995, 13). This suggests significant room for interpretation in the labeling of movements. The devil, it seems, is in the details. The growth of an armed rebellion seeking to overthrow the government and take control of the state certainly suggests a risk for democracy. But does township organizing along the lines of the civics under apartheid pose a real danger? What if civic mobilization leads to violence? The question becomes one of degree: when might popular mobilization be understood as part of a vibrant democracy and when might it be considered a threat to the state?

Looking at a period of great mobilization characterized by violence, which began roughly twenty years into the life of Italy's new democracy, Sidney Tarrow suggests that even dramatic periods of instability are productive for democracy: "For when the dust of the disorder had settled, it became clear that the boundaries of mass politics had been extended. There were changes in public policy and in the composition of the political class. New frames of meaning were introduced into what Gramsci called the 'common sense' of capitalist democracies. Most people were taking part in decisions affecting their lives, and new forms of participation had been added to the repertoire of participation. Disorder contributed to the broadening of democracy where it was strong and to its consolidation where it was weak" (1989, 1). In the mid-1960s to 1970s, when the protests were occurring, many critics worried about the threats of anarchism and utopian political ideologies, but looking back,

Tarrow is quite adamant that "disorder and democracy are not opposed." He does, however, add an important caveat that underlines some of the fears mentioned earlier. Tarrow argues that disorder is productive as long as "elites are not united around an anti-democratic project" as was the case in Germany in 1933 and in Italy in 1922 (1989, 347).

In South Africa, political and economic elites have unanimously endorsed liberal democracy and the economic gains that it has brought them (M. McDonald 2006), but violence remains a problem. As popular organizing in South Africa's poor townships once again increased in the late 1990s and protesters took to the streets, many South Africans feared the specter of unrest. Recent history seemed to suggest that demands for change and violence went hand in hand. Continuing high rates of criminal violence (Shaw 2002) have also prompted arguments to restrict civil liberties to assist in the policing of crime.[2] But the police themselves are poorly trained, underresourced, and overstretched, and as a result they often fall back on authoritarian policing practices whether in response to an armed robbery or a rowdy public protest. The majority of protest actions in South Africa since the end of apartheid have been peaceful, but protest and the threat of violence by the police or protesters are still tied together in the popular consciousness.

Within this context, the state and social movements engage in a delicate dance marked by periods of direct action, negotiation, explosion, co-optation, and resistance. Unlike many authoritarian regimes, democracies tend not to simply repress movements (Goldstone 2003, 13; Cunningham 2003; Luders 2003) but participate in a much more sophisticated set of interactions with movement actors, tolerating and undermining, encouraging, and stifling. Similarly, movements do not simply challenge the state but often prod, promote, bait, and bargain (Zuern 2006b), and the presence of potential movement allies in state offices does not make protests any less likely (Van Dyke 2003, 240). In this chapter we will investigate the resulting interplay in three parts. First, we return to the experiences of the civics to consider a range of responses to the co-optation of the national organization. Next, we investigate the strategies of postapartheid social movements, demonstrating the use of disruption and destabilization to defend and expand the discourse and practice of political and socioeconomic rights. As these movements interact with the state, many are labeled "antisystem" by state actors. Finally, the chapter closes with a consideration of two contrasting country studies, each of which offers different parallels to the South African case. Botswana, a country with a dominant-party democracy similar in certain respects to South Africa, provides an example of a regime with very low levels of contention. Argentina, on the other hand, offers an example of extraordinarily high contention and the expansion of popular demands. These cases shed light on the dangers of destabilization for new democracies as well as the opportunities for the expansion of rights. Together these discussions suggest the possibility of a contentious route to the institutionalization of a new regime and a challenge to the disciplining forces of liberal democracy.

The Civic: Caught "With Its Pens Down"

The challenges of the transition to democracy left SANCO, in the words of its president, "with its pens down" because SANCO had "not come to grips with post-liberation politics" (Hlongwane 1997, 2). At SANCO's 1997 national conference, its leadership seemed to signal a shift in its approach and a recognition that protest action might still be necessary, even in a new democracy dominated by its ally, the ANC. The theme of the conference suggested a radical agenda, "Building a Revolutionary Social Movement to Conquer Challenges of the 21st Century," and speakers warned that national and local governments were failing to address the basic needs of residents.[3] President Mlungisi Hlongwane argued that this failure was in large part a result of the government's endorsement of neoliberal economic principles and its prioritization of growth over redistribution. He stated: "It is economically and politically impossible for government to serve equally the World Bank and the electorate as equal consumers in the S[outh] A[frican] market. Our constituency is located within those who may become disgruntled, unless radical changes and the pace of delivery assumes a revolutionary character" (1997, 6). In a clear attempt to tap into what they observed as a growing restlessness and frustration, SANCO leaders said that they would not work through negotiations alone. If the government refused to respond to SANCO's concerns, mass action remained an option. In 1998, SANCO's president asserted: "It [SANCO] will not discard its tactics of protest and mass action which it used in the '80s to effectively combat apartheid" (*Sowetan*, April 20, 1998, 11). Such arguments directly contradicted SANCO's earlier rhetoric that a new era in South African politics meant a departure from revolutionary and mass-action tactics.

Still, SANCO's national office was not willing to directly challenge the ANC. When some local SANCO organizations considered fielding their own candidates to run as local government councilors, the national office threatened consequences. The local supporters of this option drew upon the successes of SANCO leaders who ran as ward councilors in 1995 and argued that SANCO could be quite successful if it became a political party (ANC 1999 [*Umrabulo*

7]). SANCO's national leaders, however, continued to defend their blanket support for the ANC. When asked about his organization's uncritical electoral support for the ANC, SANCO's president dismissed the question, arguing: "SANCO is a poor organization, we make up the poor of this country. If you do not like our method of organizing and who we elect to office and who we will support in the next elections . . . then you do not like the poor" (*Sowetan*, April 20, 1998, 11).

Despite threats from the national office, the Eastern Cape region vowed to endorse only individual candidates in the 2000 local government elections (Tofile, interview, January 22, 2001; SANCO PEDU 2000). Penrose Ntlonti, a regional executive member, argued that SANCO would support independent candidates because it needed to be accountable to its constituents (quoted in *Daily Dispatch*, July 8, 2000); he later admitted that SANCO was also frustrated that some of its candidates had been dropped from local election lists by the ANC (*Financial Mail*, September 29, 2000, 39). One Eastern Cape civic leader argued that unquestioning support for the ANC significantly threatened the civic's continued existence and democracy itself: "We find in SANCO that the more we stick within the alliance, the more we become dictatorial to our people" (anonymous Port Elizabeth civic leader 1, interview, January 2001).

In the end, none of the independent Port Elizabeth candidates won local office.[4] This failure at the polls demonstrated the continued overwhelming electoral support for the ANC. Despite considerable discontent with local government performance and the failings of numerous ANC councilors, the ANC remained the party of liberation (Zuern 2002). A local SANCO supporter argued that voters still deferred to the ANC: "People still see the ANC as the only agent to change their lives. They don't see that their lives are in their hands" (anonymous Port Elizabeth civic leader 2, interview, January 2001). The election results also suggested that SANCO members and leaders who aspired to elected office would be best served by continuing to work with and through the ANC. National leaders of SANCO therefore employed this lack of success at the polls to underscore their pronouncements that SANCO would not and should not directly challenge the ANC. In Hlongwane's address to the ANC at its 2002 national conference, he shared an accepted truth within SANCO's leadership circle: "SANCO would have no relevance if its intention is to compete with the ANC" (SAPA, December 18, 2002).[5] The national office of SANCO remained committed to its alliance with the ANC despite the impact that this had on local organization and participatory governance. For those at the top, the benefits of a continued alliance with the ANC far outweighed the ideal of independent action.

Others disagreed. SANCO's top-heavy ANC-aligned structure led to great tensions within the organization and a dramatic rupture. In 1997, Mzwanele Mayekiso, branch chairman of SANCO Alexandra, head of the SANCO Research and Development Institute (SRDI), and frequent newspaper columnist, was suspended from SANCO by a fax from the national office. The fax charged Mayekiso with "publicly challenging the policies of the organization in the mass media and consistently and brazenly defying the decisions and directive of the national executive of SANCO" (quoted in *Sunday Independent*, July 20, 1997, 5). Mayekiso had criticized SANCO's decision to support Thabo Mbeki as the next president of South Africa because SANCO had announced its support before the ANC had formally chosen its leading candidate. Mayekiso had also raised R1 million (over $200,000) on behalf of SRDI, which SANCO's national leadership claimed the right to use at its discretion. Mayekiso disagreed, arguing that the money should go directly to SANCO branches (*Sunday Tribune*, July 20, 1997, 9).

Mayekiso's dismissal led to a split within the local Alexandra branch between a large group of his supporters who were also frustrated with the policies of SANCO national and Philemon Machitela, the branch secretary. When the Gauteng Provincial leadership of SANCO criticized the national office's handling of the dispute, the national office informed the provincial leaders that a new leadership would be elected for the province. Before the elections could take place, four provincial leaders resigned, including Ali Tleane, the former general secretary of the province.[6] In another influential SANCO branch, another long-time leader became so frustrated with the civic's actions that he too resigned. Maynard Menu, the former president of SANCO Soweto who was described in the press as "one of the country's most experienced civic leaders" (*Sunday Independent*, March 29, 1998, 2), had become increasingly critical of SANCO's top-down style and raised uncomfortable questions regarding its ventures into business. After Menu's departure, SANCO falsely claimed that Menu had left to join a rival party to the ANC (Menu, interview, May 28, 1999).[7] Tleane, who left the provincial structure, was accused of not remaining loyal to the ANC and moving SANCO away from the ANC. Such accusations only increased the public perception of SANCO as not only an ANC ally but also an ANC front.[8]

At the local level of SANCO, civic leaders in many areas were working on a project of their own to strengthen their local structures; unfortunately for the national office, this generally meant distancing themselves from the national organization. In late 1997 the leadership of the Transkei region of SANCO (an ANC stronghold) broke away from the national body, citing SANCO's ties to the ANC as a major concern (Lodge 1999b, 90). In early

1998 the Northern Cape region also considered breaking away (Gumede 1998). In 1999 a number of SANCO regions in the Eastern Cape passed a vote of no confidence in their Provincial Executive Committee; the regions also agreed to oust all SANCO executives who simultaneously held political posts (*Daily Dispatch*, May 18, 1999). The national-level response to these events was once again to attempt to control local actions. SANCO's national office argued that it needed to make sure the regions had followed the proper procedures and that if they had not, their decisions would be reconsidered (Williams, interview, May 31, 1999). In less dramatic fashion, several local civic structures in various parts of the country that still had grassroots support increasingly distanced themselves from SANCO and returned to the earlier strength of the civics, their autonomy and their responsiveness to local issues.

In other areas, community members had become so frustrated with the lack of an independent civic structure that they formed new non-SANCO structures. In the East Rand, Simunye was launched along the same lines as earlier civic structures, largely to address questions of service and housing delivery. Simunye stood firmly outside the SANCO camp. At a mass meeting in Tsakane just prior to the 1997 electricity cuts, community residents encouraged by Simunye members not only shouted down SANCO leaders attempting to address the crowd but also prevented provincial government leaders (Safety and Security MEC Jessie Duarte and Development, Planning and Local Government MEC Sicelo Shiceka) from speaking (Nxumalo, interview, July 28, 1997). Clashes between law enforcement and some residents ensued (*Star*, July 28, 1997, 1). In the Vaal area, a group calling itself the Concerned Residents Committee organized a march against local councilors, demanding that they resign. Under pressure, the councilors and the mayor signed documents agreeing to the people's demands, but the legality of the documents was later challenged, and the elected leaders retained their posts (Mazibuko, interview, May 27, 1999). As these so-called popcorn civics sprang up in different parts of the country, the one consistent aspect of their organization and mobilization was a more radical approach than that taken by the SANCO civics and, importantly, a lack of affiliation to the ANC.

Room for Debate?

South Africa is often referred to as a "dominant-party democracy" because the ANC has achieved repeated and overwhelming victories in national, provincial, and local elections.[9] Although the ANC's ascension to power has occurred through great popular support rather than intimidation or fraud, the danger in any system marked by repeated single-party success is that it will lead to reduced checks on the power of the winner and fewer opportunities for opposing ideas, arguments, and policies. Such party dominance has historically allowed for both developmental and authoritarian politics (Wade 1992; Woo-Cummings 1999; Evans 2001). Either or both are possible; neither will necessarily follow great electoral success.

Under Thabo Mbeki's leadership, the ANC took on the great challenges of postapartheid governance. To do so, it centralized power within the government and the party and suppressed dissent within both. The centralizing drive of the ANC government was closely tied to the desire to improve poor service delivery and to transform all levels of government. In order to address the fragmentation of the state and to "streamline" administrative and financial systems, the office of the president was strengthened, and numerous oversight positions staffed by loyal political appointees of the president were created. In his analysis of these reforms, Anthony Butler argues: "New oversight and co-ordination mechanisms, and the highly centralized formal structure of the core executive, are understandable reactions to the provincial incapacities in policy design and implementation" (2000, 198). He adds, however, that Mbeki also demonstrated a clear unwillingness to allow those provinces and cities that had the capacity to address challenges to take control of their own reform processes. As Mbeki centralized authority in the executive, forums for transformation that were designed to encourage broad participation increasingly gave way to top-down and technocratic approaches to governance (Gevisser 2007; Heller 2000; Lodge 1999a).

South Africa's closed-list proportional representation system also works to strengthen the power of party leaders since the leading figures in each party have extensive control over their members in parliament, undermining constituent representation in the system as a whole (Mattes and Thiel 1998, 105). Thus opportunities for debate within broader party structures are all the more important for those who seek to bring about a change in policy. A revision of the ANC's constitution, however, has increased the time between ANC national conferences from three to five years. Though this change was due in part to resource constraints and was intended to match national elections, which take place every five years, it weakened a key mechanism of leadership accountability to the rank and file within the ANC (Lodge 1999b, 8–9). ANC leaders have also exhibited a general lack of tolerance for criticism of ANC policies and often argue that such criticism, whether coming from members of the Tripartite Alliance (the Congress of South African Trade Unions, COSATU;

and the South African Communist Party, SACP) or other societal actors, is an attempt to halt transformation.

Opposition parties do offer alternatives to the ANC, but because of their relative weakness, their influence has been limited largely to criticizing ANC policy. Only three opposition parties have been able to secure at least ten parliamentary seats in more than one election. These include the Democratic Alliance (DA; formerly the Democratic Party, DP), the Inkatha Freedom Party (IFP; formerly Inkatha), and the New National Party (NNP; formerly the NP), which was disbanded in 2005.[10] Each of these parties existed in some form under apartheid and, unlike the ANC, participated in state institutions. Three significant new parties have been formed since the end of apartheid. The first two, the United Democratic Movement, launched in 1997, and the Independent Democrats, launched in 2003, initially provoked great enthusiasm but have failed to offer a sustained challenge to ANC hegemony. The third, the Congress of the People, offered the strongest challenge to the ANC of the new parties, winning thirty seats in its first election in 2009 (Habib and Herzenberg 2009). These thirty seats, however, comprise less than 8 percent of the National Assembly's four hundred seats, two-thirds of which are controlled by the ANC.

At the local level, the participatory demands of the domestic antiapartheid movement are reflected in the formal institutions of the state, but the implementation of these ideals is weak. First, the Constitution of the Republic of South Africa (1996) stresses the importance of participation by stipulating that local government should "encourage the involvement of communities and community organizations in the matters of local government" (chap. 7, sec. 152, 1.e.). Second, the Local Municipal Structures Act (1998) goes even further by calling for the creation of community-staffed ward committees "to enhance participatory democracy in local government" (chapter 4, pt. 4, 72.3). These ward committees were meant to institutionalize the best of participatory democracy achieved by the civics during the antiapartheid struggle. Makgane Thobejane, in the Johannesburg City Manager's office, argued: "The new system of local government actually emphasizes organs of people's power by talking about the establishment of ward committees. So right from the ward level there will be a mechanism of representation. So basically it is about what is it that we have learned from antiapartheid structures and struggles so that we can translate it into an institutionalized form of our new[ly] achieved democracy so it becomes a regulated kind of participatory democracy" (Thobejane, interview, January 22, 2001). Despite the creation of these new institutions, many activists have argued that there is no "real" democracy at the level of local government.[11] Popular surveys have also consistently demonstrated

	1994		1999		2004		2009	
	Vote %	Seats	Vote %	Seats	Vote %	Seats	Vote %	Seats
African Christian Democratic Party (ACDP)	0.5	2	1.4	6	1.6	7	0.8	3
African National Congres (ANC)	**62.6**	**252**	**66.4**	**266**	**69.7**	**279**	**65.9**	**264**
Azanian People's Organization (AZAPO)			0.2	1	.3	1	0.2	1
Congress of the People (COPE)							**7.4**	**30**
Democratic Party (DP)/ Democratic Alliance (DA)	**1.7**	**7**	**9.6**	**38**	**12.4**	**50**	**16.7**	**67**
Federal Alliance (FA)			0.5	2				
Independent Democrats (ID)					1.7	7	0.9	4
Inkatha Freedom Party (IFP)	**10.5**	**43**	**8.6**	**34**	**7.0**	**28**	**4.6**	**18**
Minority Front (MF)	0.1	0	0.3	1	.4	2	0.3	1
National Party (NP)/ New National Party (NNP)	**20.4**	**82**	**6.9**	**28**	**1.7**	**7**		
Pan Africanist Congress of Azania (PAC)	1.2	5	0.7	3	.7	3	0.3	1
United Christian Democratic Party (UCDP)			0.8	3	.8	3	0.4	2
United Democratic Movement (UDM)			3.4	14	2.3	9	0.9	4
Vryheidsfront Plus (VF)	2.2	9	0.8	3	0.9	4	0.8	4

National Assembly election results, 1994–2009 (data from Independent Electoral Commission of South Africa [www.elections.org.za] and the Electoral Institute of South Africa [EISA; www .eisa.org.za]; table by Sumedha Senanayake)

the highest levels of citizen dissatisfaction with local rather than provincial or national government (Afrobarometer 2009b; Mattes, Davids, and Africa 2000; Taylor and Mattes 1998).[12] The Municipal Demarcation Board appointed by President Mbeki, the national ministry responsible for local government, politicians across the political spectrum, and the media have repeatedly expressed concern over the state of local government, describing it as inefficient, ineffective, and often corrupt.

Interviews with town councilors in Gauteng in 2001 and 2002, after South Africa's second local government elections and the introduction of the Municipal Structures Act, highlighted clear problems of representation through local structures. DA and IFP representatives spoke of being marginalized as non-ANC councilors. They argued that they did not have a voice in decision making and that the ANC would not accept ideas from other parties (Fuchs, interview, July 16, 2002; Ntuli, interview, July 18, 2002). A number of ANC councilors also raised concerns regarding the ANC selection process for local candidates. One councilor, who asked not to be named, argued quite passionately that the

ANC had subverted local-level democracy and made "political" rather than popular decisions: "Some of the candidates were not supposed to have been on board [serving as councilors], but they are on board now after serious intervention from senior structures of the movement" (anonymous ANC councilor, interview, January 2001). Councilors across party lines repeatedly described the ward committees as mechanisms for the government and the ruling party to disseminate information to residents (Gomati, interview, January 25, 2001; Moepi, interview, July 16, 2002) rather than forums in which residents could raise concerns to their elected representatives.[13] Some went so far as to describe ward committees as "just an advisory body" (Moedi, interview, July 19, 2002) or even a "farce" (Fuchs, interview, July 16, 2002). Studies conducted in municipalities across the country have demonstrated that the ward committee system does not provide an effective mechanism for constituents to hold their councilors to account (Bénit-Gbaffou 2008; Piper and Deacon 2008; Raga and Taylor 2005). Even when ward councilors make efforts to represent their constituents' concerns, their powers are limited by the centralization of policy making dominated by the ANC.[14] A government report investigating the state of local government reported: "In practice sector departments hardly ever consult or involve ward councilors in plans and projects" (RSA, Cooperative Governance and Traditional Affairs 2009, 15).

South Africa's Resurgent Movements

Together the centralization of state policy making, the demand for unity within the dominant party, the weakness of opposition political parties, the shortcomings of local government authorities, and SANCO's co-optation have weakened key formal avenues of interest representation for the poor majority. Instead, some of the loudest voices representing the concerns of the country's marginalized citizens have come from the extra-institutional protest actions of social movements, many of which incorporate local civics independent of SANCO. These movements, which formed within a few years of the late 1990s, comprise a range of actors including the Treatment Action Campaign (TAC), the Concerned Citizens' Forum, the Anti-Privatization Forum (APF), the Soweto Electricity Crisis Committee (SECC), the Landless People's Movement (LPM), and the Western Cape Anti-Eviction Campaign (WCAEC) (Ballard et al. 2005; Bond 2006a; Gibson 2006). Other movements, most notably Abahlali baseMjondolo ("the people who live in shacks," AbM), have since become central actors in this resurgence. These movements have received substantial local and international press attention for their demands ranging from medication for HIV/AIDS patients to land reform and redistribution. They have worked to resist housing evictions and the privatization of electricity and water supplies. Together, their actions have publicized both citizens' socioeconomic claims and the state's responses to them. They employ a range of tactics including both legal and illegal actions, but none employs violence as a central strategy to achieve its goals. Despite this fact, they have often been demonized by government officials.

The timing of this increase in popular protest, much of it coming from some of the poorest sectors of the population, coincided with the growing impact of GEAR (the government's neoliberal economic plan) in the late 1990s and Thabo Mbeki's election to the presidency in 1999. As protest actions increased with the new millennium, Mbeki warned of the potential danger that antiprivatization movements posed. He suggested that they threatened not just the ANC's policy goals but also democracy itself: "The ultra-left strives to abuse our internal democratic processes to advance its agenda against policies adopted by our most senior decision-making structures, including our national congresses" (Battersby and Phahlane 2002).[15] In his 2002 address at the opening of the Fifty-First National Conference of the ANC in Stellenbosch, Mbeki continued his attack: "The period since the 50th National Conference has confirmed that the struggle continues to decide who shall determine the national agenda. We must expect that this struggle will intensify with both ultra-left and rightwing forces battling to secure hegemony of their ideas over those of the national democratic revolution and our movement" (Mbeki 2002). The fact that Mbeki presented left- and right-wing movements together was a particularly harsh rebuke to those labeled "ultraleft." While the rightwing forces he referred to largely include those who resisted a transition to democracy and supported some form of apartheid, the ultraleft grew up in the struggle against apartheid. This statement underlined Mbeki's, and with him the government's, general lack of tolerance for alternative perspectives. But not all postapartheid movements have been regarded in the same way.

Movements such as the SECC and the WCAEC, which resisted the government's privatization policies, were consistently demonized by both government actors and much of the popular press. They were often labeled antisystem. Others that sought to work within the government's broader economic framework, such as the TAC, although still facing significant government resistance, often received greater sympathy from the domestic mainstream press and a broader international audience. The TAC proved to be more effective in challenging the antisystem label. Each of the three movements engaged in legal and illegal actions, but it is the TAC that is most often offered as a model of successful, present-day activism in a democratic South

Africa. In working to bring about greater public awareness of HIV/AIDS and greater access to treatment for people living with AIDS, the TAC employs civil disobedience, court actions, marches, and also direct action. In 2000, TAC activists engaged in a defiance campaign and illegally brought into the country five thousand capsules of Biozole, a significantly cheaper form of the patented drug Fluconazole. In response, the former South African health minister, Manto Tschabalala-Msimang, criticized the activists, saying their actions were "not acceptable in a country that is governed by the rule of law" (*Agence France-Presse*, October 19, 2000). Repeatedly frustrated by the government's refusal to provide antiretroviral drugs to HIV-positive pregnant women, the TAC filed culpable homicide charges against the minister of health and the minister of trade and industry in 2003 (Cornelius, interview, July 17, 2003; TAC 2003).

Despite these direct challenges to a reluctant state to address HIV/AIDS and to provide antiretrovirals, the TAC has been able to maintain a working relationship with some members of the ANC and the government. It has pursued an "issue-based incrementalism" (Friedman and Mottiar 2006) and has presented itself as a resource to government as it works to improve the delivery of health care. Its leading spokesperson, Zackie Achmat, has repeatedly defined himself as a loyal member of the ANC, even as he criticized ANC policies. The TAC's positive international press coverage, growing international concern regarding the impact of HIV/AIDS on the African continent, and sustained Western criticism of President Mbeki's HIV/AIDS policies also helped to increase its influence. Despite the illegal actions that have helped the TAC to press its case to a broader public, it is generally viewed as a movement that seeks critical engagement and cooperation with the state as it pursues a rights-based activism that presses the state to fulfill its legal responsibilities. The TAC's influence has even led to praise from South African state representatives. In 2005, Murphey Morobe, the head of communications in the presidency and a former UDF activist, referred to the TAC as "our conscience" as several thousand TAC supporters marched by Parliament (Maclennan 2005). Critical activists, however, have accused the TAC of working "within the corridors of power," possibly demobilizing grassroots activism, and failing to critique the government's broader macroeconomic policy (Friedman and Mottiar 2006, 38).

This last point is crucial. While the TAC's success has often been presented as a product of its organizing strategies, the charismatic personality of Zackie Achmat, and its very effective development of existing social networks (Mbali 2006), it has also worked to avoid additional government resistance by not presenting its demands in opposition to the core economic policies of the

South African government. As a result, it has not generally triggered significant concerns that it will destabilize the South African state. In South Africa, antisystem movements have been defined both by their challenge to the ruling party and by their approach to the government's economic policies. From the perspective of ANC leaders, antiprivatization means antisystem. This equation is a product of a purposeful conflation of the political regime, democracy, and the economic regime, neoliberalism. It results in the elevation of some rights, such as property rights, over others, such as the freedom of expression and dissent. This conflation will be addressed in greater detail in the final chapter. We will now focus on the actions of one of the more radical movements labeled as "ultraleft" and the reactions of state and nonstate actors.

Taking to the Streets and the Courts

The WCAEC, along with other movements such as the SECC and LPM, have consistently been accused of being both antisystem and antidemocratic.[16] Although they have made more-radical economic demands and employed a wider diversity of tactics than the TAC, they have also pursued legal courses of action. In contrast to the TAC, activists in the WCAEC have consistently experienced a difficult relationship with the majority of ANC and government officials. They have found few allies in the corridors of power, and their protest actions have repeatedly led to violence at the hands of the police. They have been defined as threatening to the regime, and their activists have been jailed. Some have been followed by men claiming to work for the National Intelligence Agency.

Formed in early 2001, the WCAEC organized to fight evictions, to address water cutoffs and excessive force employed by the police, and to demand the provision of basic services to poor communities. The organization therefore mobilizes around many of the same concerns as those raised by the SECC (discussed in chap. 2). Both joined the APF and regularly employ mass actions, popular education activities, legal challenges, and direct action campaigns. They are in many respects a direct outgrowth of the antiapartheid civic movement and the rent boycott that it championed. The individual organizations that participate in the campaign have employed a wide range of tactics largely depending on their access to the state, their economic options, and the historical context of state-society relations in their communities. All, however, faced the "Pay and Stay" cost-recovery policies laid out by the City of Cape Town: "Action will be taken against those who do not pay—the Council will not hesitate to cut off services and take legal action where necessary. Residents who do not pay will be without electricity or water and will have to pay the additional costs of reconnection fees, lawyers' fees and legal costs. They could ultimately have their houses sold (if they are ratepayers) or be evicted (if they are tenants in a Council house)" (Xali 2002, 101).

In 2002, based on a national survey, David McDonald estimated that up to 2 million people had been evicted from their homes for nonpayment, and up to 10 million had their water or electricity cut (2002, 162). This figure of 10 million people affected by postapartheid disconnections sparked considerable criticism from government officials, who argued that the overall number was far lower. In response, another study reassessed the data, including new survey material, to conclude that approximately 1.1 million people were affected by cutoffs annually (Hemson and Owusu-Ampomah 2006).[17] These figures underline the stark fact that huge numbers of South Africans have faced a service and housing crisis. Poor residents have been evicted in large numbers, and those who have remained in their homes have often been forced to live without electricity, at times even without water.

In response to these challenges, groups such as the Valhalla Park United Civic Front (a local organization of the WCAEC) have employed "strategic engagement" with the state, largely through direct contact and the development of personal relationships with local authorities ranging from the police to officials working in the housing office. This approach is in many respects similar to that taken by the TAC. The Valhalla Park civic, like the TAC, has stressed that activists reserve the right to take more-radical action when the state does not respond to or dismisses their concerns. A case in point was the civic's demand that the council build speed bumps on a main road where a number of children had been hit by passing cars. After the council repeatedly turned down the civic's request, "civic activists dug a four-meter wide and approximately one-meter deep hole across the main road in the middle of the night" (Oldfield and Stokke 2004, 15). The hole was repaired, and speed bumps were installed the next day. Activists have also employed strategies of illegal land invasions and court actions demanding their constitutional right to emergency housing, leading to a victory for the right to housing against the city of Cape Town (Oldfield and Stokke 2004, 14–16).

In contrast to Valhalla Park, residents in Mandela Park, a poorer community, have experienced a much more confrontational relationship with the state. The Mandela Park Anti-Eviction Campaign (MPAEC) has made demands consistent with those of the overall campaign but has had far less success in its attempts to engage local actors ranging from private banks to government housing officials. By early 2002 an estimated two thousand households in Khayelitsha, which includes Mandela Park, faced eviction. The MPAEC asked the government to intervene by helping to fix the houses and buying back the land from the banks. When these requests were not met, MPAEC members marched to the company that was disconnecting electricity and called for a flat rate of R10 (roughly $1.40) per month for basic services.[18] Activists held sit-ins at the National Building Society offices as well as the Khayalethu Home Loans Company. They also went to the provincial parliament. When these actions failed to bear fruit, MPAEC activists sought to physically stop authorities from evicting residents. The police responded with rubber bullets and made many arrests, further fueling tensions (Desai and Pithouse 2004, 251–56).

The MPAEC therefore engaged in the full range of actions outlined on the AEC website: "The AEC protects families from being evicted primarily by staging sit-ins and demonstrations aimed at turning away those forces that come to evict families. For those families who have already been evicted, the AEC often responds by moving them and their belongings back into their homes. Should these tactics prove unsuccessful in waving off evictions, and in those instances where the government is determined to move forward with evictions, the AEC has at times responded by rendering the contested property unlivable, saying if the people cannot have the land, then no one will" (http://www.antieviction.org.za).

The MPAEC's actions offer a direct parallel to earlier civic strategies. Writing of the 1980s, Tom Lodge has noted: "When evictions were carried out, street committees mobilized the community to oppose them or to reinstate evicted residents in their houses. The political climate became so charged that new tenants were frightened to occupy a house that had been vacated due to eviction for nonpayment of rent" (1991, 270). In the 1980s, evictions were a strategy implemented to defend the viability of the apartheid state. In the postapartheid period, they became part of the neoliberal model of cost recovery encouraged by the World Bank and embraced by the South African government as the pathway to economic growth and development. In both periods, the policy quickly led to violence. In the postapartheid period, police have clashed with protesters, and participants have been charged with violations including trespassing, public violence, and intimidation. The police and the media have employed the charged label of "terrorists" to describe activists resisting evictions. One MPAEC leader, Max Ntanyana, was repeatedly arrested; upon his release he was subject to restrictions that eerily echoed apartheid-era banning orders. He was prevented from addressing any public gathering, attending community meetings, or speaking on the radio (Ntanyana, interview, July 16, 2003).[19]

The frustration of Mandela Park activists is clear. As their attempts to work with state officials were thwarted and their popular actions repressed, the only option seemed to be to employ increasingly radical tactics.[20] As one activist observed, "The government that we have been voting for now regards us as terrorists, but we are not terrorists. We are fighting for the people. There is nothing that is related to the terrorists. Now everybody is being evicted in South Africa. The person who is rich in South Africa must stay rich. The person who is poor must stay poor. You know? But we are not going to contest the election. We rather fight outside with the government" (anonymous MPAEC activist 1, interview, July 2003). The MPAEC's actions provoked significant debate. Journalists questioned the tactics employed by the organization (Ntabazalila 2002). Government officials frequently repeated the argument that certain movements pose a threat to South Africa's new democracy and should not be tolerated. Referring to the actions of the MPAEC, the ANC deputy secretary general, Sankie Mthembi-Mahanyele, argued: "We are a young democracy. . . . We need a consensus. So we cannot behave in a manner like societies [that have been] independent for many years" (*Mail and Guardian*, August 8, 2003, 17).

This demand for consensus underlines the very reason why movements such as the WCAEC are so significant in South Africa's new democracy. Like the civics in the 1980s, the MPAEC raises the voices of the dispossessed and also offers a community service by creating a place for people to come with their problems related to evictions and water and electricity cutoffs. It seeks to offer community members a chance to participate and to make their demands heard when these options are not readily available through state institutions. Like the civics, the MPAEC has faced challenges in institutionalizing democratic practices that empower all its members. Women have, at times, been pressed into the background and have struggled to play an equal role to that of men (Pointer 2004; Miraftab 2006). But even as the MPAEC has struggled to implement the nonhierarchical democracy that many of its members envision, its actions have been crucial in drawing attention to violations of basic rights in Mandela Park and elsewhere.

The WCAEC as a whole, with all its strengths and shortcomings, has experienced important successes. Prior to the campaign's mobilization, poor people who faced eviction from their homes had little recourse even though the Constitution of South Africa protects their right to housing. The WCAEC has responded by taking to the streets but also to the courts. Ashraf Cassiem from Tafelsig (another area that experienced an acute eviction crisis) is a leading member of the campaign's legal team. Though he has no law degree, Cassiem goes to court to represent residents facing eviction. When asked in court why he was sitting on the bench set aside for lawyers, Cassiem replied that he represented residents facing eviction and that he had training in the application of the Prevention of Illegal Evictions Act. Although the judge noted that only lawyers and people without legal representation were formally allowed to address the court, he agreed that Cassiem could participate as long as he addressed the court on his own behalf and did not seek to represent others (*Mail and Guardian*, January 15, 2008). This loophole allows Cassiem to continue to assist communities affected by evictions.

Though he participates in court proceedings and praises the constitutional court for decisions such as *The Government of the Republic of South Africa v. Irene Grootboom* (Constitutional Court of South Africa 2000) that uphold the constitutional right to housing, he does not believe these processes on their own will address the needs of the people.[21] "The court is a nice place to win all these things, but when it comes to the reality of implementation of what the decision said, then the struggle begins" (Cassiem, interview, August 9, 2005). Cassiem goes to court to get the arguments of those facing eviction on the record, to postpone evictions, and to draw attention to the case in order to mobilize the community in which the eviction is to occur. For the WCAEC, participating in court proceedings is a strategy for areas not already as mobilized as Mandela Park or Valhalla Park. While the court process drags on, Cassiem and other members of the WCAEC work with the people facing eviction to mobilize their neighbors. They organize a "tea party" or a braai (barbeque) at the home of the family to be evicted so that when the police arrive, they find a full house. Sometimes this show of solidarity is enough to dissuade the police from returning to complete the eviction. Through his actions in the court, Cassiem seeks to demonstrate the unconstitutionality of evictions. Through his actions in local communities, he works to stop evictions from happening despite legal orders.

Cassiem and other WCAEC activists work to realize the socioeconomic promises of the South African Constitution. In this way, they are reinforcing the rights-based foundation of the state rather than threatening it as government actors have claimed. They are working to expand both popular aspirations and the actual practices of citizenship. For the WCAEC, working within the legal system is productive only if it is accompanied by extra-institutional actions, such as resisting evictions, building speed bumps (or ditches), and occupying unused land, that address the immediate needs of residents. Placards left on the steps of the Cape High Court after a demonstration aptly summarized a key question posed by AEC supporters to the state: "Why must we vote? What are your parties doing for us[?]" and simply: "We need houses for our kids" (http://www.abahlali.org/node/4931).

The WCAEC has also worked to overcome apartheid divisions separating African from coloured communities. It incorporates local organizations from former coloured areas such as Valhalla Park and Tafelsig with African townships such as Mandela Park in Khayelitsha. In so doing, it has faced different challengers because homes in Valhalla Park and Tafelsig are council houses, owned by the state, while those in Mandela Park are bonded houses, largely owned by the banks. The campaign has achieved concrete successes including a moratorium on evictions and service cutoffs in several townships, municipal rate exemptions for houses valued at less than R50,000 (roughly $6,850), and a ban on evictions of the elderly and the disabled (Miraftab 2006, 198). Overall, the WCAEC seeks to address immediate material needs but also to change the public conversation about rights: to put socioeconomic rights on equal footing with political and civil rights (particularly the right to private property).

The WCAEC is not alone in pursuing these aims. Other movements, including AbM, formed in 2005 in Durban, also combine direct action, non-violent protest, and court cases to demand both political and socioeconomic rights. AbM rose to national prominence by engaging in an illegal blockade of a major road after city officials abandoned an oral promise to make additional land available for community housing, granting it instead to a private corporation to build a brick factory (Pithouse 2006). The elected chairperson of AbM argued that protest was the only remaining method available to the community: "We discovered that our municipality does not listen to us when we speak to them in Zulu. We tried English. Now we realize that they will not understand Xhosa or Sotho either. The only language that they understand is when we put thousands of people on the street. We have seen the results of this and we have been encouraged. It works very well. It is the only tool that we have to emancipate our people" (Zikode 2006, 187). As the movement has grown, its members have faced police harassment, threats, violence, and detention. When the office of the city manager, Mike Sutcliffe, repeatedly denied AbM's applications to march, the movement went to court and "won a court order interdicting the City and the police from interfering with [its] rights to protest" (Pithouse 2008, 83–84).

When legislators introduced the Elimination and Prevention of Reemergence of Slums Act in the KwaZulu Natal provincial parliament, AbM took the case all the way to the constitutional court. The court declared a section of the act unconstitutional, defining the act as "irrational" due to the broad scope of powers granted to local authorities in evicting any unlawful occupier and arguing that the act would make residents of informal settlements "more vulnerable to evictions" (Constitutional Court of South Africa 2009a).[22] The implications of this ruling are significant; while it will not improve the immediate material circumstances of most shack dwellers, it has upheld their rights to not be forcibly evicted as part of the government's slum-eradication program.

Urban planning specialist Marie Huchzermeyer (2009) has argued that the act "equated the elimination of slums with the eviction of people living in them and was intended to make this much more frequent and easily facilitated." Although AbM won in court, its leaders and members have been subject to continued harassment and attacks leading to the deaths of two people in a raid on one of their meetings. After the attack, members of the movement were arrested by the police (*Mail and Guardian*, October 2, 2009; *Mercury*, October 9, 2009; *Weekender*, October 10, 2009; http://www.abahlali.org). These attacks, the actions of the police, and the state's reluctance to establish an independent inquiry into the violence against shack dwellers in Durban underscore the great challenges that the movement and all shack dwellers face (Friedman 2009b). It also demonstrates a clear lack of institutionalized democracy as the state fails to uphold the constitutional rights of citizens. AbM's experiences are unfortunately not unique. In a number of cases, increased organization and mobilization have been met with repression and the banning of gatherings planned by movements including the LPM, the APF, and the WCAEC (Eveleth 2003; McKinley 2003).

SANCO's Challenge to the Resurgent Movements

The WCAEC, the SECC, and other organizations such as AbM work to draw attention to the dire circumstances of a large sector of the population struggling to make ends meet. Although not all members of the communities they claim to represent may agree with the methods or broader goals of the movements (Sinwell 2009), their presence does importantly press the state to respond. The ANC government's response to these new movements has ranged from repression to attempts to delegitimize and marginalize them and co-opt individuals within them. When ANC activists have directly addressed the demands of the movements, it has been largely to engage in the politics of blame: to suggest that others aside from the ANC government are responsible for the problems that the movements cite, to argue that the movements themselves offer no credible solution to the problems, and to restate the argument that current government policies offer the best solutions. Desai reported that in Durban the ANC took "to the streets calling for free water, blaming water disconnections on white conservative bureaucrats" (2003, 26). The ANC has also employed its ally, SANCO, in an attempt to draw support away from more radical actors and to reinforce the state's policies and power (Zuern 2006a). This approach has met with mixed success.

In Mandela Park, SANCO has lost ground by at least one measure: popular support. In an effort to address the housing crisis and to maintain its own organization, SANCO offered to represent residents in negotiations with the ANC and the banks that owned property in Mandela Park. Although these negotiations did not lead to a positive resolution for residents, they did present returns for SANCO. As a product of its role in local negotiations, SANCO received a 20 percent share in the Khayelethu Home Loans Company, which provided finance for loans in Khayelitsha. Thereafter, when residents received letters demanding payment, these were jointly signed by Khayeluthu and SANCO (Desai and Pithouse 2004, 250). The struggle against evictions therefore also became a struggle against SANCO (Xali 2006, 129). Residents formed the MPAEC to resist the policies that SANCO sought to enforce and took over the building that it had formerly used. As the MPAEC became active in resisting evictions, tensions with SANCO increased, and MPAEC members accused SANCO of ongoing harassment and "unethical methods" (anonymous MPAEC activists 1 and 2, interviews, July 2003).

In Soweto, SANCO employed a different strategy to maintain its significance in local communities frustrated by its policies. Despite its rhetoric as a revolutionary social movement and representative of South Africa's poor, SANCO has continued to support the logic of credit-control measures even when this means widespread electricity disconnections and the installation of water-flow restrictors. The national structure of SANCO has therefore worked to support a neoliberal framework of governance in which citizenship rights become contingent upon access to financial resources. One civic leader in the Vaal summed up this perspective in stark terms: "We need to protect [the consumer] as SANCO, but you protect a consumer who is obedient" (Lehoko, interview, June 9, 2004). As residents in Soweto became increasingly desperate and angry, SANCO continued to lose support, and groups such as the SECC, which took a more radical approach, gained in popularity. SANCO's response to this challenge was to leverage its position by threatening mass action in an attempt to upstage the SECC (SAPA, June 7, 2001) while simultaneously presenting itself as a credible negotiating partner with ESKOM, the electricity utility. In 2002, SANCO participated in negotiations with ESKOM and government representatives, which led to an agreement that residents with faulty meters would pay a flat fee of R120 ($16) per month until their meters were repaired (SAPA, April 26, 2002). In areas such as Zola, within Soweto, civic leaders strategically drew attention to these agreements to try to convince community residents that SANCO rather than the SECC would find a solution to their problems (S. Monnakgotla, interview, July 15, 2002). Despite the weakness of its local branches, SANCO sought to assert itself as the primary broker between township residents and state actors.

SANCO's greatest triumph came in May 2003. ESKOM and the Ministry of Public Enterprises (headed by Jeff Radebe, a recent member of SANCO's National Executive Committee) along with the Human Rights Commission and SANCO came to an agreement to write off R1.39 billion ($190 million) in Johannesburg electricity arrears. Although this write-off was clearly in response to the influence of movements such as the SECC and the APF, SANCO rather than the SECC or the APF was included in the negotiations. SANCO presented itself as the public representative of the poor and was given at least formal credit for the write-off. A supporter of the SECC and the APF campaigns wrote: "All but moribund 12 months ago, SANCO has suddenly come to life with resources and influence from political heavyweights in national government, determined, it would seem, to counter the growing influence—and anti-neoliberalism—of SECC and the APF" (McDonald 2003).

A SANCO leader summed up SANCO's strategy regarding the challenges it faced from groups such as the SECC and the ways in which it employed its relationship with the government:

Credit goes to SANCO. . . . As a civic movement we grab those people that support Trevor [Ngwane of the SECC], look at their issues, and actually change them. We can strategize. . . . Let the credit come to SANCO, and then SANCO will take the credit back to government. It is quite a nice ball game. . . . Whilst now we confront, they deliver. The credit goes to SANCO. You take the credit back to government. You call a mass meeting, address the people, and say government has delivered. . . . That is how you deal with it. You actually strategically try to isolate them [SECC and others]. (anonymous Gauteng SANCO leader, interview, January 2004)

From the perspective of the SECC, Trevor Ngwane argued: "Earlier they [the government] responded by calling us agitators, criminals, or denying that we exist. Now they are acknowledging our existence. Now they are vicious and clever; they are gonna smash people, but they are clever enough to acknowledge that there are such organizations. They might not publicly say there is the SECC, but you can see it from their strategies that they are kind of adapting" (Ngwane, interview, July 19, 2002).

SANCO presented itself to local communities as a problem solver that could employ its relationship with the government to address residents' concerns. This argument, however, deliberately ignores the role that the SECC had played. Without pressure from the SECC and massive nonpayment,

ESKOM would never have agreed to such a large write-off. In contrast to SANCO's claimed success in Soweto, where SECC mobilized, it failed in Tshwane, where there was no group like the SECC. In Tshwane, SANCO leaders also participated in a series of negotiations with the metropolitan government council, but the council refused SANCO's request to write off outstanding arrears, arguing that effective credit-control measures were already in place (SAPA, May 12, 2003). Without popular pressure, government representatives saw no reason to address citizens' demands.

SANCO leaders in Tshwane learned from their mistakes. They began to innovate by employing some of the tactics used by groups such as the SECC and WCAEC while still working to maintain their alliance with the ANC. In order to support the ANC, SANCO leaders endorsed the government's credit-control procedures from services to housing. They therefore supported the cutting of electricity, while arguing for lifeline tariffs that would give residents access to a minimal amount of water and all paying consumers a small amount of electricity for free (Qhakaza, interview, January 15, 2004; Tshabalala, interview, January 17, 2004). SANCO branches worked with banks to try to help people get loans but were then also asked by the banks for a quid pro quo. One local civic leader commented: "The banks are honest with us, to say: 'We want to help; if you can assist in those who owe us, we will also assist you in those who need loans.' It puts us in a difficult position, but you see we must sit down and see what we can come up with" (Kutumele, interview, June 11, 2004). In order to assist residents with loans, SANCO agreed to help the banks collect their debts. This was a similar deal to that which SANCO made in Mandela Park. These arrangements with banks, government leaders, and private businesses were reportedly made in the name of SANCO's quest for "people-centered development," but whether it was the membership deal with AIG, SIH's investments, or agreements with private banks, each time the majority of the benefits seemed to accrue to leaders, largely in the form of job opportunities, rather than to the communities they claimed to represent.

In Tshwane, regional SANCO leaders did, however, realize that they could not simply rely on their alliance with the ANC to maintain their relevance. They needed to reach out to local communities and work to draw attention to their concerns. They learned from the actions of the SECC and the WCEAC that institutional politics were not enough to garner the government's attention and demand some form of change. Though SANCO as an organization stressed negotiations over protest, local leaders in Tshwane repeatedly argued that it was necessary to demonstrate their capacity for protest and even the potential to cause "damage" to draw attention to their concerns:

Contentious Democracy

I believed in our branches in SANCO actually creating damage so that the ANC can run to us and say, "Comrade!" The ANC will keep despising you if you are not acting. . . . That's why we go there and stop the [government development] project completely. And then the leadership would come to me or government would call me and say, "Look, your people on the ground are actually stopping the project," and I say, "Why? Why are they stopping the project?" "No, we don't know; they are arrogant." . . . I say, "No, they have a reason. Arrange a meeting, and then we will come and speak formally, but by the time I come to you I will have met my [people] on the ground, and I will be coming to you with concrete reasons why they stopped the project." . . . And I know, I know; I was part of stopping that project, but I will behave innocently as if I don't know. But I already know the reason. (anonymous SANCO Tshwane leader, interview, January 2004)

Regional leaders openly acknowledged that their actions contradicted SANCO policies but noted that this was simply the most effective way of bringing about change:

And therefore whilst we were supporting [cost recovery] as leaders, . . . we will treat it very sensitively, because we know that we want to achieve certain things, but it is also wrong. And therefore we will distance ourselves, not necessarily distance ourselves from the leaders [in the community], but we will distance ourselves from the act. To say that we condemn that act . . . When you are a leader and you have followers, they wouldn't necessarily do things like those without informing you. They would actually want your approval. . . . And you wouldn't say to them: "Look, invade the land." You would just say to them: "Comrade, you are a leader. Do what has to be done. Take a decision and implement." . . . We can't just distance [ourselves] from you; we can distance [ourselves] from the act that you are doing, if it is illegal, but we won't distance ourselves from you. (anonymous SANCO Tshwane leader, interview, January 2004)

SANCO leaders in Tshwane therefore navigated a careful line of supporting popular community demands and condoning and even encouraging the tactics employed by the so-called ultraleft movements such as the WCAEC and the SECC. At the same time, they presented themselves as reliable negotiators with local government authorities. This brokerage role allowed SANCO to exploit its local position as well as its alliance with the ANC. In this case, the alliance that was often an impediment was turned into a strength for SANCO Tshwane by a careful shifting of the rules of the game. SANCO could potentially capture the power of a locally based social movement by encouraging protest and harness that influence by employing its politically connected national structure.

One SANCO officer, a well-known Tshwane leader, argued that SANCO's overall role is to ease relations between township residents and the government:

"SANCO is a cushion, on both sides. . . . It works both ways. It is a cushion on the government side, but it is also a cushion on the people's side. Then it actually eases tensions" (Qhakaza, interview, June 9, 2004). SANCO Tshwane played this brokerage role. It positioned itself as an intermediary between communities and local government authorities. It offered its support to the ANC to help the party campaign in national, provincial, and local government elections and its position in local communities to help residents navigate government policies and programs. The actions of SANCO Tshwane and the arguments of its leaders also underscore the crucial role that movements such as the WCAEC and the SECC play in South Africa's new democracy. They raise voices that are otherwise not heard in the corridors of power by making it impossible for those living far from the poor townships to ignore their demands. The fact that SANCO needed to employ the methods of South Africa's radical movements also underlines the simple truth that these demands are not being addressed via formal institutional channels, even for those with connections to government.

In South Africa, significant pressure for the enforcement and expansion of socioeconomic as well as political rights is coming from outside the formal institutions of the state, but it is also changing the way those institutions operate. The 2004 national government elections took place amid great social movement mobilization demanding that government pay more attention to the needs of the poor. In response, government budgets have allocated increased funding to infrastructural investment, public work programs, and social welfare (Habib and Valodia 2006, 248). Seekings reports: "Expenditure on social assistance almost doubled from about 2 percent of GDP in 1994 (and 2000) to about 3.5 percent in 2005" (2007, 19). Although such grants did not address the central demands of movements such as the AEC and the SECC for the right to housing and basic services, they did allow the ANC government to argue that it was engaging in pro-poor policy reform. Government officials repeatedly argued that this increase in spending was not a result of increased social mobilization but rather part of a long-term plan. It is quite striking, however, that increased resources were allocated from the early years of the twenty-first century just as resurgent movements were gaining great domestic and international attention.

The Expansion of Rights in Botswana and Argentina

The cases of Botswana and Argentina demonstrate the expansion of rights in two starkly contrasting cases of contention in new democracies.

In Botswana, popular organizations are relatively weak, and levels of public contention are low. This has led some observers to characterize the country as a democracy that demonstrates the benefits of consultation over contention. Argentina, in contrast, has strong popular organizations and has experienced exceptionally high levels of contention. Contention in postapartheid South Africa is therefore closer to that in Argentina than in Botswana. All three countries are middle-income electoral democracies. Their societies are also all characterized by exceedingly high inequality (Gini coefficient of 50 or higher), but the similarities among all three end there. The following discussion evaluates arguments for consultation in Botswana and probes concerns regarding the fear of destabilization in Argentina.

Botswana, like South Africa, is a dominant-party democracy. Since independence in 1966, the Botswana Democratic Party (BDP) has controlled government. While the percentage of voters casting their ballots for the BDP has declined from a high of 80 percent in 1965 (I. Taylor 2003, 217) to just over 53 percent in 2009, the party still holds almost 80 percent of seats in parliament, forty-five of a total of fifty-seven (Independent Electoral Commission, http://www.iec.gov.bw). This is a product of the first-past-the-post electoral system and a contrast to South Africa's system, which is largely proportional.[23] State power in Botswana is centralized under a strong executive president with substantial powers of appointment. Despite its consistent control of government, the BDP never outlawed opposition parties to declare a one-party state or engaged in the extreme levels of corruption and violence that plagued several resource-rich African countries after independence. Instead it pursued a developmental course and achieved extraordinary levels of economic growth into the 1990s. But despite its upper-middle-income GDP, half the population still falls below the two-dollar-a-day poverty threshold. Economic inequality is also reportedly higher than that found in starkly unequal South Africa (UNDP 2009).[24] Botswana therefore serves as an important reminder that poverty and inequality on their own do not lead to wide-scale contention.

Analysts have repeatedly described Botswana's popular organizations as weak. Even those who argue that local organizations are playing an increasing role in politics acknowledge that "few have either many members or deep roots in society" (Carroll and Carroll 2004, 349; Holm, Molutsi, and Somoleka 1996). In contrast to the contention-based approach presented in this book, some analysts have argued that Botswana is characterized by a productive politics of consultation. This argument draws on Botswana's cultural heritage and the *kgotla*, a consultative assembly in which adult males make decisions for the community. Zibani Maundeni argues: "The dominant Tswana political culture emphasizes open discussions in each other's presence. In contrast, violent behavior is peripheral to Tswana political culture and enjoys no moral and media support" (2004, 621). According to this argument, street protests and strikes also defy the cultural norm. But strikes are discouraged by the legal system as well. Due to a requirement for an extensive arbitration process, they are, in practice, illegal (I. Taylor 2003, 226). While the *kgotla* model provides an important basis for open discussion and debate, it has historically been limited to Tswana men. Government appeals to adhere to this tradition have been employed to challenge human rights struggles organized by women and ethnic minorities (Kerr 2001, 265).

In order to evaluate the politics of consultation and contention, we will consider two pressing rights issues protected in Botswana's constitution but not consistently enforced: citizenship rights and indigenous rights. The first concerns the 1982–84 Citizenship Act, which changed the basis of citizenship rights from territory to descent. According to the new law, the citizenship of the father would determine that of the child. Children born to female citizens married to male foreigners would no longer be granted citizenship (Van Allen 2001). When initial attempts to lobby the government to change the law failed, women mobilized. In 1986 a new women's organization was launched, Emang Basadi (Stand Up, Women) (Molokomme 1991).[25] Emang Basadi's members engaged in tactics ranging from organizing workshops and conferences to writing articles for local newspapers and launching a broad political education campaign. In response, the government labeled the women as "unpatriotic" (Leslie 2006), and many citizens, including women, viewed the actions of the women's movement as "upsetting the natural order of things" and "undermining . . . government as [the] modern law maker" (Selolwane 2000, 87–88). The women's actions were a significant milestone in popular organizing because they so defiantly challenged the status quo. Their actions did not, however, lead to a quick change in legislation. In 1990, Emang Basadi supported a legal challenge to the Citizenship Act filed by Unity Dow, a lawyer and director of the Metlhaetsile Women's Information Centre. Dow was married to a U.S. citizen, and her children were thereby denied citizenship (Dow 1991). When the high court ruled that the act was unconstitutional, the government appealed. After the court of appeal upheld the high court's ruling, government officials considered calling a referendum to change the constitution in order to avoid altering the law.

The women's movement mobilized. Women marched to the passport offices, where they demanded passports for their children, and launched a campaign to increase the number of women elected to parliament. As a product of their actions, they received considerable national and international media attention, and the government finally amended the discriminatory provisions of the act in 1995 (Van Allen 2001). Agnes Ngoma Leslie comments on the movement's disruptive tactics: "In a country where protest had been seen as taboo, the protests left the government of Botswana embarrassed and afraid of the possibility of instability in its traditionally stable society" (2006, 65). One of the women who participated in the actions described the state's response: "They thought *Emang Basadi* was disrupting democracy" (quoted in Leslie 2006, 101). Emang Basadi did certainly challenge the government's practice of governance, but in so doing, it expanded discussions and implementation of women's rights in Botswana and with it democracy. Emang Basadi subsequently grew to become one of only a few organizations with a large membership that also included significant participation in rural areas (Carroll and Carroll 2004, 349). Although it has not achieved all its goals, such as a minimum 30 percent representation of women in parliament, and it has experienced a decline in organization and mobilization (Bauer 2010), it did effectively broaden the discussion of rights and forced a reluctant government to revise its policies. Emang Basadi has achieved these successes through a combination of legal strategies and popular mobilization. At key moments in the dispute over rights, popular mobilization and disruptive tactics proved to be crucial.

A second rights dispute also draws on constitutional protections, this time for the people living within the Central Kalahari Game Reserve (CKGR). In 1997 the government increased its efforts to expel the Basarwa people from the reserve. It established two villages outside the reserve, arguing that the subsistence practices of the Basarwa were incompatible with wildlife conservation (Solway 2009, 327). Just a year earlier, Vice President Festus Mogae (who became president in 1998) had described the inhabitants of the CKGR as "stone age creature[s]" who would "die out like the dodo" if they refused to accept government plans for their development (quoted in Good 2008, 124). A negotiating team made up of church, human rights, and civic groups initially pursued a consensual model of demand making and met with President Masire in 1997 but made no progress. Despite state orders to leave, many residents refused to relocate and worked with local organizations including the First People of the Kalahari and Ditshwanelo, a human rights advocacy group, to attempt to halt further evictions. Negotiations continued until late 2001 and, according to Ditshwanelo, "had almost succeeded" in developing a plan for "the sustainable use of natural resources and wildlife inside the CKGR by the Basarwa communities" (http://www.ditshwanelo.org.bw/ethnic.html). In early 2002, however, the government cut off water and other essential services to the people remaining in the CKGR. Pensions and destitute rations were withheld. People's huts were dismantled. Boreholes for water were sealed, and people were forcibly removed (Good 2008).

Survival International, a transnational NGO based in the United Kingdom, joined the campaign to draw attention to the rights violations committed by the government. The government responded by arguing that the resistance to relocations was driven by foreign interests and increased pressure on groups like Ditshwanelo to abandon the campaign. Ditshwanelo conceded, commenting that Survival's tactics were too confrontational and failed to respect the culture of Botswana (I. Taylor 2003). While Survival's campaign, designed to appeal to a Western audience, included inaccuracies and was heavily criticized within Botswana (Solway 2009), the argument for a politics of consultation over contention worked to support the government's intransigence. Government officials used cultural arguments for consensus to undermine resistance to their policy decisions, but the residents of CKGR continued their struggle by pursuing their case in court. Unity Dow, who had become Botswana's first female high court judge, was one of three judges on the case. In her judgment, she argued that this was ultimately a case of "people demanding dignity and respect" (quoted in Good 2008, 137). The high court ruled that the evictions were illegal, but only those named in the case were allowed to return. They were not allowed to bring in domestic animals, and the boreholes were not reopened (Solway 2009).[26] Although domestic mobilization did not address the immediate material needs of the people involved, the legal precedent set by the high court case and ongoing attention and debate have created a basis for further rights claims. The politics of consultation did not protect the residents of CKGR, and the cultural argument against contention was used by Ditshwanelo only after it had been forced by the government to back down. Local groups including Reteng (We are here), a multicultural association of minority groups, continue to pressure the government (Good 2008; Reteng 2008).

In the case of citizenship and of indigenous rights in Botswana, consultation was not sufficient to effect the expansion and enforcement of rights. Court actions supported by mobilization and a politics of contention proved crucial to local groups' demand making. In Argentina, in contrast, the question is not whether popular actors engaged in consultation or contention. Argentina experienced extraordinary levels of contentious action in the wake of its 2001 financial crisis. This action was remarkable even among the Latin American countries caught in a wave of mobilization in the last decades.[27] The Argentine case therefore raises questions concerning the stability of new democratic regimes in the wake of such extreme levels of protest. Do high levels of protest lead to the breakdown of democracy as the proponents of democratic consolidation feared?

In Argentina, *piqueteros* (picketers) and *cacerolazos* (pot bangers), among others, took to the streets in record numbers. The protesters included members of the middle class, workers, the unemployed, and the urban poor. Mobilization in Argentina, as in South Africa, was fueled by the economic impact of neoliberal economic policies as well as the shortcomings of democratic representation. In both cases, protesters responded to the contradictions of the formal political rights offered by electoral democracy and the lack of socioeconomic rights they experienced as a product of free-market policies. In 1989, just six years after Argentina's return to electoral democracy, Carlos Menem was elected to tackle the country's economic crisis and embarked on a path of radical economic reform. Although the reform program successfully ended hyperinflation, in less than a decade the country was once again beset by economic crisis (Schamis 2002). Market-oriented reforms cut the public sector and led to a dramatic increase in unemployment. The official poverty rate, which had ranged from 17 to 20 percent at the beginning of Menem's time in office, rose to 33 percent in 2001 and over 50 percent in 2002 (Alcañiz and Scheier 2007, 162).[28] At the end of 2001, massive antigovernment protests led to serial presidential resignations and five different presidents in less than two weeks. In 2002, after President Eduardo Duhalde announced that he would leave office early, presidential elections were rescheduled four times amid conflict over electoral rules (Levitsky and Murillo 2005b).

This series of events offered a dramatic challenge to Argentina's weak democratic institutions, but the country's formal democratic system did not collapse. The presidential election of 2003, although strongly contested, led to the victory of Néstor Kirchner over former president Menem, who withdrew, fearing an overwhelming defeat in the second round of voting.[29] Steven Levitsky and María Victoria Murillo summarize the turbulent period: "Between 1989 and 2003, Argentine politics seemed to go full circle: from basket case to international poster child, and back to basket case. . . . Yet the 2001–2002 crisis broke with past patterns in an important way. The armed forces, which had toppled six governments between 1930 and 1976, remained on the sidelines, and core democratic institutions remained intact. Amid the worst economic crisis in its history, Argentine democracy proved to be strikingly robust" (2005b, 1).

The regime survived despite the massive mobilization that led to violence and numerous deaths. Protesters banged pots, blocked roads, and even physically attacked politicians under the slogan *Que se vayan todos* (All of them must go). Although a wide array of protesters actively encouraged the collapse of governments, many also sought to redefine not only government policies but also the practices of governance. One petition read: "We are your neighbors.

We have been banging pots almost without a pause since that historic 19th of December, when we went out to the streets even though nobody had called for us. Why did we do it? To make all of them get out. All of them? Yes. But not our democracy. We say that they must all get out, so that justice can return. And to be able to build together a life with dignity in this country that has been looted and abused" (quoted in Villalón 2007, 147).

Many protesters organized outside the conventional channels of institutional politics, transcending both political parties and unions to create new organizational forms and new alliances. The *piquetero* movements gave new political saliency to the chronically unemployed poor, who demanded government-based unemployment relief (Epstein 2006). Neighborhood assemblies brought together largely middle-class residents in participatory democratic organizations (Swampa and Corral 2006), and barter clubs transcended market principles to pursue ideals of solidarity and mutual aid (Bombal and Luzzi 2006). Protesters employed broadly inclusive labels such as "citizen" or "person" as they made demands and decried the failures of their elected representatives (Armony and Armony 2005). Each of these forms of organization along with actions such as crowds rattling their keys at banks (*llaverazos*), the public shaming of officials in front of their homes (*escraches*), and the pot banging (*cacerolazos*) expressed great popular frustration but also demanded more-democratic institutions that would enhance the accountability of public officials (Peruzzotti 2005).

This dramatic period of mobilization was, however, relatively short lived. Participation in neighborhood assemblies declined over the course of 2002 as "the significant burdens of active participation took their toll on assemblies, leaving only a nucleus of neighborhood members and leftist party activists" (Peruzzotti 2005, 248). Barter clubs, after including record numbers of participants in early 2002, struggled to maintain the organizational principles necessary for their effective functioning (Bombal and Luzzi 2006). Public support for continuing *piquetero* mobilization that blocked traffic also dropped markedly, and the government stepped in with "measured repression" as the economic crisis subsided (Epstein 2006, 110–11). Despite a return to economic growth, by 2004 poverty and indigence rates as well as urban unemployment rates had not fallen below the levels of October 2001, and social inequalities had not been reduced (Wolff 2009, 1010).

The decrease in active organization was a result not of dramatic socioeconomic change but rather of a promise of political change. Presidential elections held early in 2003 worked to reorient debate around the functioning of political institutions. Despite the destabilizing impact that mobilization had on Argentine politics, the 2003 runoff was between two Peronist candidates.

Kirchner challenged former president Menem, promising to listen to the people and to address some of the demands made by the protesters (Wolff 2009). He called for "a normal Argentina" as well as "a more just country" (Armony and Armony 2005, 48). In the end, no antiestablishment party won even 2 percent of the vote (Levitsky and Murillo 2005a, 41). This was a significant defeat for those who had hoped that such incredible popular mobilization and outrage at politicians and parties would lead to the introduction of a radical new style of politics. It was, instead, a victory for the centrist tendencies of liberal democracy and the resilience of Peronism and clientelism in Argentina. As society demobilized, many of the surviving local associations became institutionalized, allowing them to participate in policy-making decisions but weakening their challenge to government. The mobilization of the *piquetero* organizations dramatically increased cash transfers to the unemployed: from approximately one hundred thousand government subsidies under Menem to two million under Duhalde (2002–3) after the height of the protests. Under Kirchner the number of cash transfers remained high (Alcañiz and Scheier 2007, 160). These transfers offered vital resources to the poor but also provided opportunities to reestablish networks of political patronage that had collapsed in the run up to the 2001 mass actions (Ayero 2005).

Neither Botswana nor Argentina offers a model of the easy extension of rights or the clear enforcement of a broadly accountable democratic system, but each does provide examples of the role of protest in challenging unresponsive governments and demanding the extension of basic rights. Argentina is a case of the survival of democratic institutions despite high levels of popular protest that destabilized successive governments. Protest actions drew attention to political and economic demands, expanding understandings of which rights and protections were necessary within a capitalist economy. In an effort to address the demands of the people and to quell protest, government leaders were forced to accept the need for social welfare programs such as transfers to the unemployed, a system that had been dismantled under Menem's neoliberal reforms.

The Argentine case cannot be generalized to argue that all new democracies could survive such high levels of protest, disruption, and also violence. What the case does demonstrate, however, is the resilience of one democracy despite its weak institutions. It also offers further support to the argument that contention can work both to demonstrate the weaknesses of existing democratic systems and to press for greater accountability. The actions of popular organizations offered an important check on state power in South Africa, Botswana, and Argentina. In each case, the new institutions of democracy had failed to adequately constrain state power and to enforce the protection of citizen's rights. Popular mobilization on its own could not, however, address the shortcomings of liberal democracy.

The Contentious Institutionalization of a New Democracy

Contention and some level of destabilization are necessary to expand popular understandings of rights and to press states to respect and enforce them. Despite the dramatically different political histories of South Africa, Botswana, and Argentina and the wide range of popular mobilization in their young democracies, in each case movements' actions to destabilize political power were crucial to the expansion of rights. This conclusion, although commonly accepted in discussions of movements under authoritarian regimes, is often challenged in young democracies, with the argument that disorder and violence will threaten weak institutions. But though each state warned of the need to quell protest, disorder actually promoted democracy. In South Africa, the rise of protest led to the expansion of demands and new challenges to the government's cost-recovery programs that forced it to work to reduce the financial burden placed on the poor. The expanding dialogue has reinforced key rights enshrined in the South African Constitution such as the right to housing and the freedom of expression. The lesson that each of these cases suggests is straightforward: the protection and expansion of political and socio-economic rights requires not just action within government institutions but also mobilization outside them.

Each democracy is defined by the ongoing interactions between government institutions and any popular organizations seeking to represent marginalized communities outside of government and party structures. Activists such as those within the SECC, WCAEC, and AbM at times deliberately break the rules to draw attention to their demands. Though these actors clearly press the government, most also act in ways that reflect their respect for constitutional democracy. All three South African movements repeatedly requested permits for demonstrations and filed legal cases when they had access to legal counsel and the funds to pay for their services. The actions of participants in some illegal activities do not, on their own, indicate that these actors are a threat to the long-term stability of the state. But the actions of a state that works to undermine peaceful movements by restricting opportunities for protest or allowing the police to harass protesters do signal a significant challenge to the institutionalization of a democratic regime. In this way, social movements offer an important test for any new democracy.

In cases such as South Africa, where the most engaged debates are occurring outside institutionalized politics, increased social movement activity suggests the potential for a vibrant democracy because it provides a vital check on centralized state power. South Africa does not fit the model of an elite-negotiated transition to democracy (O'Donnell and Schmitter 1986) because of the central role that popular mobilization played in bringing about change and pressing it forward. It also does not meet the definition of a comprehensive social revolution (Skocpol 1979; Goodwin 2001) because of the relatively slower pace and lesser degree of change that occurred (Zuern 2006b). As a result, Elizabeth Wood (2001) has labeled South Africa's transition an "insurgent path to democracy." Revolutionary means were employed to achieve a democratic regime. The postapartheid period in South Africa suggests a continuing contentious path to the institutionalization of the new democratic regime, one in which the definition of that new regime is contested by popular actors, and the processes of revising it are extra-institutional as well as bureaucratic. Argentina has experienced a similarly contentious process that has worked to draw attention both to the material needs of the protesters and to their demands for a more democratic and participatory process. In Botswana growing concerns over the centralization of power suggest that increased movement activity may be necessary to expand and enforce rights.

What we are seeing in South Africa and Argentina and to a far lesser extent in Botswana is a contentious process of institutionalization. This process is spurred by the contradictions of inequality and liberal democracy. Such a perspective turns much of the debate concerning the institutionalization of democracy on its head. It presents contentious forces as not merely challenging and threatening the old but also participating in the construction of something new. This is not to argue that these movements will necessarily achieve their short-term goals, but their actions do raise concerns expressed by marginalized citizens in each country and thereby contribute to the construction of a democratic system. In an era of growing mobilization around socioeconomic concerns, democracy will be defined both by representatives within formal state institutions and by those on the streets who are excluded or ignored by those very institutions. In the final chapter, we return to this debate over the very meaning of democracy.

6

Substantive Democracy

> The process towards democracy must be shaped by the singular reality
> that those whose democratic participation is at issue are the ordinary
> people of Africa. . . . So long as this fact is kept steadily in focus, democ-
> racy will evolve in ways that will enhance its meaning . . . But it will be
> quite different from the contemporary version of liberal democracy, in-
> deed, different enough to elicit suspicion and even hostility from the
> international community that currently supports African democratiza-
> tion. If, however, African democracy follows the line of least resistance
> to Western liberalism, it will achieve only the democracy of alienation.
>
> Claude Ake, "The Unique Case of African Democracy"

laude Ake offered this prescient warning in the early 1990s,
a time of great enthusiasm for a new wave of democ-
racies on the African continent and beyond. His argument cuts to a central
challenge commonly overlooked in discussions of democratization: when
ordinary people mobilize for democracy, they often demand a very different
system from that which domestic elites, dominant international organizations, and powerful states, such as the United States, work to support. This
leads to a fundamental contradiction that lies at the core of democracy's future
prospects.

Two distinct approaches outline the debate: procedural measurements of
electoral democracy and popular understandings of substantive democracy.
Each creates a framework that determines the relevant and necessary components for the successful institutionalization of a democratic system. One leads
to a starkly different evaluation of existing democracies than the other. On
one hand, electoral democracy is measured by a relatively minimal set of
procedural criteria (Dahl 1971; Dalton, Shin, and Jou 2007). For the sake of

parsimony, clarity, and comparability, regimes are classified according to their formal institutional procedures and legally guaranteed rights. Democracy with adjectives, such as popular descriptions of South Africa's democracy as "shrunken" or Chile's as "low fat," are discouraged since they weaken analytic clarity and reduce comparability (Collier and Levitsky 1997). Procedural definitions make the task of measurement easier by emphasizing the conduct of elections and the formal codification of basic political and civil rights rather than citizens' direct and messy experiences interacting with their government or seeking to act on their promised rights. On the other hand, in South Africa, popular understandings of democracy expressed by the civics, resurgent social movements, and many ordinary people have suggested that such a minimalist understanding robs democracy of its key content, because it reduces the discussion of rights not only to deprioritize but also to effectively ignore socioeconomic rights. Substantive understandings of democracy define socioeconomic rights as central to democracy's success (Zuern 2009).

In contrast to the dominant model that focuses on formal procedures for liberal democracy, substantive approaches draw on a broader ideal of democracy as liberation. This understanding includes basic socioeconomic rights as well as the freedom for citizens and their representatives to determine a country's policies without external interference. In South Africa, the struggle against apartheid was commonly understood as a struggle for liberation. South Africans have also repeatedly associated democracy with the provision of basic material needs. In 1995, "91.3 per cent of respondents equated democracy with 'equal access to houses, jobs and a decent income.'" Although a majority of South Africans associated democracy with political competition and participation, "their endorsement of these political goods was far less ringing than the almost unanimous association of democracy with improved material welfare" (Bratton and Mattes 2001, 454–55). This early postapartheid understanding of democracy is a direct product of the history and struggle that preceded it (Chipkin 2003; Salazar 2002).

South Africa, because of apartheid, is often inaccurately presented as an exceptional case on the continent. Despite South Africans' preferences for substantive democracy, prominent analysts of African democratization have employed survey research to argue that Africans overall have embraced liberal democracy: "Africans, like people in other parts of the world, *see democracy in liberal and procedural terms*. Africans clearly put the protection of civil liberties uppermost in their definition of democracy *across time and space*" (Bratton and Cho 2006, 14, emphasis in original). But the data on which these findings are based are contradictory. When the survey question is asked one way, respondents favor procedural understandings; when it is asked another way, the majority offer substantive understandings. As we will see, South Africa is not, in fact, exceptional, and its domestic debates over democracy illuminate contradictions faced by many regimes across the continent and beyond.

Democracy as Liberation

In his discussion of modern statecraft, James Scott employs the term *techne* to describe the scientific knowledge that is presented as precise, comprehensive, reliable, impersonal, and universally applicable (1998, 320). The benefits of such knowledge are clear. It allows the development and teaching of technical skills in verifiable steps that encourages researchers and practitioners to learn from and build off one another, but it also works to reinforce the trusted model and can thereby constrain experimentation and penalize difference. Procedural definitions are best understood as a key component of what might be called the *techne* of democracy. *Techne* allows a certain quantitative precision that suggests objectivity and facilitates the dissemination of knowledge. It also describes much of the expertise that has driven the pursuit for modernization (Ferguson 2006), reinforcing the need for the world's so-called late developers to catch up with early industrializers and emulate their successes.

Freedom House's database of rankings offers an important example of the *techne* of democracy, for it offers a procedural measure, including in the definition of democracy a range of civil and political freedoms. Its indicators provide a basis for the comparison of regimes (2010), but in some cases the rankings appear to be at odds with the experiences of people living under the regimes in question. South Africa, for example, was largely labeled as "partly free" throughout the 1970s and 1980s despite the stark brutality of apartheid and the national state of emergency in place from 1986 to 1990. Despite incredible repression within Zimbabwe in the first decade of the new millennium, Cuba continued to receive a slightly lower score until 2009. This remained the case even after Zimbabweans experienced Operation Murambatsvina (take out the trash) in 2005, a government slum-demolition program that demolished thousands of shantytowns with little warning. The United Nations estimated that the program, which was part of a larger campaign of terror against perceived opposition supporters, affected 2.4 million people and left 700,000 without homes and/or livelihoods (Tibaijuka 2005, 7). In its rankings, Freedom House includes economic freedoms within civil rights, thus allowing regimes with some degree of market economy to appear freer than those that place restrictions on the market. Despite arguments for the need to separate political and economic factors in discussions of democracy, these measurements include some rights that address economic concerns, such as property rights, while excluding others, such as the right to a living wage. This approach thereby reinforces the World Bank's understanding of good governance as necessarily requiring liberal democracy and capitalism and effectively limits the role of ordinary citizens in defining their democratic system.

The pursuit of a universally applicable measure also suggests that the concept of democracy can be separated from its largely European roots. Promoters of universal models often point to ancient Greece or Rome, or for liberal democracy, to American struggles for political and civil rights. Western understandings of democracy are thereby repackaged as universal. The participatory ideals of African village communities or ancient Indian republics, however, while forming an important basis for African (Dong'Aroga 1999) or South Asian discussions of democracy, do not often register in Western debates. In the Freedom House rankings, the European states as well as Australia, New Zealand, Canada, and the United States receive the highest scores for democracy, while most of the remaining countries receive far lower scores. Though many regimes do deserve low scores, the overall picture of rankings suggests more of a telos than a diversity of possible models. Discussions of democracy's universal applicability thereby work to mask the privileging of certain historical trajectories and present-day ideals over others.

In contrast to the universally applicable *techne*, Scott offers *metis*: contextual knowledge that challenges standard operating procedures and clear, replicable frameworks and instead adapts to consider the immediate circumstances of a problem or project (1998, 313–16). As the methods of *techne* have become the favored approach to debating democracy in most policy and academic circles, *metis* has less frequently drawn attention beyond local audiences. The concept of *metis*, however, lies far closer to the ideal of a democratic regime as one that innovates in response to the interests and arguments of its citizens. Popular understandings and expectations of democratic regimes are by definition part of *metis*. Such understandings are a product of historical practices as well as the successes and failures of local struggles for democracy. It is from these experiences that substantive understandings are derived.

Material demands played a significant role in mobilizing protest for democracy in South Africa. Across much of the African continent, the impact of economic reforms required by structural-adjustment loan conditionalities also spurred protest. This correlation between material demands, in some cases including resistance to externally mandated economic reform, and calls for regime change has led a number of African social scientists, such as Peter Ekeh

(1997) and Eghosa Osaghae (2005), to refer to the transformations that occurred across the continent from the late 1980s not as democratization processes but instead as quests for liberation. This movement for a "second liberation," following the first movement for liberation from colonial rule, parallels the earlier demands for independence in important respects: popular agitation was in both cases focused on the expansion of political rights and the improvement of socioeconomic conditions and included demands that Africans be free to define their own future without external interference or control.

Although the first generation of liberation movements did achieve political independence for former colonies, they generally failed to bring about strong rights-based regimes, significant socioeconomic gains for the majority, or an end to external interference in most countries. Prodemocracy activists hoped that this second movement for liberation would be more successful. The idea came from citizens who were frustrated by their governments and their regimes. Writing of the Zairian context, Georges Nzongola-Ntalaja argues: "The concept of 'second independence' was developed, not by social scientists, but by ordinary people in the Kwilu region of western Zaire [Democratic Republic of the Congo]. For the people, independence was meaningless without a better standard of living, greater civil liberties, and the promise of a better life for their children" (quoted in Osaghae 2005, 5).

This ideal of a second liberation is far more encompassing than that of democratization as it is generally employed by western social scientists. Proponents of a second liberation see democracy and broader socioeconomic development as mutually dependent, each unobtainable without the other. But they also take an additional step to address broader concerns for independence. As Osaghae argues, "liberation was used to describe the [re]assertion of [African] initiative and authenticity to rid the state, society and economy of foreign domination and psychological fixation or colonial mentality" (2005, 4). This notion of liberation includes a psychological process of decolonization and a struggle to bring local knowledge to the fore to empower formerly colonized societies (Biko 1978; Fanon 1961; Okere, Njoku, and Devisch 2005). The term "democratization" as it is commonly employed therefore fails to capture the full essence of this transition because it offers liberal democracy as its goal. In contrast, liberation seeks substantive democracy.

Ake's warning regarding the alienating potential of liberal democracy is crucial to understanding the challenges facing any new regime. If the pursuit of democracy is viewed by many as a process of liberation, external pressure to adopt a particular set of institutions and policies will dramatically undermine and delegitimize both the process and its outcome. Although African quests for liberation and democratization, like liberal democracy, emphasize basic freedoms, they are also fundamentally concerned with the removal of internal and external structures of power created under colonial and apartheid rule that were often merely adapted by the postcolonial or postapartheid state.

Lessons from South Africa

During the struggle against apartheid, the civics echoed the words of the Freedom Charter by working to bring together material struggles and demands for political and civil rights. Within the context of a repressive apartheid state, the civics organized to respond to the harsh realities of life for urban Africans and focused on issues ranging from high rents and the need for adequate housing to forced removals and police brutality. They provided a central opportunity for ordinary residents to participate in local politics, and by developing locally based organizations across the country, they formed a key component of the national movement for liberation. The civics also established a basis for demands for participatory democracy. Although material struggles often offered the immediate incentive for organizing, local organizations also worked to include large numbers of township residents in struggles for political and civil rights. Liberation and the necessary dismantling of the most divisive and discriminatory aspects of the apartheid system operated in tandem with the pursuit of a popular, participatory democracy.

In the postapartheid period, resurgent social movements continue to press for the socioeconomic rights that liberal democracy has failed to achieve. When government leaders deride these movements as "antisystem," they engage in a purposeful equation of political and economic regimes. "Antisystem" is presented as "antidemocratic," but its application to movements resisting privatization suggests that the system to which members of government are referring is actually that of neoliberalism. As a result, the defense of neoliberal economic policy has often trumped the democratic rights of protesters. This conflation of economic and political systems is exactly what defenders of procedural democracy seek to avoid, but when measurements of electoral democracy include property rights within civil rights and governments studiously work to defend these rights, the functioning of the economic regime cannot be separated from that of the political regime.

Civic activists and the leaders of postapartheid social movements have consistently repeated a number of central expectations regarding South African democracy. First, the struggle for liberation and democracy raised demands that citizens should be consulted by their leaders in a relatively participatory system. Liberation and democracy were also expected to provide the basis for addressing material inequality and to target assistance to poor black South Africans, whose life chances have been dramatically reduced by the institutionalization of inequality under apartheid. The most common complaints coming from activists in the postapartheid period have focused on these twin goals of liberation: consultation and participation along with the reduction of inequality and poverty.

The first oft-repeated concern is that elected leaders have failed to consult their constituencies or respond to their demands. South Africans have consistently expressed the lowest levels of support for the tier of local government and have critiqued the functioning of ward committees meant to offer opportunities for participatory democracy. This dissatisfaction is due to the general failure of local government officials to respond to citizens' demands. The second consistent argument is that service delivery and economic policies more broadly have not effectively addressed South Africa's stark inequalities. Activists have commonly pointed to councilors who were "not delivering" and demanded that those who do not deliver "come and account" to the community (anonymous Sowetan independent civic activist, interview, January 2001). Representatives of social movements as varied as the TAC, which has at times successfully negotiated with the government, and the more radical SECC and WCAEC, which have experienced a more adversarial relationship with government officials, have all described delivery failures as a failure of democracy.[1] Leaders of these organizations have argued that these delivery failures more generally as well as government engagement with citizens' demands in particular indicate a stark nonresponsiveness to the needs of the majority of citizens. In a 2006 interview, Trevor Ngwane of the SECC critiqued "bourgeois democracy" and argued that his organization's struggle was to find a councilor who would repeat the demands of the people at council meetings to make the material needs of the majority central to policy debates. Otherwise, he argued, the government could not consider itself a democracy (interview, August 8, 2006). Despite their stark differences, the TAC and the SECC both sought to improve democracy and delivery together, which they view as inextricably linked.

These substantive demands have been voiced by community leaders, both those who describe themselves as generally supporting the ANC and those who accuse many ANC leaders of "selling out" the struggle. Although civic and postapartheid social movement leaders do not represent all South Africans or even all poor black South Africans, they do represent a powerful understanding of democracy that resonates within the ANC-supporting majority as well as a growing minority more critical of the ANC (Mangcu 2005). Afrobarometer's 2005 findings support this argument: almost one in four South Africans surveyed stated they had joined a march or demonstration (Bratton and Cho 2006, 36).[2] This suggests that many citizens engage in extra-institutional means of political participation and that the demands made by social movements are fairly broadly supported. Significantly, the ANC still describes itself as a "liberation movement" and defines its goals in terms of the "National Democratic Revolution," which aims to address apartheid's political as well as material inequalities (ANC 2005; Butler 2007; Marwala 2007).

Finally, South African citizens' substantive understandings of democracy are supported by their constitution. The constitution enshrines justiciable socioeconomic rights, including access to land, housing, health-care services, food, water, and education, next to civil and political rights in its bill of rights. The constitutional court has upheld these rights in cases such as *The Government of South Africa v. Irene Grootboom* (2000) and *The Minister of Health v. Treatment Action Campaign* (2002). In the first case, the court held that the state's housing policy was unconstitutional when it failed to provide temporary shelter to homeless people. In the second case, the court ruled that the state must provide the antiretroviral drug Nevirapine to HIV-positive mothers to prevent the transmission of HIV to the newborn. More recently, the court has upheld the basic rights of squatters in *Abahlali baseMjondolo v. Premier of the Province of KwaZulu-Natal and Others* (2009a). Concluding his review of South Africans' socioeconomic rights and the state's responsibility to meet them in practice, Tseliso Thipanyane argued: "Failing to do so, especially in relation to the realization of economic and social rights for the poor, would mean that democracy and human rights are nothing but a myth and illusion" (2005, 240). Together, South Africa's history of struggle, its ruling party's rhetoric, and its constitutional provisions have reinforced citizens' continuing emphasis on substantive understandings of democracy.

When the Institute for Democracy in South Africa (IDASA), perhaps the best-known democracy advocacy and research organization in South Africa, designed its "Democracy Index," it developed the key components of its definition with a clear eye to the South African context. Though noting that many researchers argued against including socioeconomic rights in measures of democracy, IDASA, in the words of its executive director and one of its senior researchers, "knew it had to be there." They explained that "South Africans in their own working definition of democracy blended the procedural aspects that liberal democrats tend to emphasize with the social and economic outcomes that social democrats and democratic socialists preferred to attach weight to. Thus, for IDASA, far from being 'overburdening,' social justice represents a cornerstone of democracy" (Calland and Graham 2005, 9). Unsurprisingly, of

IDASA's five key measures—participation, elections, accountability, political freedoms, and human dignity—South Africa scored highest in elections and lowest on human dignity. The study's substantivist approach therefore highlights key aspects of people's daily experiences that a proceduralist account would miss. Adding human dignity to the composite assessment of democracy lowers South Africa's score and offers a significant opportunity to bridge the gap between many external analysts' praise and local citizens' criticisms of their regime.

African Perceptions of Democracy

Looking beyond South Africa, Afrobarometer surveys of the attitudes of ordinary Africans across a range of liberalizing sub-Saharan countries (from twelve countries in 1999–2001 to twenty by the end of 2009) offer a comprehensive look at popular opinion.[3] In the most wide-ranging discussion of Afrobarometer findings, Bratton, Mattes, and Gyimah-Boadi analyze the results from the first round of surveys. Though the authors argue that the majority of Africans surveyed understand democracy in "procedural terms by referring to the protection of civil liberties, participation in decision making, voting in elections, and governance reforms" (2005, 69–70), other findings in the same survey challenge this conclusion. The argument for procedural understandings is based on an open-ended question to which respondents could give up to three responses in ten of the twelve countries surveyed. Looking just at a comparison of first responses, as they were available in all twelve countries, the authors argue that over half the respondents offered procedural understandings.

When the same respondents were asked the question in a different way, their responses favored substantive understandings:

An alternate, structured question gives rise to dissonant results. Because "people associate democracy with many diverse meanings," respondents were asked to say which items on a list of political and economic attributes were "essential . . . for a society to be called democratic." . . . Only in Zimbabwe do respondents rate political procedures and socio-economic substance as equally essential to their conception of democracy, though they come close in Botswana and Zambia. . . . In seven other countries, and especially Tanzania and South Africa (but also Mali and Nigeria), respondents report that substantive features are significantly more essential than procedural ones. . . . At a minimum, therefore, expectations of what democracy should do also include material components of economic delivery and social equity. (Bratton, Mattes, and Gyimah-Boadi 2005, 87)

This contrasting evidence supporting first proceduralists' and then substantivists' claims suggests that the authors' conclusion that respondents define democracy in liberal terms is at best a bit hasty.[4] The responses to both types of questions concerning the meaning of democracy might best be understood to suggest that procedural and substantive understandings, at the very least, exist side by side. As the authors break down the responses, it becomes clear that elites, those who worry less about access to basic material goods on a regular basis, make up a significant proportion of proceduralists. In contrast, nonelites are more likely to understand democracy in substantive terms. The surveys also found that 80 percent of respondents "think that a democratic society should ensure education and employment for all" (Bratton, Mattes, and Gyimah-Boadi 2005, 275), clearly a substantive claim.

Turning specifically to an investigation of the poor, as measured by an indicator of "lived poverty" that considers access to food, fuel, water, heath care, electricity, and income, a later study focuses on how survey respondents perceive their regimes. Bratton finds that the poor are less likely than the well-to-do to express satisfaction with their democracies and even less likely to believe that their regime is a full democracy or one with minor problems. This leads him to conclude that "poverty is the single most important social factor shaping popular assessments about the quality of African democracies" (Bratton 2006, 19). This finding is particularly significant given the recent Afrobarometer (2009a) survey results, which, despite an increase in popular support for democracy as preferable to other kinds of government, show an average decline in satisfaction with the way in which democracy actually works.[5]

Together these findings suggest growing frustration with practical experiences of democracy, particularly among the poor. People's expectations are not being matched by the reality of governance. Although some degree of disenchantment with the practical application of an ideal is to be expected, growing disillusionment suggests an important challenge for new, formally democratic regimes. This challenge is not rooted in antisystem movements but rather in the lack of accessible, fully functioning democratic institutions. The failures of democratic institutions, in turn, encourage mobilization that makes popular disillusionment visible. Afrobarometer's survey results also demonstrate that destitute people are far more likely than their wealthier counterparts to seek to address their demands to the regime via informal rather than formal channels (Bratton 2006, 17). This underscores the difficulties that the poor experience or expect to experience in accessing the state and the benefits that their regime formally offers. It suggests that economic inequality creates political inequality leading to cumulative, even durable, inequality.

Afrobarometer's analytic separation of political and economic factors and strong support for procedural democracy works to support an ideological separation of political and economic goods. It reinforces the model of liberal democracy that Ake challenged, in which democracy is expected to legitimate the market and diminish concerns about economic inequality. But their own survey findings challenge this approach. As the results of the alternative wording of the meanings of democracy question suggested, substantive understandings of democracy are actually more popular in the majority of states surveyed. The survey results also importantly demonstrate that the majority of respondents are particularly concerned with the unequal burdens that reforms place on different political and economic classes and the growing inequality that has resulted (Bratton, Mattes, and Gyimah-Boadi 2005, 124; Bratton and Cho 2006, 12). This inequality forms the basis for demands for substantive democracy.

South Africa's Lack of Exceptionalism

South Africa's struggle for democracy was commonly understood as a process of liberation similar to many other struggles across the continent. The significant difference between South Africa and most other African countries lies not in the meaning of liberation but in the sequencing of the process. South Africans define 1994 as the culmination of a struggle for democracy and against exclusive white rule. They therefore have pursued two forms of liberation simultaneously. Many other Africans speak of two distinct processes of liberation: the first from colonial rule, the second from autocratic African rule. As a result of apartheid, South Africa is an extreme but not an exceptional case on the continent. Apartheid was in practice an extension of colonial rule in South Africa and therefore offers parallels to experiences of both colonialism and authoritarianism across the continent.

The majority of African countries struggled with various forms of postcolonial exclusion and repression, and most engaged in transitions to some form of multiparty system around the same time that South Africa instituted its new democracy. Although the pre-1990 regimes on the continent were quite diverse from South Africa's racialized but multiparty apartheid system to Ghana's military rule under Rawlings and Tanzania's one-party state under Nyerere, by 2010 the overwhelming majority of African regimes were multiparty systems that formally grant basic political and civil rights to their citizens. The practice and enforcement of these rights does, however, vary widely. While regimes experimented with different economic systems in the past, from the variously defined systems of African socialism to capitalism, all have instituted market economies since their return to electoral democracy. Across much of the continent, the poor played a significant role in protests that ushered in political change, but when elections were held in countries ranging from

Ghana to Zambia and Kenya, "virtually all political parties of any significance campaigned on an adjustment-friendly platform" (Abrahamsen 2001, 98). In South Africa the ANC also instituted stringent economic reforms after 1994. Across the continent, despite the demands of the poor, political leaders seem to have concluded that their political and economic survival depended on such reforms, a significant indication of the power of international financial institutions and the states that lead them.

Nowhere on the continent have the ideals of liberation been achieved. Although South Africa is often presented as one of the more successful cases of both political and economic reform, roughly half its citizens remain unsatisfied with the democratic system in place (Afrobarometer 2009b).[6] This suggests a sharp disjuncture between the international measurement tools that are most commonly employed by analysts to gauge the strength of democracy and popular understandings of what a democracy must entail in order to be a "real democracy." As a product of apartheid and postapartheid economic policies, South Africa faces an extremely high rate of economic inequality. But here, too, South Africa stands as an extreme rather than an exception. Basic indicators suggest that inequality is on the rise across much of the continent; countries that have been marked by low inequality such as Tanzania have seen increases in recent years, and others with extremely high inequality such as Botswana and Namibia, with the highest recorded in the world, have failed to bring about any significant reduction (Ndlovu 2007; Mutagwaba 2009; Good 2008; Melber 2007; UNDP 2009). As a result of neoliberal economic reforms, the majority of African countries will likely be faced with the growing challenge of addressing economic inequality.

Service Delivery and Democracy

The ANC government, in power since 1994, has consistently promised to pursue both economic growth and redistribution. Even as it shifted from the RDP (Redistribution and Development Programme) to GEAR (Growth, Employment, and Redistribution), it continued to offer at least rhetorical assurances that it would work to address South Africa's great economic inequality. Despite the government's promises, the policies of GEAR prioritized growth and worked to reign in spending while pursuing the privatization of several industries. Analysts accused the ANC of "talking left and walking right" (Bond 2006b) as economic inequality and unemployment increased. But in the early years of the new millennium, social expenditure also increased considerably. This coincided with the dramatic resurgence of a range of social movements and the government's improved economic balance sheet. In response, social support grants to children, the disabled, and the elderly have risen as has spending on education and health care.[7] Further privatization has been taken off the table. These actions have marked a significant shift in South Africa's approach to social welfare, but something else has been occurring as well.

During his time in office, President Mbeki centralized power in the executive and demonized movements that challenged his economic policies by labeling them "ultraleft." The president's undermining of political contestation was not confined to those he labeled as antisystem but spread to his opponents on a wide range of issues. As he attempted to maintain control of the state and defend his policy decisions, he removed members of government who defied him (Feinstein 2007) and aggressively protected his supporters against all critics. As a result, he lost the support of much of his key constituency: the intelligentsia and the urban middle and upper-middle classes (Gevisser 2007), and his approval ratings dropped precipitously in 2007, leading up to the ANC party elections.[8] This shift was a product of several factors, but most importantly the sense that Mbeki was defying popularly accepted and expected democratic norms (Habib 2008).

Mbeki's shortcomings opened the door for South Africa's embattled Jacob Zuma to become both the leader of the ANC and the president of the country. Despite corruption charges and an earlier rape trial in which he was acquitted, Zuma achieved two election victories. The second, and less dramatic, was as the ANC's candidate for the presidency of South Africa in April 2009. Given the ANC's dominance, there was never any doubt that its chosen presidential candidate would assume office. Zuma's first election victory, for the presidency of the ANC in late 2007, however, was a political earthquake. Mbeki, who had been president of the ANC since 1999, ran to retain his leadership of the party against his rival. Many powerful players in the ANC came out in support of Mbeki, arguing that Zuma's personal scandals would tarnish the reputation of the party and the country and that Mbeki had demonstrated solid leadership. But the rank and file of the party voted to oust Mbeki. In the most bitterly contested ANC election in decades, ordinary members of the ANC engaged their leaders from the floor, and Zuma won an overwhelming victory. The heated and open debate offered promising signs for democratic engagement within the ANC (Friedman 2007), even as analysts worried where President Zuma might lead South Africa (Hassim 2009). Despite what had to be a rather humbling, even humiliating, experience for Thabo Mbeki, once the ANC leadership announced its decision to recall him from the presidency in 2008, Mbeki went on national television to announce that he would step down.

Substantive Democracy

Kgalema Motlanthe was appointed by the ANC as interim president until elections were held the following year, and Zuma became the president of South Africa in May 2009.

Zuma's first few months in office were hardly quiet. In July and August, so-called service delivery protests spread to several townships across the country. By the end of August the number of such protests in 2009 had significantly exceeded those of the past few years, including 2005, a year of widespread protests (RSA, Cooperative Governance and Traditional Affairs 2009, 12). Thandakukhanya, outside Piet Retief in Mpumalanga province, was the site of one of the first large protests after Zuma became president. Several residents who had previously met as the Committee of 13, which was formed to address concerns over the allocation of housing, joined with other community members to elect the thirty-member Concerned Group. In a memorandum sent to the provincial premier, David Mabuza, the group stated its purpose: "To request the office of the premier to facilitate an urgent investigation to our local Mkhondo municipality in connection with the following high rate of alleged corruption happening within the municipality" (reproduced in Sinwell et al. 2009, 9–11). The memorandum detailed residents' concerns and demands including the call for more-transparent and accountable local government. It made specific requests for the minutes of municipal committee meetings, a clear accounting of the use of funds allocated from national and provincial government, the qualifications of administrative hires, and the procedures regarding the allocation of houses and the determination of rates to be paid by residents.

Echoing many previous civic demands, the memorandum called for "proper consultation in terms of resource distribution and infrastructure" and recommended that local councilors be suspended pending the outcome of investigations.[9] The demands made in this memorandum reflect those submitted in a previous memorandum delivered to the local town hall and sent to the premier. On June 22 the Concerned Group met with the premier and asked that the local councilors be suspended. Premier David Mabuza promised to come to the area for an open forum the following Sunday to respond to the community's concerns but argued he could not suspend the councilors until investigations had been conducted. On the agreed upon date, the premier failed to visit the township but sent representatives to meet with community members (Sinwell et al. 2009, 2). In July, residents staged another march, which the Concerned Group was unable to control. Some protesters burned tires and blocked roads. Cars belonging to the municipality, a health clinic, and a public library were burned; two protesters were killed, reportedly by police and security forces (*Times*, December 26, 2009).

Similar demands not just for the delivery of services but most importantly for government accountability were repeated in townships across the country. In Thokoza and Diepsloot in Gauteng, Khayelitsha in the Western Cape, Duncan Village in the Eastern Cape, and elsewhere, citizens took to the streets. As the protests grew, two areas received the greatest media attention: Siyathemba and Sakhile, both in Mpumalanga. Protests in Siyathemba township outside Balfour began with a march to the local municipal offices. When the municipality failed to respond, a community meeting was held, but clashes erupted between the police and residents after the police fired rubber bullets and teargas in an attempt to disperse the crowd (Sinwell et al. 2009, 5). Some protesters also blocked roads and looted foreign-owned shops. In response to the protests and the destruction that ensued, President Zuma surprised residents by briefly visiting the township and promising to listen to their concerns. In Sakhile, described as a "battlefield" by the local press (*Sowetan*, October 14, 2009), residents promised to continue their protests, including the barricading of roads and the burning of government buildings, until the president also came to resolve their issues (*Mail and Guardian*, October 15, 2009). Sakhile township residents demanded the "right to elect their own representatives," instead of ANC party structures determining candidates for local office, and called for an inquiry into alleged corruption. Protests and the police response led to significant destruction of property and the injury of at least fourteen people (*Mail and Guardian*, October 16, 2009). Although President Zuma did not visit Sakhile, ANC officials came to the area and, in a surprise move, fired the municipal mayor and her entire committee just days ahead of a presidential meeting with all the country's mayors and municipal managers (*Sunday Independent*, October 25, 2009, 1).

In response to the protests in Siyathemba and Sakhile, the Zuma administration has signaled a willingness to listen, but it is not clear whether this is simply a stopgap response to growing unrest and violence or a concerted effort to address the demands for improved governance. In stark contrast to Mbeki, who repeatedly attempted to silence the movements that challenged his policies, Zuma has sought to present himself as someone who will engage citizens' concerns.[10] Zuma condemned the destruction of property and violence that became part of the wave of protests, but in a dramatic change of tone from Mbeki, he also noted the role that protest plays in supporting democracy: "This is our heritage. It is what makes South Africa the vibrant democracy it is today and will continue to be in the future" (quoted in *Mail and Guardian*, November 9, 2009). Yunis Carrim, the deputy minister of cooperative governance and traditional affairs, argued that the protests "signaled the failure of the ward committee system and other methods of public participation in municipalities"

(*City Press*, October 18, 2009). His ministry tabled a report arguing that the protests indicate an "escalating loss of confidence in governance." The report continued to assert that "a culture of patronage and nepotism is now so widespread in many municipalities that the formal municipal accountability system is ineffective and inaccessible to many citizens" (RSA, Cooperative Governance and Traditional Affairs 2009, 11). In response to the protests, the ANC began an audit of local councilors in late 2009, but the audit itself remained internal to the ANC and excluded local communities (*Mail and Guardian*, October 23, 2009).

Although the protests drew important attention to the demands for accountable government, most were able to attract attention only by blocking roads and destroying property and through the corresponding police responses, which included rubber bullets and teargas. The news media ran pictures of burning tire blockades, damaged public buildings, and police taking aim at protesters. This immediately raised the question of the "civility" or "civicness" of the protesters. How could protesters destroy public buildings when they claimed to be agitating for better public-service delivery? How could protesters press for more-responsible government when they were proving to be irresponsible themselves? Minister in the presidency Trevor Manuel in a talk at the Graduate School of Public and Development Management in Johannesburg condemned the protesters' actions, arguing that a behavioral change was necessary for development (October 26, 2009). This argument that citizens must be more civil and must work to support state-based initiatives has long been employed to challenge the legitimacy of popular demands. It suggests, once again, that the public must defer to the expertise of technocrats and policy makers. It also deliberately ignores the question as to what opportunities ordinary citizens have at their disposal for participation and engagement with their elected representatives. In its review of four protests in mid-2009, the Centre for Sociological Research at the University of Johannesburg found that each protest "only occurred after unsuccessful attempts by community members to engage with local authorities over issues of failed service delivery" (Sinwell et al. 2009, 1). Arguments concerning the need for behavioral change to allow for development to take root ignore the demands of the protesters for democratic accountability. Instead, they frame citizens' actions as merely "service-delivery protests" that might be addressed with minimal infrastructural improvements.

In these cases, as with the overwhelming majority of protests discussed in this book, residents first sought to employ institutional routes to petition government, but government actors failed to engage their requests by meeting with local residents, listening to their concerns, and working to address them. In each case, protest actions began with organized nonviolent marches. Those that later turned to violence tended to do so as a product of interactions with local authorities, particularly the police. Trevor Manuel's argument concerning the need for a certain degree of popular civility in order for democracy to function echoes the arguments of civil society analysts such as Robert Putnam (1993, 2000). While this argument may be convenient for a government minister seeking to institute his model of development, it is based upon a misunderstanding of how democracy is established and deepened. Democracy is not a product of good behavior but rather of protracted struggles that often meet with great resistance from those who seek to defend their privilege (Foweraker and Landman 1997, 243).

Zhekele Maya, a member of the Dipaliseng Youth Forum in Balfour, summed up the importance of social mobilization, arguing that "protest is a democratic right" in South Africa today, but it only became a right "through a culture of defiance" (Centre for Sociological Research workshop, October 30, 2009). Ideally, residents' questions and concerns would be addressed by an effective public administration overseen by accountable elected officials, but every study of local government in South Africa, by government and nongovernmental actors, has repeatedly demonstrated that this is often not the case. In this context, the discourse of civility suggests that citizens should accept a lack of accountability when their petitions are ignored and government offices offer no response to residents' questions and concerns. It is exactly the perceived "uncivil" actions that draw attention to claims for democracy.

In response to protesters' demands, Zuma has initiated a review of local government, but the question remains as to whether this review will differ from the many that have come before and have brought little change in local government accountability. Although the new president has not changed the ANC's overall economic-policy framework, he has pledged to work to improve existing social programs and to give greater voice to a wide range of actors in South African society. While the changes over the last decade in South Africa have not led to a fundamental restructuring of power, they have opened the door to the creation of a more substantive democratic system.

Substantive Democracy

Critics of substantive democracy have argued that such definitions reduce the analytic power of the concept. Although this may be true for analyses that seek to investigate the interaction of political and economic variables, such as the impact of regime type on poverty, it is not the case when concerns for the future of democracy are at stake. The exclusion of socio-economic criteria from our understanding of democracy threatens to divorce analysis from the concerns of ordinary people and suggests that material inequality does not effect political equality. On this latter question, classics of American democracy such as Tocqueville's *Democracy in America* ([1835] 2003) and Robert Dahl's *Who Governs?* (1961) are unequivocal. Both assume dispersed rather than durable inequalities for democracy to function. In cases where inequalities become reinforcing and durable, democracy is deeply compromised as the poor lose access to the institutions and rights that their democratic constitutions promise. This occurs not only because the wealthy have superior resources to influence elected officials on contentious issues but also because they can work to set the agenda, determining which issues are relevant for debate and which should simply be taken off the table. By supporting liberal democracy, which defines property rights as fundamental, wealthy citizens can work to limit the scope of discussion since radical redistributive programs to address durable inequalities can easily be labeled antidemocratic.

Poverty, defined as a lack of material resources, is clearly connected to social exclusion and to political exclusion as well. Amartya Sen refers to Adam Smith in underlining the importance of "being able to appear in public without shame and being able to take part in the life of the community" (2006, 35). This can be difficult where a lack of financial means separates the poor or the very poor from their wealthier fellow citizens, affecting the events that they are able to attend and their role in those at which they are present. Poverty encourages social and political exclusion when the poor are looked down upon, when participation in public debate requires access to a range of informational experiences that are out of reach for most people with limited finances, and when policy debates occur in arenas that the poor cannot access due to high entrance costs. In her discussion of basic human capabilities, Martha Nussbaum (2006) lists key criteria for active public engagement, which are often assumed but rarely stated; these include good health, freedom of movement, and basic education. South Africans have added secure housing, ability to care for children, a decent neighborhood, supportive social relationships, and resources to deal with emergency situations to this list of basic necessities (Wright, Noble, and Magasela 2007). Basic rights such as housing, education, health, and freedom of movement do not simply involve a government's "failure to impede" but require "affirmative material and institutional support" (Nussbaum 2006, 54) in order for citizens to take advantage of them. The impact of the absence of these necessities is demonstrated in survey findings that the poor are less likely than their wealthier counterparts to attempt to access formal institutions such as government offices.

South African understandings of democracy, emerging from a legacy of apartheid, build on a basic-capabilities approach. Apartheid and colonialism in South Africa and colonialism and many postcolonial regimes across the continent have worked to entrench poverty and deny the majority of Africans the opportunity to participate in meaningful political processes in their countries. As a result, "substantivists" do not reside in South Africa alone but may well span the continent. Afrobarometer's findings suggest that Tanzanians, Malians, and Nigerians among others favor substantive understandings of democracy. Looking at Nigeria, the other continental giant next to South Africa, with a starkly different political history, Michael Bratton and Peter Lewis (2005, 31) argue: "There is . . . little doubt that economic delivery is a core component in the basic calculus that Nigerian citizens first use to judge how much democracy their leaders are supplying."

The legitimacy of democratic institutions is undermined when ordinary people lose faith in what their democracy actually offers them and become alienated from a regime, institutions, and processes that fail to fully include them because of barriers placed in their way by poverty. Although the South African and the Nigerian regimes are starkly different, the challenges presented to both are similar in one fundamental respect: in both cases support for democracy is undermined by the perception that the system is designed to meet the needs of the wealthy much more than those of the poor. In South Africa, first the civics and later a rising chorus of resurgent social movements have sought to press government to address economic inequality through policy changes and political inequality through the construction of a more-inclusive democratic regime. Through the construction of a politics of necessity, they have mobilized and demanded a democratic regime that protects not just civil and political but also socioeconomic rights. It is this full set of human rights that activists have in mind when arguing: "We are fighting for our rights all the time" (Ndabazandile, interview, July 16, 2003). Support for substantive democracy in African states ranging from Tanzania to Nigeria suggests a basis for possible mobilization to press for the expansion of democracy and rights.

The struggle to move beyond a narrow understanding of democracy is also a struggle to resist alienation. In South Africa, movements have challenged the postapartheid government for undermining their democratic rights through the enforcement of neoliberal economic policies and the use of state power and even violence to implement them. Though the constitution supports their demands, the government often has not. Their fight has not been against democracy but it has been waged against the structures of power that they believe have inhibited their democracy. Social movement struggles in South Africa and elsewhere have achieved many successes. They have empowered people to demand their rights and expanded popular discussions of necessary rights. For many South African activists, the changes in policy have been productive, and a departure from the centralization of power under Mbeki was definitely welcomed, but they also argue that much more needs to be done.[11] Substantive democracy is a goal that has yet to be achieved. At the end of one of our discussions, I asked Ashraf Cassiem if he thought he could successfully work to bring about more dramatic change in the political and economic structures of power that have resisted substantive democracy. His response suggested he was certainly going to try: "We who are in Africa, who have to live here, we don't have money to travel by plane to Europe if we don't like what we see. We have to be living here. We have to be struggling. I mean four hundred years, it's a long time to be struggling for freedom, and I mean, four hundred more is not going to make a difference. And I think people have this will. This is South Africa, and people are strong" (Cassiem, interview, August 9, 2005).

Notes

Introduction

1. Freedom House has reported declines in basic indicators of civil and political rights across a range of regimes from 2006 to 2009 (2010).

2. Firebaugh (2003, 160) demonstrates an increase in average within-nation regional inequality in Western Europe, Eastern Europe, Latin America, and Asia as well as the "Western off-shoots": Australia, Canada, New Zealand, and the United States. Nearly global increases in inequality since 1982 did level off in most countries in the early years of the new millennium (Galbraith 2008).

3. Depending on how measures are constructed, Gini coefficient scores can vary significantly between sources. For this reason, the only scores that are compared cross-nationally here are taken from the UNDP.

4. "Of all the novel things which attracted my attention during my stay in the United States, none struck me more forcibly than the equality of social conditions. I had no difficulty in discovering the extraordinary influence this fundamental fact exerts upon the progress of society; it set up a particular direction to public attitudes, a certain style to the laws, fresh guidelines to governing authorities, and individual habits to those governed. . . . As I studied American society, I increasingly viewed this equality of social conditions as the factor which generated all the others and I discovered that it represented a central focus in which all my observations constantly ended" (Tocqueville [1835] 2003, 11).

5. According to the UNDP, the following countries (listed in order of their human development score) have Gini coefficients of 50 or greater: Chile, Argentina, Panama, Brazil, Colombia, Ecuador, Dominican Republic, Suriname, Paraguay, Honduras, Bolivia, Cape Verde, Guatemala, Nicaragua, Botswana, Namibia, South Africa, Comoros, Swaziland, Angola, Papua New Guinea, Haiti, Lesotho, Zambia, Liberia (2009, 195–98).

6. Interestingly, the differences between inequalities in major U.S., Latin American, and African cities are not as great as countrywide statistics might suggest. UN

Habitat reported on the United States in 2008: "Major metropolitan areas, such as Atlanta, New Orleans, Washington, D.C., Miami, and New York, have the highest levels of inequality in the country, similar to those of Abidjan, Nairobi, Buenos Aires, and Santiago (Gini coefficient of more than 0.50 [on a scale of 0 to 1])" (65).

7. By 2007, Uruguay's inequality had risen to 46.2. Brazil, Bolivia, and Colombia had the highest inequality respectively in the early 1990s. By 2007, Brazil had reduced its inequality coefficient to 55; Bolivia remained largely unchanged at 58.2, and Colombia assumed the role of highest inequality in the region at 58.5. For comparison, inequality in the United States in 2007 measured 40.8 (Gaspirini, Cruces, and Tornarolli 2009; UNDP 2009).

8. Among Uruguayans, 80 percent perceived democracy as "preferable to any other form of government," while only 50 percent of Brazilians did (Karl 2000, 155–56).

9. Foweraker and Landman argue, in contrast, that civil and political rights develop together, citing Anthony Giddens, *The Nation-State and Violence*: "Civil rights thus have been, from the very early phases of capitalist development, bound up with the very definition of what counts as 'political'" (1997, 9).

10. Because of poor data in South Africa prior to the early 1990s and poor data across much of the rest of the continent, it is impossible to argue that South Africa's inequality is currently one of the highest on the continent and to determine how this has changed over time. Even the most casual observer visiting South Africa, however, will be shocked by the contrast between the visible poverty of the majority and the incredible and often ostentatious wealth of a small and increasingly racially diverse elite.

11. The surveyed countries include Botswana, Ghana, Lesotho, Malawi, Mali, Namibia, Nigeria, South Africa, Tanzania, Uganda, Zambia, and Zimbabwe.

12. Bratton and his colleagues describe South Africans as "hard core substantivists" (Bratton, Mattes, and Gyimah-Boadi 2005, 218).

13. Trevor Manuel (minister of finance from 1996 to 2009, minister in the presidency in charge of the National Planning Commission from 2009) noted that almost 50 percent of young African men and women have never had a job (2009).

14. "African population" is used here to refer to those who were defined as "black" under apartheid. Other population groups under the apartheid framework were those defined as "white," "Indian," or "coloured." "Black" is employed to include all those formerly classified as African, Indian, or coloured.

15. After reviewing different data sources, Simkins (2004) concluded: "All the evidence we have, suitably interpreted, indicates that inequality, as measured by the Gini coefficient, increased by a substantial margin between 1995 and 2001." Leibbrandt et al. (2010, 32) and the South African government (RSA, Presidency 2009, 25), employing more recent data, agree that inequality has increased markedly since the end of apartheid. The government reported an increase of 3.9 from 1995 to 2008, while Leibbrandt et al. calculated an increase of 4 from 1993 to 2008.

16. South Africa does not have a national poverty line. The government currently collects data on those living with less than 283, 388, and 524 rand a month. Depending on the measure employed, 40 or even 50 percent of the population would qualify as

living in poverty (Woolard and Leibbrant 2006, 26; J. H. Martins 2007; Wright, Noble, and Magasela 2007; South African Institute of Race Relations [SAIRR] 2009).

Chapter 1. Community Organizing in South Africa

1. In some communities in the Eastern Cape, such as Port Elizabeth and Uitenhage, civics actually took over local government offices through boardroom coups in the early 1990s.

2. The Population Registration Act (1950), repealed in 1991.

3. The Suppression of Communism Act (1950), repealed in 1990.

4. The Group Areas Act (1950), repealed in 1991; the Bantu Authorities Act (1951), repealed in 1984; the Promotion of Bantu Self-Government Act (1959), repealed in 1994.

5. The Natives (Co-ordination of Documents) Act (1952) and the Natives Laws Amendment Act (1952), both repealed in 1986.

6. The Prohibition of Mixed Marriages Act (1949) and the Immorality Act (1950), both repealed in 1986.

7. Criminal Law Amendment Act (1953), repealed in 1982.

8. Separate Amenities Act (1953), repealed in 1990; Bantu Education Act (1953), repealed in 1991; the Extension of University Education Act (1959), repealed in 1994.

9. The Native Labour (Settlement of Disputes) Act (1953), repealed in 1981; the Industrial Conciliation Act (1956), repealed in 1995.

10. The Riotous Assemblies Act (1956), repealed in part in 1982.

11. Robert Sobukwe and others left the ANC in 1959 to form the PAC. This move was in opposition to the ANC alliance with white, Indian, and coloured organizations under the Freedom Charter.

12. On March 21, 1960, the South Africa police fired on protesters, leaving sixty-nine dead and many more injured. Today the date is commemorated with a public holiday: Human Rights Day.

13. In its 1978–79 Strategic Review, the ANC evaluated its political and military strategy and acknowledged both its lack of political organization within South Africa and the urgent need for such organization. Barrell (1992) argues that by 1965 the ANC's domestic underground organization had been destroyed by the apartheid state.

14. Another youth, Mbuyisa Makhubo, eighteen, picked up Hector's body. Sam Nzima captured the moment in the now-famous picture of Mbuyisa carrying Hector and Hector's sister, Antoinette, seventeen, running alongside. (Though the public memorial in Soweto spells his name Peterson, the family goes by Pieterson [Baines 2007].) Today, June 16 is a national holiday: National Youth Day.

15. In 1977 the Soweto branch of the Black People's Convention called for a meeting to form a civic organization (Lodge 1983, 353); the result was the creation of the Soweto Committee of Ten, a group composed of individuals endorsing several different ideological perspectives but generally dominated by adherents to black consciousness.

16. In March 1980, PEBCO claimed twenty thousand registered members, but this number probably included active supporters rather than paid-up members (*Cape Herald*, March 15, 1980, 9).

17. In the early 1980s, Botha addressed the UN General Assembly and traveled across the United States and Canada speaking about the community-based struggle against apartheid (*Eastern Province Herald*, October 2, 1981).

18. Although Buthelezi did speak out against apartheid's injustices, he also participated in and benefited from the apartheid system in his position as leader of the KwaZulu homeland and leader of Inkatha, which by its definition as a Zulu cultural organization fit into the logic of separate development under apartheid.

19. Both Sowetan civic organizers and those from Port Elizabeth commented on the cooperative relationship that existed between the two organizations. Comrades from Soweto visited PEBCO shortly after its launch to share ideas and discuss strategies.

20. New organizations were formed across the country, including the East Rand People's Organization outside Johannesburg and the Uitenhage Black Civic Organization near Port Elizabeth as well as the Cape Areas Housing Action Committee, the Western Cape Civic Association, and the Federation of Cape Civic Associations in the Western Cape and the Durban Housing Action Committee and the Joint Rent Action Committee in the Durban area.

21. The 1977 Community Councils Act called for the establishment of community councils; by November 1981, 227 community councils had been established (SAIRR 1981, 248). The Black Local Authorities Act of 1982 later replaced administration boards and community councils with black local authorities to be introduced in November 1983.

22. The UDF was formally launched on August 20–21, 1983, in Mitchell's Plain, a black working-class suburb of Cape Town. Another broad front, the National Forum, was formed outside Johannesburg a few months earlier. In contrast to the UDF, this coalition of organizations (which included a number of the same organizations as the UDF) broadly supported the principles of black consciousness (Murray 1987; Lodge 1991).

23. Slogan printed in five languages on the cover of the UDF National Launch pamphlet (UDF 1983).

24. Shubane argues that this was actually a poor showing for the SCA. While 10 percent of registered voters voted in the 1983 elections, this was more than the 6 percent turnout for the 1978 elections (Shubane 1991, 264).

25. These included the Vaal Civic Association (VCA), the Cradock Residents' Association (CRADORA), and the Grahamstown Civic Action Association.

26. PEBCO's original constitution specifically endorses black consciousness (and ignores the ANC's nonracialist discourse) by stating: "Membership shall be open to Blacks only" (PEBCO n.d., [4a]).

27. This is particularly true as civic leaders look back on the earlier days from the vantage point of postapartheid South Africa (after the ANC gained control of government).

28. PEBCO leaders among others used these terms to indicate their contempt for the councils and those serving on them (*Evening Post*, October 25, 1979, 3; October 31, 1979, 2).

29. The police sought to justify their actions by claiming that Twala was part of a gang breaking into a liquor store.

30. All dollar amounts are given in U.S. dollars at the exchange rate at the time. Given different costs of living between and within the two countries as well as fluctuating exchange rates, these figures are meant only as a rough approximation of value.

31. The Delmas treason trial lasted three years, during which time the accused were kept in detention. At the end of the trial in 1988, only five of the twenty-two defendants received jail sentences; these five—Popo Molefe, Patrick Lekota, Moses Chikane, Tom Manthata, and Gcinumuzi Malindi—had their sentences overturned by the appellate division of the supreme court in December 1989.

32. In many areas, the court did find evidence that COSAS or youth organizations were involved in violent acts.

33. From September 1984 to May 1986, 12 councilors and many more policemen were killed. Over 200 councilors lost their homes or businesses; over 814 black policemen lost their homes. By May 1985, 257 councilors had resigned (Price 1991, 197).

34. The domestic opposition was now led by the unions that were still able to function as legal organizations under the banner of the Congress of South African Trade Unions (COSATU). These unions added political demands to their own labor demands as strike activity reached new heights (SAIRR 1988–89, xxx).

35. These social movements are not "new" in the sense often discussed in the literature on social movements (Offe 1985) because they are not postmaterial movements. They are "new" in the South African sense because they are postapartheid movements.

Chapter 2. Material Inequality and Political Rights

1. Political "conscientizing" also included encouragement to support particular movements rather than others. In the case of the ANC, a civic leader and ANC member argued: "People saw civics as bread and butter. Once people were highly politicized, people became involved in ANC politics. . . . ANC underground operatives would enter organizations and begin to 'conscientize' people toward ANC politics and bring that particular understanding to the fore" (Lephunya, interview, July 24, 1997).

2. Rent boycotts entailed a withholding of payment for both rent and service charges. Township residents were billed for both by their local authority on the same bill, so the two items together were commonly referred to as "rent" payments.

3. In Wattville in the East Rand, for example, East Rand Administration Board officials raided homes in April 1984. The strategy was cold and simple: homes were raided, any furniture and belongings were placed outside the house, and the doors of the houses were locked (*Sowetan*, April 17, 1984, 2). In Soweto, state agents added

another tactic. In dawn raids during which residents were woken from sleep, defaulters were made to sign documents (which they often did not understand) promising to pay rent. In some cases, those pursued by the authorities owed less than R50 (roughly $24) (*Sowetan*, February 19, 1988, 3).

4. The UN calculated a coefficient of 57.8 in 2007 (UNDP 2009, 197). This is much lower than the figures presented by the South African government, which show an increase of 64.0 in 1995 to 67.9 in 2008 (RSA, Presidency 2009, 25).

5. By 2000 the HDI score for white South Africans had declined from its high in 1990 but remained close to .9 (on a scale of 0 to 1). Africans still had not achieved a score of .7 (UNDP 2003, 41). As a whole, South Africa's HDI score has declined since 1995, largely due to a decrease in life expectancy as a result of HIV/AIDS.

6. Ironically, while civic structures in poor townships worked to encourage payments to local municipalities in the mid-1990s, the wealthy (formerly all white) Johannesburg suburb of Sandton began its own boycott action. This was in response to an approximately 240 percent increase in its (formerly incredibly low) rates, which was meant to bring the area in line with the rest of Johannesburg. The boycott gained widespread support after Liberty Life (the largest corporation in the area) announced its support. As part of the action, most residents only paid for services. At the same time, nearby Alexandra residents were responding to civic calls to pay for rates and services. The Alexandra civic even went so far as to organize a march in support of payment (*Business Day*, September 6, 1996, 1).

7. In most areas, local government offices were unable to offer accurate reports concerning the rate of payment, because their record keeping was so poor.

8. Longtime civic activist Daniel Sandi criticized the government Masakhane program for not involving the civics directly. He argued that local civic structures should have been the ones to coordinate Masakhane, noting that you need to "set a thief to catch a thief," meaning that the same people who campaigned against the old government and asked residents not to pay should go back to their communities and argue that it was now time to pay (Sandi, interview, August 5, 1997).

9. The group of civic supporters was made up mainly of elderly women and men in ANC shirts (*Eastern Province Herald*, July 21, 1995, 1).

10. A February 1997 Human Sciences Research Council (HSRC) poll indicated that 53 percent of respondents nationally disagreed with the statement that those who fail to pay rent and service charges should be evicted and deprived of services. Blacks much more so than whites (who were not generally subject to such actions) disagreed with the use of evictions and service cuts. The HSRC reported that only 35 percent of Africans, 42 percent of "coloureds," and 25 percent of Indians supported such drastic actions (1997). Popular responses in the communities where such cuts occurred in mid-1997 indicate that in the face of cuts within their own communities, an even lower percentage of residents seemed to support them.

11. Large government offices were among some of the most significant debtors but were not among those cut. On August 11, 1997, almost a week after cuts began in other areas, government departments in Greater Johannesburg paid R4.8 million (just over

$1 million). Their accounts were already sixty days in arrears, the criterion used for cutoffs in areas such as KwaThema (*Star*, August 12, 1997, 1).

12. Speaking from his own experience growing up in Alexandra township, a so-called black spot next to the wealthy white suburbs of Johannesburg, Mark Mathabane notes: "Our aspirations as individuals, our capacity to dream and to create, our hopes for the future as a nation united, had been ruthlessly stunted by whites who possessed our lives from birth to death" (1986, 234–35).

Chapter 3. Power to the People!

1. Mandela described his original plan: "The idea was to set up organizational machinery that would allow the ANC to make decisions at the highest level, which could then be swiftly transmitted to the organization as a whole without calling a meeting. In other words, it would allow an illegal organization to continue to function and enable leaders who were banned to continue to lead. The M-Plan was designed to allow the organization to recruit new members, respond to local and national problems, and maintain regular contact between the membership and the underground leadership" (1994, 126).

2. In Grahamstown the civic formed an anti-crime committee in part to draw the attention of the authorities away from other structures: "We used to have meetings with the security people around. We were not scared, because we were talking about ways of combating crime. Meanwhile . . . in our street and area committees, people were talking of reforming the structures . . . but when [the security people] meet us at the executive level, we talked about crime . . . and they were busy writing" (Zake, interview, August 7, 1997).

3. A 1984 HSRC survey of attitudes toward various organizations (cited in Swilling 1988, 108) shows the greatest support in the townships for the ANC and the UDF (and its affiliates). The most popular reason for supporting the UDF was that it "fights for democracy" (35.6 percent). The second and third most popular reasons were respectively "solves our problems" (17.1 percent) and "represents all groups" (12.7 percent).

4. One civic leader in Soweto explained the way in which councilors attempted to use their leverage and the limits of that leverage. As a union member, he spoke to several councilors in 1982 in an effort to procure land for workers' accommodations. Eventually, he did obtain land for these accommodations; shortly thereafter the councilors approached him to campaign for them in the elections. One councilor promised him a house in return for his support in the elections. When local ANC cadres heard of his meeting with the council, the cadres paid the former union leader a visit to express their concern that he might campaign for the council. He believed that the only thing for him to do was to leave Soweto until the elections were over. This made him inaccessible to the councilors and left no doubt in the minds of opposition forces that he did not campaign for the council. When he returned, the councilor who had made the promise of housing referred to him as a "dirty youngster." The councilor was later killed in the rising township violence (anonymous Sowetan civic leader 1, interview, July 1997).

5. Winnie Mandela later denied having made the statement, but the Associated Press claimed to have the comments on tape.

6. In Port Elizabeth, for example, a strong motivation for the formation of street committees was the need to control the militant youth (Lanegran 1997, 224). Such concerns were also clearly expressed in other townships, particularly Alexandra. Father Ronald Cairns, who worked with Alexandra civic leaders during the turbulent late 1980s, echoed the arguments of many township residents. Although he voiced criticisms of some civic actions, he argued: "The organization itself in its leadership level, I really think thirsted to serve the people to the best of their ability. What happens beneath that, individuals, small civic committees, and bodies, what they get up to isn't always in the control of the leadership" (Cairns, interview, June 23, 1997).

7. The other two PEBCO leaders were Sipho Hashe and Champion Galela.

8. The other Cradock leaders were Fort Calata and Sparrow Mkhoto; Sicelo Mhlawuli, the fourth victim, was a civic leader in Oudshoorn.

9. The five were Moses Mayekiso (chairperson of AAC), Paul Tshabalala (deputy chair), Obed Bapela (public secretary), Richard Mdakane (general secretary), and Mzwanele Mayekiso (organizer). They were accused of treason and of attempting to seize control of the township. All five were acquitted in 1989, but as in many similar cases, they were still subject to state restrictions on their movements and activities.

10. After 1990, with the beginning of South Africa's formal transition process, state officials made a remarkable admission by acknowledging the potential usefulness of informal court structures (Seekings 1992b, 187–88).

11. In an example of total defiance toward the state, the Dobsonville branch of the Soweto civic subverted the waiting-list process and occupied and allocated new council houses to homeless families that had been waiting for housing for years (Murray 1987, 427). Residents claimed that even once they were on the waiting list, they were asked to pay a bribe to get accommodations. They also argued that councilor's girlfriends often seemed to be the first to receive housing (SCA 1987, 3).

12. The minister of planning, provincial affairs and national housing, Hernus Kriel, noted that six townships in the Cape, sixteen in the Orange Free State, and seven in the Transvaal had their services cut by March 1991. By June 1991 the Vaal townships (Boiphatong, Bophelong, Sebokeng, Sharpeville, and Zamdela) all had their electricity cut (SAIRR 1991/92, 355); by November the numbers had further increased. The *Star* reported that hundreds of thousands of township dwellers were living without electricity (November 13, 1990, 3), some of whom illegally reconnected their supplies (*Star*, November 18, 1990, 4). In August the town council of Carolina in the Eastern Transvaal, controlled by the Conservative Party, went so far as to cut water, sewerage, refuse removal, and water supplies to the nearby township of Silobela (*Star*, August 30, 1990, 1) and resumed services only after receiving payment for water arrears from the TPA.

13. The discussion of negotiations during the early transition period focuses on civics in the Transvaal region. Civics in other areas of the country were less involved in negotiations due to either the weakness of their structures (e.g., Natal) or the strength of the ANC at the local level (e.g., Eastern Cape). In the case of the Port Elizabeth One

City Forum, PEPCO, though an early champion of the one-city initiative, was plagued by internal rivalries in the early 1990s, giving the ANC the opportunity to take control of local negotiations.

14. All present and past civic leaders interviewed regarding the SPD negotiation process repeatedly stressed the importance of reporting back both through local street-committee meetings as well as larger meetings at venues such as Orlando stadium. Respondents underlined the need for the people to endorse any agreements if they were ever to be successfully implemented. After the August 1990 reports back to the community, the majority of township residents supported the agreement. Only a small but vocal group of younger Sowetans called for rejection of the accord (Swilling and Shubane 1990, 40).

15. In January 1992 a new agreement was signed between the SCA and the local authorities that set the tariff for services at R55 (roughly $20) per month, a rate that would increase as services also improved. By April 1992, Issac Mogase, the chairman of the SCA, announced the resumption of the rent and service boycott in response to a lack of improvement in services and growing allegations of corruption within the local council (SAIRR 1992/93, 433).

16. For an extensive discussion of participatory democratic practices in postapartheid civic structures, see Heller and Ntlokonkulu 2001.

17. The EZLN did, however, encourage abstention in the 2000 presidential elections. Marcos has argued that democracy "is much more than an electoral contest or the alternation of power" (quoted in Swords 2008, 299).

18. Speaking at the rally, Garrick Leton, a MOSOP leader, stressed the material basis of the movement: "We are asking for the restoration of our environment, we are asking for the basic necessities of life: water, electricity, education; but above all we are asking for the right to self-determination so that we can be responsible for our resources and our environment" (quoted in Cooper 1999, 195).

19. MOSOP advocated Ogoni nationalism and even had a flag and a national anthem (Obi 2000, 71).

20. The *New York Times* began its story on Shell in Nigeria with the following words: "Royal Dutch Shell, the big oil company, agreed to pay $15.5 million to settle a case accusing it of taking part in human rights abuses in the Niger Delta in the early 1990s, a striking sum given that the company has denied any wrongdoing" (June 9, 2009).

Chapter 4. Disciplining Dissent

1. Tarrow (1994, 74–75; 1996, 56–58) looks at differences in short-term and long-term changes in opportunity but does not address the question of whether groups can effectively respond to or influence these shifts in the short term.

2. In early 1990, the national political climate in South Africa became substantially freer, but many civic leaders were still subject to various restrictions on their activities, considerable harassment, and even violence from state authorities.

3. The Alexandra Civic Organization (ACO) was officially launched in December 1989 after five leading civic organizers were released from detention. The Vosloorus Civic was established in early 1990 and drew tremendous support within the community. The civic continued to draw clear lines between the residents of the township and anyone in the pay of the state.

4. Daniel Sandi, a prominent civic leader during the 1980s and 1990s, claims that 2,000 local-level, 120 subregional-level, and 13 regional-level civic structures existed in South Africa in 1992 (1994, 1). The number of local branches is, however, an estimate based on claims made by the various regions.

5. Between 1987 and 1992, Kagiso Trust invested almost R4 million ($1.6 million) in civic organizations and their projects (Seekings, Shubane, and Simon 1993, 12).

6. External funding also had some unintended side effects. The most problematic of these was a decline in both accountability of leaders to local residents and volunteerism. Once outsiders became the most important suppliers of resources to civics, leaders were forced to consider and in some cases prioritize funders' concerns over those of the community. Similarly, once outside funding paid for certain staff positions, competition for such positions increased, and former volunteers often felt that paid civic organizers should now be responsible for the vast majority of civic work (Seekings, Shubane, and Simon 1993, 33–44).

7. While nationwide violence declined dramatically after the 1994 elections, violence connected to political conflict continued in KwaZulu-Natal (R. Taylor 2002).

8. For Coetzee and de Kock's confessions, see Gobodo-Madikezela 2003; Pauw 1997.

9. Such definitions of friend and foe were often quite contradictory and based on stereotypes and rumors. One civic leader offered a surprising example of such stereotypes in his description of "what Zulus are like": "The only mistake about them is they are such shallow-minded people. They are mostly immigrants; a lot had no wives or children. . . . As I am saying, they are quite shallow minded; even the question of being politically party-minded, they never had such things, and that's why they were simply drawn in, because the leader of Inkatha could just simply come and say, 'I am going to address the Zulus,' and then they just go there as Zulus only to find that they are now politically captured. You can even go inside [the hostels] today and ask them what they were fighting for and they can't tell you. They will just say to you that once an instruction has been given then they took care of it. That is how they are. . . . They just take instructions, that's how they are" (Mbata, interview, July 17, 1997). Interestingly, the interviewee, a civic leader and an ANC supporter, is also Zulu.

10. This argument was made most strongly by two ANC Midlands leaders: Blade Nzimande and Mpume Sikhosana (who was also a local civic leader) (1991, 1992a) and was met with strong disagreement from other civic leaders (Nkosi 1991; Mayekiso 1992), prompting the two ANC leaders to defend their arguments once again (Nzimande and Sikhosana 1992b, 1992c).

11. The following comment is widely representative of statements made by numerous civic leaders across the country: "The civic remains autonomous of state and

business institutions including political parties and movements. . . . Civics will play a community watchdog role on democracy, even in a democratic South Africa" (Sandi 1993, 1).

12. In Alexandra, for instance, ANC leaders attempted to unify the competing civic associations into a single group allied with the party. One local ANC leader who was part of this failed attempt echoed the ANC's contradictory approach to the civics by arguing for their independence while seeking to define parameters for their actions. He underlined that the ANC "need[s] the civics" (Ngidi, interview, July 15, 1997). Another elected ANC official argued: "[SANCO's] chances are slim. . . . The ANC must take the lead" (L. Twala, interview, July 7, 1997).

13. SANCO was not a member of the Tripartite Alliance. Because of SANCO's weak and uncertain role as a national civic structure, it was never invited to become a formal alliance member but has instead been viewed as an unofficial partner. SANCO is therefore referred to as the "plus one" of the alliance, a term that many civic leaders feel indicates a lack of respect for SANCO.

14. The Soweto civic is perhaps the strongest exception here as far as SANCO's support is concerned. Its base has traditionally been drawn from slightly more conservative house, rather than shack, dwellers.

15. SANCO's third national president traced the weakening of the civic structures to this decision, which he described as a "somersault" for the organization (Hlongwane, interview, June 9, 2004).

16. Three Sowetan women working with the NGO Women for Peace argued that there really was no discernible difference between the civics and the ANC in their section of the township: "The civic is the same as the ANC; they are the ANC" (V. Monnakgotla, interview, July 28, 1997; also Mtimkulu and Rajuili, both interviewed on July 28, 1997).

17. SANCO's 1997 constitution (SANCO 1997a), which all local SANCO branches were required to adopt, included a listing of SANCO's goals (this was a shorter, more succinct listing than that provided in the previous constitution [SANCO 1992]): "1.3 Now therefore we commit ourselves to strive for the following: 1) the improvement of living conditions; 2) the eradication of poverty, homelessness and insecurity; 3) the building of an united community and country; 4) the promotion of socioeconomic and political justice for all; 5) the creation of empowerment structures; 6) job creation, wealth creation and distribution of resources; 7) social security and comfort for all; 8) the implementation of the freedoms and securities enshrined in the Constitution including freedom of speech, freedom of movement, freedom of association and equality for all. 9) To actively and conscientiously promote the participation of youth and women in all its activities; and 10) The implementation of the reconstruction and development program (RDP)."

18. Unfortunately for the workers recruited by the civic, once the rather dilapidated station was cleaned up, a new tendering process was initiated to provide cleaning services. The lowest tender (which employed the fewest number of workers) won, and those hired by the civic lost their jobs (Tseleii, interview, May 19, 1999).

19. An executive member of SANCO and the ANC Gauteng legislature's chief whip argued that much of the tension between local SANCO and ANC branches boiled down to "access to resources." "Once the leader of [the] ANC says SANCO is not supposed to be there, it is not really because he doesn't believe that SANCO should be there, he is just simply saying that he wants to have the dominant view in terms of access to resources and . . . patronage. That has been the problem throughout the country" (Mdakane, interview, January 16, 2004).

20. SANCO's earlier motto was "People centered development, and democratic local government for all" (SANCO 1992, 1). In 1997, after the completion of local government elections across South Africa, the second part of the motto was dropped.

21. SANCO's national president underlined the organization's limited business experience: "We thought having a company is similar to opening a bottle store, which in a few months' time, you will begin to benefit from the proceeds of sales and thus have sustainability financially. . . . What we did not realize was that entering into long-term investments without resources, without capital, it meant that you have to approach banks and enter into long-term debts, then use those resources to invest in long-term investment which takes many years before you can realize any value or liquidity from those companies" (Hlongwane, interview, June 9, 2004).

22. The Gauteng Province also had an investment arm of its own, Sinamandla, which entered into a joint venture with a local bank and derived some profit. In SANCO Gauteng, as at the national level, SANCO leaders found it incredibly difficult to access any financial support from Sinamandla and complained that they were not involved in any important financial decision making within Sinamandla (Tleane, interview, June 3, 1999).

23. SANCO had initially promised fifty-four centers around the country by the end of the decade.

24. A SANCO leader in the East Rand lamented: "As comrades, I don't think we did our work thoroughly [to] discuss the question of the constitution, because there are some clauses of the new constitution that are contradicting and frustrating us" (Magazi, interview, August 22, 1997).

25. The community liaison officer for the Vaal CEDC admitted that many local residents "don't actually know what is happening in the CEDC" (Letsela, interview, May 27, 1999).

26. The breakdown of the membership fee was the following: R13.42 to AIG for the funeral insurance scheme, R3.16 for administrative costs (paid to the national office), R3.42 to the post office, R2.00 for the recruiter, R2.00 for each level of SANCO (national, provincial, regional, branch) (SANCO 1997c, 8).

27. A SANCO ward chair in Soshanguve explained the incentives for people to join: "Some join because they want to assist other people. Some join because they think they can benefit, someone can stand for them in case of trouble. It varies from individual to individual. Some join because they want power to rule. There are multiple reasons" (Mgidi, interview, June 11, 2004).

28. This plan was criticized by no lesser ANC member than Nelson Mandela, who argued that such an action ran counter to the aims of the negotiation process. In response to the ANC's strongly critical statements and behind-the-scenes discussions, the civics backed down and entered into negotiations with the banks.

29. In the Gauteng province, SANCO's general secretary boasted: "Branches are involved in all the campaigns that are taking place at local level now. In certain areas, the ANC might be weak and our branches will go and take up the ANC campaign, be part of the election committee, whatever [is necessary] at local level. The whole province, our entire working committee, which are the fifteen elected leadership, is being deployed into the different election committees of the ANC" (Matila, interview, May 19, 1999).

30. Interestingly, SANCO's national president agreed with these criticisms. He argued that SANCO's top-down structure "kills innovation within our regions and branches, and as such, it makes us a highly powerful body at the national level without necessarily serving the true agenda of what our structures on the ground require" (Hlongwane, interview, June 9, 2004).

31. Decalo reports that "a World Bank delegation was at the time ensconced in a Cotonou hotel watching the conference proceedings and prodding Kérékou to compromise" (1997, 54).

32. In the March 1995 legislative elections, "voters removed two-thirds of the incumbent deputies, electing new members from 17 political parties" (Magnusson 1999, 222).

33. A substantial number of people voted to retain Pinochet in office. Schneider demonstrates the class-based dimension of the vote: "The cumulative vote against Pinochet in Santiago's poorer districts was closer to 65 percent. In wealthy Las Condes, Pinochet won 75 percent of the vote. In impoverished La Pintana, he lost, 68 percent to 32 percent" (1995, 193).

34. From 1990 to 2010, Chile's government was led by different parties belonging to the center-left Concertación coalition. In 2010, Sebastián Piñera of the right-leaning Coalition for Change won the presidency.

35. Policymaking in Chile does, however, remain highly centralized (Teichman 2009, 83).

36. Posner argues: "Though the PC [Communist Party] eventually abandoned the via armada and supported an electoral exit from authoritarianism, it never overcame its political isolation. Thus, with the PS-Almeyda joining and the PC excluded from the dominant AD [Democratic Alliance, forerunner to the Concertación], those political elements most strongly committed to promoting popular sector organization and participation were destined to have virtually no influence in shaping the terms of the transition" (2004, 66).

37. One senior official offered a telling explanation of why local organizations should not be included in policy making, even concerning questions of poverty alleviation: "We are responsible for the [World] Bank loan for this program, not the NGOs, so why should they be involved?" (quoted in Teichman 2009, 78). The World Bank eventually pressured the Chilean government to allow some monitoring and evaluation of poverty-relief programs by NGOs.

Chapter 5. Contentious Democracy

1. Cost recovery forms a central pillar of the World Bank's discourse of adjustment and good governance (Abrahamsen 2001).

2. In Alexandra, one civic leader who had helped turn in a few minor criminals explained the dangers of doing so, as alleged criminals, even if apprehended by the police, were often quickly back on the street: "[Then he] comes back to you the next day and points a finger at you. You find yourself in a situation where you don't know what you have to do next time, if you find a criminal" (Langa, interview, June 19, 1997).

3. SANCO's suggestion was that block tariffs should be implemented for services such as electricity and water. The first block, in the case of water, fifty liters, would be free. Anything beyond that amount would be charged to the consumer. SANCO suggested that as consumption rates increased so should the charge per block. Those who consumed the most would therefore be required to pay the highest rates per block (Williams, interview, May 10, 1999).

4. Nine candidates ran in the Port Elizabeth area with local SANCO support. One of the candidates summed up his conclusions by arguing: "The is the fault of the system in a way, it is so party-politically based" (Gamble, interview, January 22, 2001).

5. In a further attempt to calm any ANC concerns regarding SANCO's loyalty, Hlongwane pledged that SANCO would not accept any expelled ANC members into its ranks: "SANCO also has a warning to all opportunists. SANCO has closed its door to all people who were expelled from the ANC and who have jumped to SANCO" (SAPA, December 18, 2002).

6. SANCO's national office argued that these provincial leaders had already been cited by SANCO for not following national resolutions, adding that a "veil of corruption" hung over Ali Tleane in particular (Williams, interview, May 10, 1999). These allegations came only after the resignation of the provincial leaders and pointed to a smear campaign on the part of SANCO's leaders against those that had defied their directions. Tleane was mayor of Tembisa-Kempton Park until May 1996, when he was replaced by the ANC after it became public that he was not paying for his services and continued to support a flat-rate payment system (Lodge 1999b, 50).

7. Another SANCO Soweto civic leader explained his decision to leave SANCO: "SANCO is not a civic movement [anymore]. . . . It is aligned with a political party" (Hlatuta, interview, January 27, 2001).

8. In a move designed to create a civic body that would be truly independent of any political party, Mayekiso, Tleane, and Menu along with a large group of supporters launched the National Association of Residents and Civic Organizations (NARCO) in 1998. Although local structures were launched in several townships across the country, the organization failed to generate wide support and soon declined.

9. Dominant-party democracy is commonly defined as one characterized by "electoral dominance for a prolonged and uninterrupted period, dominance in the formation of governments, and dominance in determining the public agenda" (Giliomee 1998, 128).

10. The NP won a majority of seats in Parliament throughout the apartheid period (1948–89). In 1997 it was renamed the New National Party and merged with the DP in 2000 to create the DA. After leaving the DA in 2001, it formed an alliance with the ANC and voted to disband in 2005. All NNP members of Parliament became members of the ANC as allowed by the parliamentary floor-crossing legislation in effect at the time.

11. Activists echoed complaints frequently heard from township residents since the mid-1990s. One resident of a poor area of Soweto noted: "[Our] councilor doesn't want educated people. He wants to tell people what to do. This leads to disputes" (K. Twala, interview, July 21, 1997).

12. In Afrobarometer's 2008 survey, 64 percent of respondents noted that local councilors "never" or "only sometimes" "try their best to listen to what people like you have to say." Again, 64 percent said local council is "very badly" or "fairly badly" following procedures "allowing citizens like yourself to participate in council's decisions" (Afrobarometer 2009b).

13. One councilor described the ward committee as her "eyes and ears" (Bapela, interview, January 26, 2001).

14. Some councilors have apparently been quite honest with their constituents as to who they expect will hold them to account for their actions: "The last councilor, when as the residents we call him, he will just tell you: 'No, I have never been elected by you, the residents. I have been elected by the ANC'" (Bozo, interview, January 23, 2001). The councilor in question was elected via the proportional representation list, not as a ward councilor.

15. This statement was made on the eve of a COSATU-organized antiprivatization strike in September 2002. COSATU was often presented as being hijacked by ultraleft movements (*Cape Argus*, October 3, 2002), and movement activists such as Trevor Ngwane spoke of "win[ning] COSATU away from the ANC" (Ngwane, interview, July 19, 2002). COSATU was pressured by the ANC to distance itself from actors such as the APF. The APF, which had offices in COSATU house in downtown Johannesburg, was eventually evicted.

16. In the case of the LPM, tensions between the state and the movement increased markedly as the LPM organized a campaign to draw attention to landlessness during the World Summit on Sustainable Development held in Johannesburg in 2002: "Before the 'Week of the Landless,' there had been a lot of interference by the state in the movement . . . direct harassment . . . arrests of activists, initially on fairly minor charges of destruction of property, contravention of the Regulations of Gatherings Act. . . . Then as the movement grows and the struggle becomes more prominent, then we start to see more serious charges of assaults . . . arson . . . murder. So there has been an escalation of direct state police harassment and victimization" (Hargreaves, interview, July 15, 1997).

17. In Gauteng province, the total number of households without access to electricity has increased markedly from just over 420,000 in 2001 to 740,000 in 2009 (RSA, Cooperative Governance and Traditional Affairs 2009, 46).

18. Due to large swings in the exchange rate for the Rand to the U.S. dollar, all post-2000 equivalencies are calculated at R7.3 to $1, the average for the decade, not including the erratic year 2002.

19. Max Livingstone Ntanyana's court order from the High Court of South Africa (Cape of Good Hope Provincial Division) dated May 12, 2003, placed the following conditions on his release: he could not leave his place of residence from 6:00 p.m. to 6:00 a.m., he could not "attend or address any public meeting," and he could not "participate directly or indirectly in the activities of the Anti-Eviction Campaign."

20. In his November 11, 2005, column in *ANC Today* (no. 45), President Mbeki contrasted patriots with those who destroy public property and with this action seek to destroy the democratic state: "The genuine patriots who fought for our liberation, who are engaged in struggle to strengthen the democratic state as a social instrument to serve the masses of the working people, know that the destruction of public property, valuable assets owned by the people, can only serve the interests of those who want to weaken the democratic state, against the interests of the people."

21. Irene Grootboom died in 2008, still living in her shack eight years after the landmark judgment on socioeconomic rights (*Mail and Guardian*, August 8, 2008).

22. Another example of poor people's activism in the courts is the Phiri water case: *Lindiwe Mazibuko v. City of Johannesburg*. Residents of Phiri, Soweto, went to court to demand a minimum of fifty liters of free water per person per day and to challenge the constitutionality of prepaid water meters piloted in Phiri. Although the South Gauteng High Court had granted an order of fifty liters per day, this was amended by the supreme court of appeal and the case went to the constitutional court. In what many activists saw as a significant setback for the pursuit of socioeconomic rights through legal means, the constitutional court ruled that it was not the role of the courts to determine policy such as the amount of water that should be supplied for free and that prepaid meters were "neither unfair or discriminatory" (Constitutional Court of South Africa 2009b).

23. Seats in South Africa's National Assembly are determined by proportional representation; the president is elected by the National Assembly. At the level of local government, a hybrid system exists within which half the representatives are elected via a proportional-representation party-list system and half are first-past-the-post constituency elections.

24. The UNDP (2009) estimates a Gini score of 61.0 for Botswana, higher than South Africa's stark inequality score of 57.8.

25. Emang Basadi's objectives as defined in its founding constitution are (1) "to identify the problems and issues related to women through discussion and research, particularly participatory research"; (2) "to chang[e] the socioeconomic and legal position of women in Botswana"; (3) "to mobilize and increase awareness among women and the public in general"; (4) "to highlight the role of and enhance concrete recognition of women's participation in national development"; and (5) "to work toward greater social equality" (Molokomme 1991, 848–49).

26. In 2009 six CKGR residents were convicted of illegally hunting; the government had not issued any hunting licenses to residents since 2001 (*Economist*, August 8 2009).

27. This wave of new movements includes challenges to water privatizations and gas pipeline investments in Bolivia, the MST in Brazil, Afro-Colombians resisting displacement, and the Zapatistas in Mexico, among others (Stahler-Sholk, Vanden, and Kuecker 2007).

28. In his pursuit of a market economy, Menem also undermined democratic institutions that threatened his reforms by circumventing the legislature and stacking the supreme court with loyalists (Helmke 2005).

29. Levitsky and Murillo (2008) argue that the regime not only remained democratic but actually improved in some areas with the 2007 election of Cristina Kirchner.

Chapter 6. Substantive Democracy

Part of this chapter originally appeared in the journal *Democratization* 16.3 (Zuern 2009).

1. Delivery is generally understood by community activists not simply as building roads or houses but doing so in consultation with local residents in order to consider their needs. One member of the local SANCO branch in New Brighton summed up often repeated frustrations with development projects that forced people to move without considering their transportation costs, access to services, jobs, family, and security: "We want the project, but we do not want it the way it is going on" (Gebengana, interview, January 23, 2001).

2. This number decreased to 19 percent in 2008, an expected decline because the survey did not coincide with elections as did the previous one (Afrobarometer 2009b).

3. The first round, 1999–2001, included the following countries: Botswana, Ghana, Lesotho, Malawi, Mali, Namibia, Nigeria, South Africa, Tanzania, Uganda, Zambia, Zimbabwe. The fourth round also included: Benin, Burkina Faso, Cape Verde, Kenya, Liberia, Madagascar, Mozambique and Senegal.

4. Unfortunately, the question regarding which attributes are essential for a society to be considered democratic was not included in either the third (2005) or fourth (2008) round of surveys. The first question was repeated in 2005 but not in 2008.

5. Support for democracy over other kinds of government increased from an average of 68 percent in 1999 to 72 percent in 2008 across eleven countries. Satisfaction with the way democracy works in practice declined from 61 percent in 1999 to 56 percent in 2008 (Afrobarometer 2009a, 2, 7).

6. Forty-six percent of South Africans say they are not very satisfied or not at all satisfied with democracy in South Africa (Afrobarometer 2009b).

7. In July 2009, social development minister Edna Molewa reported to parliament that an estimated 13 million South Africans received social assistance benefits (http://www.southafrica.info/about/social/grants-060709.htm). According to Statistics South Africa (2007), increased government spending on social issues has corresponded with a relatively small improvement in living conditions.

8. In December 2006, 53 percent of those polled believed Mbeki was doing a "good job"; in June 2007 this number was basically unchanged at 54 percent. By September 2007 only 40 percent approved of the job Mbeki was doing. Disapproval ratings rose more steadily from 31 to 36 to 48 percent over the same period as fewer people were unsure about how they felt about Mbeki (Angus Reid Global Monitor 2007).

9. In order to address any accusations that they were motivated by opposition parties or the desire to attain local government office, the memorandum to the premier argued that the group's members were also members of the ANC: "We are in no position to be elected as councilors and we are mostly working, but cannot sit and fold our arms while the municipality is misusing the rate payers' money" (reproduced in Sinwell et al. 2009).

10. In an attempt to address citizens' many concerns, the Zuma administration set up a presidential hotline that was quickly overwhelmed by callers. Complaints ranged from the unresponsiveness of government departments to unfair labor practices and housing shortages (http://www.iol.co.za, December 3, 2009).

11. At a workshop organized by the Centre for Sociological Research at the University of Johannesburg, Trevor Ngwane referred to the changes at Polokwane as a change of racing jockeys, from Mbeki to Zuma, but decried the problem of the "same old tired horse" (October 30, 2009).

References

Interviews Cited

Anonymous ANC councilor. January 2001.
Anonymous MPAEC activist 1. July 2003.
Anonymous MPAEC activist 2. July 2003.
Anonymous Port Elizabeth civic leader 1. January 2001.
Anonymous Port Elizabeth civic leader 2. January 2001.
Anonymous SANCO Evaton member. August 1997
Anonymous SANCO Gauteng leader. January 2004.
Anonymous SANCO Tshwane leader. January 2004.
Anonymous Sowetan civic leader 1. July 1997.
Anonymous Sowetan civic leader 2. July 1997.
Anonymous Sowetan independent civic activist. January 2001.
Anonymous Vaal civic leader. August 1997.
Bapela, Constance. Alexandra Ward councilor. January 26, 2001.
Bozo, James. SANCO Kwazakhele. January 23, 2001.
Buthelezi, Pule. Former SCA general secretary and Northern Metro councilor. July 22, 1997.
Cairns, Ronald. St. Huberts Catholic Church priest. June 23, 1997.
Cassiem, Ashraf. Western Cape Anti-Eviction Campaign activist. August 9, 2005.
Cornelius, Rukia. Treatment Action Campaign. July 17, 2003.
Fuchs, A. J. Alexandra, Morningside, Marlboro ward councilor. July 16, 2002.
Gamble, Barry. SANCO Walmer executive committee and independent candidate in the 2000 local government elections. January 22, 2001.
Gebengana, Isaac. SANCO New Brighton. January 23, 2001.
Gomati, Morgan. Meadowlands ward councilor. January 25, 2001.
Goniwe, Mbulelo. Former CRADORA organizer. August 8, 1997.
Hargreaves, Samantha. National Land Committee, Gender Program. July 15, 2003.
Hlatuta, Green. Soweto Civic Organization president. January 27, 2001.

Hlongwane, Mlungisi. SANCO national president. June 9, 2004.

Hortop, Peter. Meadowlands parish priest. July 22, 1997.

Kobese, Fiks. SANCO Eastern Cape head of safety and security. August 6, 1997.

Kutumele, Jan. SANCO Mamelodi West coordinator. June 11, 2004.

Langa, Grace. SANCO Marlboro area committee chairperson. June 19, 1997.

Lehoko, White. SANCO Vaal regional secretary. June 9, 2004.

Lephoto, Lucas. Vaal CEDC director. May 27, 1999.

Lephunya, Pat. Former SCA secretary and UDF organizer. July 24, 1997.

Letsela, Jacob. Vaal CEDC community liaison officer. May 27, 1999.

Machitela, Philemon. SANCO Alexandra secretary. June 10, 1997.

Magazi, Ntsiki. SANCO East Rand head of governance and democratization. August 22, 1997.

Makgubutlane, Issac. SANCO KwaThema chairperson. August 25, 1997.

Mali, Aubery. SANCO Eastern Cape media officer. August 5, 1997.

Maluleka, Richard Fanyana. SANCO Wattville chairperson. August 31, 1997.

Matila, Toenka. SANCO Gauteng general secretary. May 19, 1999.

Mayekiso, Moses. Former SANCO national president, SANCO Investment Holdings. August 19, 1997.

Mayekiso, Mzonke. Alexandra Civic Organization organizer. May 25, 1999.

Mayekiso, Mzwanele. SANCO Research and Development Institute president. May 27, 1997.

Mazibuko, Mandla. SANCO Vaal deputy secretary. August 24, 1997; May 27, 1999.

Mbalukwana, Richard. SANCO Vincent Tshabalala Area Committee secretary. June 27, 1997.

Mbata, Sam. SANCO Naledi chairperson. July 17, 1997.

Mdakane, Richard. Gauteng ANC chief whip, SANCO Gauteng chairperson. January 16, 2004.

Mene, Moppo. Cradock mayor. August 8, 1997.

Menu, Maynard. Soweto Civic Organization president. May 28, 1999.

Mgidi, Julius. SANCO Soshanguve chairperson. June 11, 2004.

Mhlongo, Ben. Alexsan Resource Center. July 1, 1997.

Mngomezulu, Linda. SANCO national secretary general. January 14, 2004.

Modise, Segale Phil. SANCO Dobsonville secretary. July 18, 1997.

Moedi, Vuyisile. Diepkloof ward councilor and SANCO Soweto deputy president. July 19, 2002.

Moepi, Rebecca. Meadowlands ward councilor. July 16, 2002.

Mokoena, Oamaki. SANCO Bophelong branch chairperson. August 29, 1997.

Molefe, Shadrack. SANCO Meadowlands branch secretary. July 16, 1997.

Monnakgotla, Sugar. Zola ward councilor. July 15, 2002.

Monnakgotla, Virginia. Women for Peace. July 28, 1997.

Mothibe, Mary. SANCO Joe Modise area committee secretary. June 19, 1997.

Mothung, Abel. Vaal CEDC business development officer. May 27, 1999.

Mqobe, Sasil. SANCO Eastern Cape treasurer. August 6, 1997.

Mtimkulu, Lauretta. Women for Peace. July 28, 1997.

Ndabazandile, Chris. Mandela Park Anti-Eviction Campaign activist. July 16, 2003.

Ngidi, Justice. Sandton mayor. July 15, 1997.

Ngwane, Trevor. Anti-Privatization Forum activist. July 19, 2002; August 8, 2006.

Ntanyana, Max. Mandela Park Anti-Eviction Campaign activist. July 16, 2003.

Ntingani, Nkele. SANCO Greater Johannesburg chairperson and ANC Eastern Metropolitan Sub-Structure chairperson. June 25, 1997.

Ntuli, M. P. Jeppestown ward councilor. July 18, 2002.

Nxumalo, Aubrey. SANCO East Rand chairperson. July 28, 1997.

Pashe, Patience. Women for Peace. July 3, 1997.

Qhakaza, Lucas. SANCO Gauteng organizing secretary. January 15, 2004; June 9, 2004.

Raisa, Joel. SANCO Katlehong chairperson. July 30, 1997.

Rajuili, Gloria. Women for Peace. July 28, 1997.

Sandi, Ntsokolo Daniel. SANCO Eastern Cape president and ANC Western Region District Council chairperson. August 5, 1997.

Schabala, David. SANCO Evaton Branch deputy secretary. August 28, 1997.

Shegoak, Sutherland. SANCO Meadowlands zone 1 chairperson. July 16, 1997.

Sibisi, Bneki. Vosloorus Branch chairperson. July 31, 1997.

Thobejane, Makgane. Greater Johannesburg Metropolitan Council, Office of the City Manager, labor relations specialist. January 22, 2001.

Tleane, Ali. SANCO Gauteng general secretary (1997) and NARCO national secretary (1999). July 8, 1997; June 3, 1999.

Tofile, Mike. SANCO Port Elizabeth president. August 5, 1997; May 18, 1999; January 22, 2001.

Tseleii, Emmanuel. SANCO Soweto secretary. July 11, 1997; May 19, 1999.

Tshabalala, Jabulani. SANCO Tshwane regional secretary. January 17, 2004.

Twala, Kaizer. SANCO Freedom Charter branch chairperson. July 21, 1997.

Twala, Linda. Alexandra councilor. July 7, 1997.

Williams, Donovan. SANCO assistant to president. May 10, 1999; May 31, 1999.

Zake, Lizo. SANCO Albany secretary general. August 7, 1997.

South African Newspapers

Business Day
Cape Argus
Cape Herald
Cape Times
Citizen
City Press
Daily Dispatch
Eastern Province Herald
Evening Post
Financial Mail

Mail and Guardian
Mercury
New Nation
Post
Rand Daily Mail
Sowetan
Star
Sunday Independent
Sunday Times
Sunday Tribune
Times
Weekender
Weekend Post
Weekly Mail (*Mail and Guardian* from 1995)

Books and Articles

Abel, Richard L. 1995. *Politics by Other Means: Law in the Struggle against Apartheid, 1980–1994*. New York: Routledge.

Abrahamsen, Rita. 2001. *Disciplining Democracy: Development Discourse and Good Governance in Africa*. London: Zed Books.

African National Congress (ANC). 1985. Internal Commission Report. ANC National Consultative Conference, June 16–23, Zambia. Robben Island Mayibuye Archives, University of the Western Cape, Bellville, South Africa.

———. 1991. The African National Congress and Its Relationship to Civics. Political Education Discussion Paper no. 3, Robben Island Mayibuye Archives, University of the Western Cape, Bellville, South Africa.

———. 1996–. *Umrabulo*. http://www.anc.org.za/ancdocs/pubs/umrabulo/index.html.

———. 2001–. *ANC Today*. http://www.anc.org.za/ancdocs/anctoday/index.html.

———. 2005. Consolidated Report on the Strategic Context of the National Democratic Revolution and the State of Organisation. ANC National General Council, June 29–July 3, University of Pretoria, Tshwane. http://www.anc.org.za/ancdocs/ngcouncils/2005.

Afrobarometer. 2004. South Africa: A Decade of Democracy, 2004 Summary of Results. http://www.afrobarometer.org.

———. 2009a. Neither Consolidating nor Fully Democratic: The Evolution of African Political Regimes, 1999–2008. Briefing Paper no. 67. http://www.afrobarometer.org.

———. 2009b. Summary of Results, Round 4 Afrobarometer Survey in South Africa. http://www.afrobarometer.org.

Agacino, Rafael. 2003. Chile Thirty Years after the Coup: Chiaroscuro, Illusions, and Cracks in a Mature Counterrevolution. Translated by María Madrigal. *Latin American Perspectives* 30.5:41–69.

Ake, Claude. 1993. The Unique Case of African Democracy. *International Affairs* 69.2: 239–44.

———. 1996. *Democracy and Development in Africa.* Washington, DC: Brookings Institution.

Alcañiz, Isabella, and Melissa Scheier. 2007. New Social Movements with Old Party Politics: The MTL *Piqueteros* and the Communist Party in Argentina. *Latin American Perspectives* 34.2:157–71.

Alence, Rod. 2004. South Africa after Apartheid: The First Decade. *Journal of Democracy* 15.3:78–92.

Alexander, Neville. 2002. *An Ordinary Country: Issues in the Transition from Apartheid to Democracy in South Africa.* Pietermaritzberg: University of Natal Press.

Alexandra Action Committee (AAC). 1986. Another Massacre in Alexandra. Flyer, Historical Papers, University of the Witwatersrand, Johannesburg, South Africa.

———. 1989. Operation Clean-Up Campaign. Flyer, Historical Papers, University of the Witwatersrand, Johannesburg, South Africa.

Almeida, Paul. 2007. Defensive Mobilization: Popular Movements against Economic Adjustment Policies in Latin America. *Latin American Perspectives* 34.3:123–39.

Alvarez, Sonia, Evelina Dagnino, and Arturo Escobar. 1998. Introduction: The Cultural and the Political in Latin American Social Movements. In *Cultures of Politics, Politics of Cultures: Re-Visioning Latin American Social Movements*, edited by Sonia Alvarez, Evelina Dagnino, and Arturo Escobar, 1–29. Boulder, CO: Westview Press.

Alvarez, Sonia, and Arturo Escobar. 1992. Conclusion: Theoretical and Political Horizons of Change in Contemporary Latin American Social Movements. In *The Making of Social Movements in Latin America: Identity, Strategy, and Democracy*, edited by Arturo Escobar and Sonia Alvarez, 317–30. Boulder, CO: Westview Press.

Amuwo, 'Kunle. 2003. The State and the Politics of Democratic Consolidation in Benin, 1990–1999. In *Political Liberalization and Democratization in Africa*, edited by Julius Omozuanvbo Ihonvbere and John Mukum Mbaku, 141–77. Westport, CT: Praeger.

Angus Reid Global Monitor. 2007. Support for Mbeki Falls in South Africa. October 28. http://www.angus-reid.com.

Appadurai, Arjun. 2004. The Capacity to Aspire: Culture and the Terms of Recognition. In *Culture and Public Action*, edited by Vijayendra Rao and Michael Walton, 59–84. Stanford, CA: Stanford University Press.

Arat, Zehra. 1999. Human Rights and Democracy: Expanding or Contracting? *Polity* 32:119–44.

Armony, Ariel, and Victor Armony. 2005. Indictments, Myths and Citizen Mobilization in Argentina: A Discourse Analysis. *Latin American Politics and Society* 47.4: 27–54.

Atkinson, Doreen. 2007. Taking to the Streets: Has Developmental Local Government Failed in South Africa? In *State of the Nation: South Africa 2007*, edited by Sakhela Buhlungu, John Daniel, Roger Southall, and Jessica Lutchman, 53–77. Cape Town: Human Sciences Research Council.

Avritzer, Leonardo. 2002. *Democracy and the Public Space in Latin America*. Princeton, NJ: Princeton University Press.

Ayero, Javier. 2005. Protest and Politics in Contemporary Argentina. In *Argentine Democracy: The Politics of Institutional Weakness*, edited by Steven Levitsky and María Victoria Murillo, 250–68. University Park: Pennsylvania State University Press.

Bachrach, Peter. 1967. *The Theory of Democratic Elitism: A Critique*. Boston: Little, Brown.

Baines, Gary. 2007. The Master Narrative of South Africa's Liberation Struggle: Remembering and Forgetting June 16, 1976. *International Journal of African Historical Studies* 40.2:283–302.

Ballard, Richard, Adam Habib, Imraan Valodia, and Elke Zuern. 2005. Globalization, Marginalization and Contemporary Social Movements in South Africa. *African Affairs* 104.417:615–34.

Barmeyer, Niels. 2003. The Guerilla Movement as Project: An Assessment of Community Involvement in the EZLN. *Latin American Perspectives* 30.1:122–38.

———. 2008. Taking on the State: Resistance, Education and Other Challenges Facing the Zapatista Autonomy Project. *Identities: Global Studies in Culture and Power* 15:506–27.

Barrell, Howard. 1990. *MK: The ANC's Armed Struggle*. Johannesburg: Penguin Forum Series.

———. 1992. The ANC's Strategic Review of 1978–79. *Journal of Southern African Studies* 18.1:64–92.

Battersby, John, and Charles Phahlane. 2002. Mbeki Draws Line in Dealing with "Ultra-Left." *Saturday Star*, September 27.

Bauer, Gretchen. 2010. "Cows Will Lead the Herd into a Precipice": Where Are the Women MPs in Botswana? *Botswana Notes and Records* 42.

Bénit-Gbaffou, Claire. 2008. Are Practices of Local Participation Sidelining the Institutional Participatory Channels? Reflections from Johannesburg. *Transformation* 66/67:1–33.

Bermeo, Nancy. 2009. Does Electoral Democracy Boost Economic Equality? *Journal of Democracy* 20.4:21–35.

Biko, Steve. 1978. *I Write What I Like: Steve Biko; A Selection of His Writings*. Edited by Aelred Stubbs. London: Bowerdean Press.

Bob, Clifford. 2005. *The Marketing of Rebellion: Insurgents, Media, and International Activism*. New York: Cambridge University Press.

Bombal, Inés González, and Mariana Luzzi. 2006. Middle-Class Use of Barter Clubs: A Real Alternative or Just Survival? In *Broken Promises? The Argentine Crisis and Argentine Democracy*, edited by Edward Epstein and David Pion-Berlin, 141–60. Lanham, MD: Lexington Books.

Bond, Patrick. 2006a. Johannesburg's Resurgent Social Movements. In *Challenging Hegemony: Social Movements and the Quest for a New Humanism in Post-Apartheid South Africa*, edited by Nigel Gibson, 103–28. Trenton, NJ: Africa World Press.

———. 2006b. *Talk Left, Walk Right: South Africa's Frustrated Global Reforms*. Durban: University of KwaZulu-Natal Press.

Bozzoli, Belinda. 2004. *Theatres of Struggle and the End of Apartheid*. Athens: Ohio University Press.

Bratton, Michael. 2006. Poor People and Democratic Citizenship in Africa. Afrobarometer Working Paper 56. http://www.afrobarometer.org.

Bratton, Michael, and Wonbin Cho. 2006. Where Is Africa Going? Views from Below: A Compendium of Trends in Public Opinion in 12 African Countries, 1999–2006. Afrobarometer Working Paper 60. http://www.afrobarometer.org.

Bratton, Michael, and Peter Lewis. 2005. The Durability of Political Goods? Evidence from Nigeria's New Democracy. Afrobarometer Working Paper 48. http://www.afrobarometer.org.

Bratton, Michael, and Robert Mattes. 2001. Support for Democracy in Africa: Intrinsic or Instrumental? *British Journal of Political Science* 31.4:447–74.

Bratton, Michael, Robert Mattes, and E. Gyimah-Boadi. 2005. *Public Opinion, Democracy and Market Reform in Africa*. New York: Cambridge University Press.

Bratton, Michael, and Nicolas van de Walle. 1997. *Democratic Experiments in Africa: Regime Transitions in Comparative Perspective*. New York: Cambridge University Press.

Bresnahan, Rosalind. 2003. Introduction: Chile since 1990; The Contradictions of Neoliberal Democratization. *Latin American Perspectives* 30.5:3–15.

Buhlungu, Sakhela. 2006. Upstarts or Bearers of Tradition? The Anti-Privatization Forum of Gauteng. In *Globalization, Marginalization and New Social Movements in Post Apartheid South Africa*, edited by Richard Ballard, Adam Habib, and Imraan Valodia, 67–88. Durban: University of KwaZulu-Natal Press.

Butler, Anthony. 2000. Is South Africa Heading Towards Authoritarian Rule? Instability Myths and Expectations Traps in a New Democracy. *Politikon* 27.2:189–205.

———. 2007. The State of the African National Congress. In *State of the Nation: South Africa 2007*, edited by Sakhela Buhlungu, John Daniel, Roger Southall, and Jessica Lutchman, 35–52. Cape Town: Human Sciences Research Council Press.

Cadena-Roa, Jorge. 2009. Contentious Politics in Mexico: Democratization and Mobilizations after NAFTA. In *Contentious Politics in North America: National Protest and Transnational Collaboration under Continental Integration*, edited by Jeffrey Ayres and Laura Macdonald, 114–31. New York: Palgrave Macmillan.

Caldeira, Teresa, and James Holston. 1999. Democracy and Violence in Brazil. *Comparative Studies in Society and History* 41:691–729.

Calland, Richard, and Paul Graham. 2005. Debate and Democracy: Why Measure Democracy in South Africa? In *Democracy in the Time of Mbeki*, edited by Richard Calland and Paul Graham, 3–20. Cape Town: Institute for Democracy in South Africa.

Canel, Eduardo. 1992. Democratization and the Decline of Urban Social Movements in Uruguay: A Political-Institutional Account. In *The Making of Social Movements in Latin America*, edited by Arturo Escobar and Sonia Alvarez, 276–90. Boulder, CO: Westview Press.

Carroll, Terrance, and Barbara Wake Carroll. 2004. The Rapid Emergence of Civil Society in Botswana. *Commonwealth and Comparative Politics* 42.3:333–55.

Carter, Charles Edward. 1991. Comrades and Community: Politics and the Construction of Hegemony in Alexandra Township, South Africa, 1984–1987. PhD diss., Mansfield College, Oxford University.

Casanova, Pablo González. 2005. The Zapatista "Caracoles": Networks of Resistance and Autonomy. *Socialism and Democracy* 19.3:79–92.

Castells, Manuel. 1983. *The City and the Grassroots: A Cross-Cultural Theory of Urban Social Movements*. Berkeley: University of California Press.

Cayford, Steven. 1996. The Ogoni Uprising: Oil, Human Rights, and a Democratic Alternative in Nigeria. *Africa Today* 43.2:183–98.

Chatterjee, Partha. 2004. *The Politics of the Governed: Reflections on Popular Politics in Most of the World*. New York: Columbia University Press.

Chen, Shaohua, and Martin Ravallion. 2008. The Developing World Is Poorer Than We Thought, but No Less Successful in the Fight against Poverty. Policy Research Working Paper 4703, World Bank Development Research Group, Washington, DC. http://econ.worldbank.org.

Cherry, Janet. 2000. Hegemony, Democracy and Civil Society: Political Participation in Kwazakele Township, 1980–1993. In *From Comrades to Citizens: The South African Civics Movement and the Transition to Democracy*, edited by Glenn Adler and Jonny Steinberg, 86–113. New York: St. Martin's Press.

Cherry, Janet, Chris Jones, and Jeremy Seekings. 2000. Democratization and Politics in South African Townships. *International Journal of Urban and Regional Research* 24.4:889–905.

Chipkin, Ivor. 2003. The South African Nation. *Transformation: Critical Perspectives on Southern Africa* 51:25–47.

Coleman, Max, and David Webster. 1986. Repression and Detentions in South Africa. In *South African Review 3*, edited by South African Research Service, 111–36. Johannesburg: Ravan Press.

Collier, David, and Steven Levitsky. 1997. Democracy with Adjectives: Conceptual Innovation in Comparative Research. *World Politics* 49.3:430–51.

Collinge, Jo-Anne. 1986. The United Democratic Front. In *South African Review 3*, edited by South African Research Service, 248–66. Johannesburg: Ravan Press.

———. 1991. Civics: Local Government from Below. *Work in Progress* 74 (May): 8–11. http://www.disa.ukzn.ac.za.

Congress of the People. 1955. The Freedom Charter. http://www.anc.org.za/ancdocs/history/charter.html.

Constitutional Court of South Africa. 2000. *The Government of the Republic of South Africa, the Premier of the Province of the Western Cape, Cape Metropolitan Council and Oostenberg Municipality v. Irene Grootboom and Others, CCT 11/00*. Decided on October 4, 2000. http://www.saflii.org/za/cases/ZACC.

———. 2002. *The Minister of Health, Member of the Executive Council for Health, Eastern Cape, Free State, Gauteng, KwaZulu-Natal, Mpumalanga, Northern Cape, Northern Province and North West v. Treatment Action Campaign, Dr. Haroom*

Saloojee, and Children's Rights Centre, CCT 8/02. Decided on July 5, 2002. http://www.saflii.org/za/cases/ZACC.

——. 2009a. *Abahlali baseMjondolo Movement of South Africa and Sibusiso Zikode v. Premier of the Province of KwaZulu-Natal, Member of the Executive Council for Local Government, Housing and Traditional Affairs, KwaZulu-Natal, Minister of Human Settlements and Minister of Rural Development and Law Reform, CCT 12/09.* Decided on October 14, 2009. http://www.saflii.org/za/cases/ZACC.

——. 2009b. *Lindiwe Mazibuko, Grace Munyai, Jennifer Makoatsane, Sophia Malekutu and Vusimuzi Park v. City of Johannesburg, Johannesburg Water (Pty) Ltd., and Minister for Water Affairs and Forestry, CCT 39/09.* Decided on October 8, 2009. http://www.saflii.org/za/cases/ZACC.

Cooper, Joshua. 1999. The Ogoni Struggle for Human Rights and a Civil Society in Nigeria. In *Nonviolent Social Movements: A Geographical Perspective*, edited by Stephen Zunes, Lester Kurtz, and Sarah Beth Asher, 189–202. Malden, MA: Blackwell.

Cornia, Giovanni Andrea, and Julius Court. 2001. *Inequality, Growth and Poverty in the Era of Liberalization and Globalization.* Helsinki: United Nations University, World Institute for Development Economics Research.

Cunningham, David. 2003. State versus Social Movement: FBI Counterintelligence against the New Left. In *States, Parties and Social Movements*, edited by Jack Goldstone, 45–76. New York: Cambridge University Press.

Dagnino, Evelina. 1998. Culture, Citizenship, and Democracy: Changing Discourses and Practices of the Latin American Left. In *Cultures of Politics, Politics of Cultures: Re-Visioning Latin American Social Movements*, edited by Sonia Alvarez, Evelina Dagnino, and Arturo Escobar, 33–63. Boulder, CO: Westview Press.

Dahl, Robert. 1961. *Who Governs? Democracy and Power in an American City.* New Haven, CT: Yale University Press.

——. 1971. *Polyarchy: Participation and Opposition.* New Haven, CT: Yale University Press.

Dalton, Russell, Doh Shin, and Willy Jou. 2007. Understanding Democracy: Data from Unlikely Places. *Journal of Democracy* 18.4:142–56.

Daniels, Glenda. 1991. Beyond Protest Politics. *Work in Progress* 76 (July): 13–15. http://www.disa.ukzn.ac.za.

Decalo, Samuel. 1997. Benin: First of the New Democracies. In *Political Reform in Francophone Africa*, edited by John Clark and David Gardinier, 43–61. Boulder, CO: Westview Press.

Delmas Treason Trial. 1988. Judgment. Historical Papers, University of the Witwatersrand, Johannesburg, South Africa.

——. n.d. Defense Material. Historical Papers, University of the Witwatersrand, Johannesburg, South Africa.

Desai, Ashwin. 2002. *We Are the Poors: Community Struggles in Post-Apartheid South Africa.* New York: Monthly Review Press.

——. 2003. Neoliberalism and Resistance in South Africa. *Monthly Review* 54.8: 16–28.

Desai, Ashwin, and Richard Pithouse. 2004. "But We Were Thousands": Dispossession,

Resistance, Repossession and Repression in Mandela Park. *Journal of Asian and African Studies* 39:239–69.

Díaz-Barriga, Miguel. 1998. Beyond the Domestic and the Public: Colonas Participation in Urban Movements in Mexico City. In *Cultures of Politics, Politics of Cultures: Re-Visioning Latin American Social Movements*, edited by Sonia Alvarez, Evelina Dagnino, and Arturo Escobar, 252–77. Boulder, CO: Westview Press.

Dong'Aroga, Joseph. 1999. The Idea of Democracy in African Tales. *Research in African Literatures* 30.1:140–53.

Dow, Unity. 1991. Gender Equality under the Botswana Constitution. In *Putting Women on the Agenda*, edited by Susan Bazilli, 256–61. Johannesburg: Ravan Press.

Eaton, Kent. 2004. Risky Business: Decentralization from Above in Chile and Uruguay. *Comparative Politics* 37.1:1–22.

Egan, Anthony, and Alex Wafer. 2006. Dynamics of a "Mini-Mass Movement": Origins, Identity and Ideological Pluralism in the Soweto Electricity Crisis Committee. In *Voices of Protest: Social Movements in Post-Apartheid South Africa*, edited by Richard Ballard, Adam Habib, and Imraan Valodia, 45–65. Durban: University of KwaZulu-Natal Press.

Ekeh, Peter. 1997. The Concept of Second Liberation and the Prospects of Democracy in Africa: A Nigerian Context. In *Dilemmas of Democracy in Nigeria*, edited by Paul Beckett and Crawford Young, 83–110. Rochester, NY: University of Rochester Press.

Ellis, Stephen. 1998. The Historical Significance of South Africa's Third Force. *Journal of Southern African Studies* 24.2:261–99.

Epstein, Edward. 2006. The Piquetero Movement in Greater Buenos Aires: Political Protests by the Unemployed Poor during the Crisis. In *Broken Promises? The Argentine Crisis and Argentine Democracy*, edited by Edward Epstein and David Pion-Berlin, 97–115. Lanham, MD: Lexington Books.

Esteva, Gustavo. 2001. The Meaning and Scope of the Struggle for Autonomy. *Latin American Perspectives* 28.2:120–48.

Evans, Peter. 2001. *Embedded Autonomy: States and Industrial Transformation*. Princeton, NJ: Princeton University Press.

Eveleth, Ann. 2003. Criminalising Dissent: Experiences of the Landless People's Movement and the National Land Committee during the WSSD. In *The Right to Dissent: Freedom of Expression, Assembly and Demonstration in South Africa*, edited by Simon Kimani Ndung'u, 84–91. Johannesburg: Freedom of Expression Institute.

Fanon, Franz. 1961. *The Wretched of the Earth*. New York: Grove Press.

Fatton, Robert, Jr. 1995. Africa in the Age of Democratization: The Civic Limitations of Civil Society. *African Studies Review* 38.2:67–99.

Federation of Cape Civic Associations. 1980. Newsletter, no. 1.1. Robben Island Mayibuye Archives, University of the Western Cape, Bellville, South Africa.

Feinstein, Andrew. 2007. *After the Party: A Personal and Political Journey inside the ANC*. Johannesburg: Jonathan Ball.

Ferguson, James. 2006. *Global Shadows: Africa in the Neoliberal World Order.* Durham, NC: Duke University Press.

Firebaugh, Glenn. 2003. *The New Geography of Global Income Inequality.* Cambridge, MA: Harvard University Press.

Foucault, Michel. 1995. *Discipline and Punish: The Birth of the Prison.* New York: Vintage Books.

Foweraker, Joe, and Todd Landman. 1997. *Citizenship Rights and Social Movements: A Comparative and Statistical Analysis.* Oxford: Oxford University Press.

Frankel, Philip. 2001. *An Ordinary Atrocity: Sharpeville and Its Massacre.* New Haven, CT: Yale University Press.

Frankel, Philip, et al. 1987. Socio-Economic Conditions, Rent Boycotts and the Local Government Crisis: A Vaal Triangle Field Study. Historical Papers, University of the Witwatersrand, Johannesburg, South Africa.

Freedom House. 2010. Freedom in the World 2010: Global Erosion of Freedom. http://freedomhouse.org.

Friedman, Steven. 1992. Bonaparte at the Barricades: The Colonization of Civil Society. *Theoria* 79:83–95.

———. 2007. No, Dear, That's Not Mob Rule—It's Called Democracy. *Mail and Guardian*, December 17.

———. 2009a. An Accidental Advance? South Africa's 2009 Elections. *Journal of Democracy* 20.4:108–122.

———. 2009b. Call on the State President to Restore the Credibility of Our Democracy by Establishing an Independent Commission of Inquire into Violence against Shackdwellers in Durban. Statement by the Centre for the Study of Democracy, Rhodes University/University of Johannesburg. In author's possession.

Friedman, Steven, and Shauna Mottiar. 2006. Seeking the High Ground: The Treatment Action Campaign and the Politics of Morality. In *Voices of Protest: Social Movements in Post-Apartheid South Africa*, edited by Richard Ballard, Adam Habib, and Imraan Valodia, 23–44. Durban: University of KwaZulu-Natal Press.

Galbraith, James. 2009. Inequality, Unemployment and Growth: New Measures for Old Controversies. *Journal of Economic Inequality* 7.2:189–206.

García, María Elena. 2005. *Making Indigenous Citizens: Identities, Education and Multicultural Development in Peru.* Stanford, CA: Stanford University Press.

Garretón, Manuel Antonio. 2003. *Incomplete Democracy: Political Democratization in Chile and Latin America.* Chapel Hill: University of North Carolina Press.

Gaspirini, Leonardo, Guillermo Cruces, and Leopoldo Tornarolli. 2009. Recent Trends in Income Inequality in Latin America. ECINEQ Working Paper Series 132, Society for the Study of Economic Inequality, Palma de Mallorca, Spain. http://ideas.repec.org/search.html.

Gay, Robert. 1994. *Popular Organization and Democracy in Rio de Janeiro: A Tale of Two Favelas.* Philadelphia: Temple University Press.

Gazibo, Mamoudou. 2005. Foreign Aid and Democratization: Benin and Niger Compared. *African Studies Review* 48.3:67–87.

Gevisser, Mark. 2007. *Thabo Mbeki: The Dream Deferred.* Johannesburg: Jonathan Ball.

Gibson, Nigel. 2006. Calling Everything into Question: Broken Promises, Social Movements and Emergent Intellectual Currents in Post-Apartheid South Africa. In *Challenging Hegemony: Social Movements and the Quest for a New Humanism in Post-Apartheid South Africa*, edited by Nigel Gibson, 1–53. Trenton, NJ: Africa World Press.

Giddens, Anthony. 1987. *The Nation-State and Violence.* Vol. 2 of *A Contemporary Critique of Historical Materialism.* Berkeley: University of California Press.

Gilbreth, Chris, and Gerardo Otero. 2001. Democratization in Mexico: The Zapatista Uprising and Civil Society. *Latin American Perspectives* 28.4:7–29.

Giliomee. Hermann. 1998. South Africa's Emerging Dominant-Party Regime. *Journal of Democracy* 9.4:128–42.

Gisselquist, Rachel. 2008. Democratic Transition and Democratic Survival in Benin. *Democratization* 15.4:789–814.

Gobodo-Madikezela, Pumla. *A Human Being Died that Night: A South African Story of Forgiveness.* Boston: Houghton Mifflin.

Goldstone, Jack. 1998. Social Movements or Revolutions? On the Evolution and Outcomes of Collective Action. In *From Contention to Democracy*, edited by Marco G. Giugni, Doug McAdam, and Charles Tilly, 125–68. Lanham, MD: Rowman and Littlefield.

———. 2003. Introduction: Bridging Institutionalized and Noninstitutionalized Politics. In *States, Parties and Social Movements*, edited by Jack Goldstone, 1–26. New York: Cambridge University Press.

Good, Kenneth. 2008. *Diamonds, Dispossession and Democracy.* Oxford: James Currey.

Goodwin, Jeff. 2001. *No Other Way Out: States and Revolutionary Movements, 1945–1991.* New York: Cambridge University Press.

Goodwin, Jeff, and James Jasper. 2004. Caught in a Winding, Snarling Vine: The Structural Bias of Political Process Theory. In *Rethinking Social Movements: Structure, Meaning and Emotion*, edited by Jeff Goodwin and James Jasper, 3–30. Lanham, MD: Rowman and Littlefield.

Guelke, Adrian. 2000. Interpretations of Political Violence during South Africa's Transition. *Politikon* 27.2:239–54.

Gumede, William. 1998. Implosion on Main Street. *Siyaya* 1:50–51.

Gunther, Richard, P. Nikiforos Diamandouros, and Hans-Jürgen Puhle, eds. 1995. *The Politics of Democratic Consolidation: Southern Europe in Comparative Perspective.* Baltimore: Johns Hopkins University Press.

Habib, Adam. 2008. Substantive Uncertainty: South Africa's Democracy Becomes Dynamic. *African Analyst* 3:2:79–98.

Habib, Adam, and Collette Schultz Herzenberg. 2009. Democratization and Parliamentary Opposition in Contemporary South Africa: The 2009 National and Provincial Elections in Perspective. Manuscript. In author's possession.

Habib, Adam, and Vishnu Padayachee. 2000. Economic Policy and Power Relations in South Africa's Transition to Democracy. *World Development* 28.2:245–61.

Habib, Adam, and Imraan Valodia. 2006. Reconstructing a Social Movement in an Era of Globalization: A Case Study of COSATU. In *Voices of Protest: Social Movements in Post-Apartheid South Africa*, edited by Richard Ballard, Adam Habib, and Imraan Valodia, 225–53. Durban: University of KwaZulu-Natal Press.

Harvey, Neil. 1998. *The Chiapas Rebellion: The Struggle for Land and Democracy*. Durham, NC: Duke University Press.

Hassim, Shireen. 2009. Democracy's Shadows: Sexual Rights and Gender Politics in the Rape Trial of Jacob Zuma. *African Studies* 68.1:57–77.

Heilbrunn, John R. 1993. Social Origins of National Conferences in Benin and Togo. *Journal of Modern African Studies* 31.2:277–99.

———. 1999. Corruption, Democracy and Reform in Benin. In *The Self-Restraining State: Power and Accountability in New Democracies*, edited by Andreas Schedler, Larry Diamond, and Marc Plattner, 227–43. Boulder, CO: Lynne Rienner.

Heller, Patrick. 2000. "Technocratic Creep" Threatens Local Government Reform. *Synopsis* 4.1:1–2, 12.

Heller, Patrick, and Libhongo Ntlokonkulu. 2001. *A Civic Movement, or a Movement of Civics? The South African National Civic Organization (SANCO) in the Post-Apartheid Period*. Research Report 84, Centre for Policy Studies, Johannesburg.

Helliker, Kirk, Andre Roux, and Roland White. 1989. "Asithengi" Recent Consumer Boycotts. In *South African Review 4*, edited by Glenn Moss and Ingrid Obery, 33–52. Johannesburg: Ravan Press.

Hellman, Judith Adler. 1994. Mexican Popular Movements, Clientelism and the Process of Democratization. *Latin American Perspectives* 21.2:124–42.

Helmke, Gretchen. 2005. Enduring Uncertainly: Court-Executive Relations in Argentina in the 1990s and Beyond. In *Argentine Democracy: The Politics of Institutional Weakness*, edited by Steven Levitsky and María Victoria Murillo, 139–62. University Park: Pennsylvania State University Press.

Hemson, David, and Kwame Owusu-Ampomah. 2006. The "Vexed Question": Interruptions, Cut-Offs and Water Services in South Africa. In *South African Social Attitudes: Changing Times, Diverse Voices*, edited by Udesh Pillay, Benjamin Roberts, and Stephen Rule, 150–75. Cape Town: HSRC Press.

Heynes, Barbara. 2005. Emerging Inequalities in Central and Eastern Europe. *Annual Review of Sociology* 31:163–97.

Hipsher, Patricia. 1996. Democratization and the Decline of Urban Social Movements in Chile and Spain. *Comparative Politics* 28.3:273–97.

Hlongwane, Mlungisi. 1997. Building a Revolutionary Social Movement to Conquer Challenges of the 21st Century. Presidential Address, SANCO 2nd National Conference, April 16–20. In author's possession.

Holm, John, Patrick Molutsi, and Gloria Somoleka. 1996. The Development of Civil Society in a Democratic State: The Botswana Model. *African Studies Review* 39.2: 43–69.

Holston, James. 1999. Spaces of Insurgent Citizenship. In *Cities and Citizenship*, edited by James Holston, 155–73. Durham, NC: Duke University Press.

Holzner, Claudio. 2006. Clientelism and Democracy in Mexico: The Role of Strong and Weak Networks. In *Latin American Social Movements: Globalization, Democratization and Transnational Networks*, edited by Hank Johnston and Paul Almeida, 77–94. New York: Rowman and Littlefield.

Huchzermeyer, Marie. 2009. Ruling in Abahlali Case Lays Solid Foundation to Build On. *Business Day* (Johannesburg), November 4.

Human Awareness Programme. 1981. Soweto: An Assessment. *Change Newsletter*. Historical Papers, University of the Witwatersrand, Johannesburg, South Africa.

Human Rights Watch. 1995. Nigeria—The Ogoni Crisis: A Case-Study of Military Repression in Southeastern Nigeria. *Human Rights Watch Africa Report* 7.5.

Human Sciences Research Council (HSRC). 1997. Media release, October 20. http://www.hsrc.ac.za.

Ikelegbe, Augustine. 2001. Civil Society, Oil and Conflict in the Niger Delta Region of Nigeria: Ramifications of Civil Society for a Regional Resource Struggle. *Journal of Modern African Studies* 39.3:437–469.

International Monetary Fund. 2007. *World Economic Outlook: Globalization and Inequality*. http://tinyurl.com/yehro6q.

Karis, Thomas G., and Gail M. Gerhart. 1997. *From Protest to Challenge: A Documentary History of African Politics in South Africa, 1882–1990*. Vol. 5, *Nadir and Resurgence, 1964–1979*. Bloomington: Indiana University Press.

Karl, Terry Lynn. 2000. Economic Inequality and Democratic Instability. *Journal of Democracy* 11.1:149–56.

Kerr, David. 2001. Media Democracy in Botswana: The *Kgotla* as Myth, Practice and Post-Colonial Communication Paradigm. In *Media, Democracy and Renewal in Southern Africa*, edited by Keyan Tomaselli and Hopeton Dunn, 255–68. Colorado Springs: International Academic.

Khunou, Grace. 2002. "Massive Cutoffs": Cost Recovery and Electricity Service in Diepkloof, Soweto. In *Cost Recovery and the Crisis of Service Delivery*, edited by David McDonald and John Pape, 61–80. Cape Town: HSRC Press.

Klopp, Jacqueline, and Elke Zuern. 2007. The Politics of Violence in Democratization. *Comparative Politics* 39.2:127–46.

Lanegran, Kimberly Rae. 1997. Social Movements, Democratization, and Civil Society: The Case of the South African Civic Associations. PhD diss., University of Florida.

Leibbrandt, Murray, Ingrid Woolard, Arden Finn, and Jonathan Argent. 2010. Trends in South African Distribution and Poverty since the Fall of Apartheid. OECD Social, Employment and Migration Working Papers 101. OECD Publishing. http://www.irinnews.org/pdf/saincome.pdf.

Leslie, Agnes Ngoma. 2006. *Social Movements and Democracy in Africa: The Impact of Women's Struggles for Equal Rights in Botswana*. New York: Routledge.

Levitsky, Steven, and María Victoria Murillo. 2005a. Building Castles in the Sand: The Politics of Institutional Weakness in Argentina. In *Argentine Democracy: The Politics of Institutional Weakness*, edited by Steven Levitsky and María Victoria Murillo, 21–44. University Park: Pennsylvania State University Press.

———. 2005b. Introduction. In *Argentine Democracy: The Politics of Institutional Weakness*, edited by Steven Levitsky and María Victoria Murillo, 1–18. University Park: Pennsylvania State University Press.

———. 2008. Argentina: From Kirchner to Kirchner. *Journal of Democracy* 19.2:16–30.

Lewis, Peter. 1999. Nigeria: An End to the Permanent Transition? *Journal of Democracy* 10.1:141–56.

Leysens, Anthony J. 2004. Marginalisation in Southern Africa: Transformation from Below? Afrobarometer Working Paper 37. http://www.afrobarometer.org.

Linz, Juan, and Alfred Stepan. 1996. *Problems of Democratic Transition and Consolidation: Southern Europe, South America and Post-Communist Europe*. Baltimore: Johns Hopkins University Press.

Lodge, Tom. 1983. *Black Politics in South Africa since 1945*. Johannesburg: Ravan Press.

———. 1989. The United Democratic Front: Leadership and Ideology. In *Can South Africa Survive? Five Minutes to Midnight*, edited by John Brewer, 206–30. New York: St. Martin's Press.

———. 1991. Rebellion: The Turning of the Tide. In *All, Here, and Now: Black Politics in South Africa in the 1980s*, edited by Tom Lodge and Bill Nasson, 23–204. New York: Ford Foundation.

———. 1999a. Policy Process within the African National Congress and the Tripartite Alliance. *Politikon: South African Journal of Political Studies* 26.1:5–32.

———. 1999b. *South African Politics since 1994*. Cape Town: David Philip.

Lopez, Linda. 2005. Advancing Human Rights Policy: Does Grassroots Mobilization and Community Dispute Resolution Matter? Insights from Chiapas, Mexico. *Review of Policy Research* 22.1:77–92.

Lucas, Justine. 2000. Civic Organization in Alexandra in the Early 1990s: An Ethnographic Approach. In *From Comrades to Citizens: The South African Civics Movement and the Transition to Democracy*, edited by Glenn Adler and Jonny Steinberg, 145–74. New York: St. Martin's Press.

Lucero, José Antonio. 2008. *Voices of Struggle, Struggles of Voice: Indigenous Representation and Social Movements in the Andes*. Pittsburgh: University of Pittsburgh Press.

Luders, Joseph. 2003. Countermovements, the State, and the Intensity of Racial Contention in the American South. In *States, Parties and Social Movements*, edited by Jack Goldstone, 27–44. New York: Cambridge University Press.

Lukose, Ritty. 2005. Empty Citizenship: Protesting Politics in the Era of Globalization. *Cultural Anthropology* 20.4:506–33.

Maclennan. Ben. 2005. Aids Activists Are Govt's "Conscience." Press release. South African Press Agency, February 16. In author's possession.

Magnusson, Bruce. 1999. Testing Democracy in Benin: Experiments in Institutional Reform. In *State, Conflict and Democracy in Africa*, edited by Richard Joseph, 217–37. Boulder, CO: Lynne Rienner.

Mainwaring, Scott, Guillermo O'Donnell, and J. Samuel Valenzuela, eds. 1992. *Issues in Democratic Consolidation: The New South American Democracies in Comparative Perspective*. Notre Dame, IN: University of Norte Dame Press.

Mamdani, Mahmood. 1996. *Citizen and Subject: Contemporary Africa and the Legacy of Late Colonialism.* Princeton, NJ: Princeton University Press.

Mandela, Nelson. 1994. *Long Walk to Freedom.* New York: Little, Brown.

Mangcu, Xolela. 2005. Citizens and Democracy: The People Shall Govern—Or Shall They? In *Democracy in the Time of Mbeki,* edited by Richard Calland and Paul Graham, 71–80. Cape Town: Institute for Democracy in South Africa.

Manuel, Trevor. 2009. Planning in the South African Government and State: Public Accountability and Governance. Address to the Graduate School of Public and Development Management, University of the Witwatersrand, Johannesburg, South Africa, October 26. In author's possession.

Marcos, Subcomandante. 1995. *Shadows of Tender Fury: The Letters and Communiqués of Subcomandante Marcos and the Zapatista Army of National Liberation.* Translated by Frank Bardacke, Leslie López, and the Watsonville, California Human Rights Committee. New York: Monthly Review Press.

Marshall, T. H., and Tom Bottomore. 1992. *Citizenship and Social Class.* Sterling, VA: Pluto Press.

Martins, Johan H. 2007. Household Budgets as a Social Indicator of Poverty and Inequality in South Africa. *Social Indicators Research* 81:203–21.

Martins, Mônica Dias, 2000. The MST Challenge to Neoliberalism. *Latin American Perspectives* 27.5:33–45.

Marwala, Tshilidzi. 2007. The Anatomy of Capital and the National Democratic Revolution. *Umrabulo* 29:57–59.

Marx, Anthony. 1992. *Lessons of Struggle: South African Internal Opposition, 1960–1990.* New York: Oxford University Press.

Mashabela, Harry. [1987] 2006. *A People on the Boil: Reflections on Soweto.* Johannesburg: Jacana Media and Guyo Buguni.

Mathabane, Mark. 1998. *Kaffir Boy: The True Story of a Black Youth's Coming of Age in Apartheid South Africa.* New York: Free Press.

Mattes, Robert, Yul Derek Davids, and Cherrel Africa. 2000. Views of Democracy in South Africa and the Region: Trends and Comparisons. Afrobarometer Working Paper 8. http://www.afrobarometer.org.

Mattes, Robert, and Hermann Thiel. 1998. Consolidation and Public Opinion in South Africa. *Journal of Democracy* 9.1:95–110.

Maundeni, Zibani. 2004. Mutual Criticism and State/Society Interaction in Botswana. *Journal of Modern African Studies* 42.4:619–636.

Mayekiso, Mzwanele. 1992. Hands off the Civics and Civil Society: A Response to Blade Nzimande. *Work in Progress* 81 (April): 21. http://www.disa.ukzn.ac.za.

———. 1996a. SANCO and Politics—Then and Now. *New Nation,* December 13.

———. 1996b. *Township Politics: Civic Struggles for a New South Africa.* New York: Monthly Review Press.

Mbali, Mandisa. 2006. TAC in the History of Patient-Driven Activism: The Case of Historicizing South Africa's New Social Movements. In *Challenging Hegemony:*

Social Movements and the Quest for a New Humanism in Post-Apartheid South Africa, edited by Nigel Gibson, 129–55. Trenton, NJ: Africa World Press.

Mbeki, Thabo. 1998. Statement of the Deputy President Thabo Mbeki at the Opening of the Debate in the National Assembly on "Reconciliation and Nation Building." Cape Town, May 29. http://www.anc.org.za/ancdocs/history.mbeki.

———. 2002. Statement of the President of the African National Congress. ANC Policy Conference, Kempton Park, September 27. http://www.anc.org.za/ancdocs/history.mbeki.

McAdam, Doug. 1982. *Political Process and the Development of Black Insurgency, 1930–1970*. Chicago: University of Chicago Press.

———. 1996. Conceptual Origins, Current Problems, Future Directions. In *Comparative Perspectives on Social Movements: Political Opportunities, Mobilizing Structures, and Cultural Framings*, edited by Doug McAdam, John D. McCarthy, and Mayer N. Zald, 23–40. New York: Cambridge University Press.

McAdam, Doug, Sidney Tarrow, and Charles Tilly. 2001. *Dynamics of Contention*. New York: Cambridge University Press.

McCarthy, John, and Mayer N. Zald. 1973. *The Trend of Social Movements in America: Professionalization and Resource Mobilization*. Morristown, NJ: General Learning.

McDonald, David. 2002. The Bell Tolls for Thee: Cost Recovery, Cutoffs, and the Affordability of Municipal Services in South Africa. In *Cost Recovery and the Crisis of Service Delivery*, edited by David McDonald and John Pape, 161–79. Cape Town: HSRC Press.

———. 2003. More Carrot, Less Stick. *Mail and Guardian*, May 26.

McDonald, Michael. 2006. *Why Race Matters in South Africa*. Cambridge, MA: Harvard University Press.

McKinley, Dale T. 2003. Trying to "Kill" the Messenger and Failing: Experiences of the Anti-Privatisation Forum during the WSSD. In *The Right to Dissent: Freedom of Expression, Assembly and Demonstration in South Africa*, edited by Simon Kimani Ndung'u, 92–100. Johannesburg: Freedom of Expression Institute.

Melber, Henning. 2007. Poverty, Politics, Power and Privilege: Namibia's Black Economic Elite Formation. In *Transitions in Namibia: Which Changes for Whom?* edited by Henning Melber, 110–29. Uppsala, Sweden: Nordiska Afrikainstitutet.

Melucci, Alberto. 1985. The Symbolic Challenge of Contemporary Movements. *Social Research* 52.4:789–816.

———. 1989. *Nomads of the Present*. Philadelphia: Temple University Press.

———. 1998. Third World or Planetary Conflicts? In *Cultures of Politics, Politics of Cultures: Re-Visioning Latin American Social Movements*, edited by Sonia Alvarez, Evelina Dagnino, and Arturo Escobar, 422–29. Boulder, CO: Westview Press.

Miraftab, Faranak. 2006. Feminist Praxis, Citizenship and Informal Politics: Reflections on South Africa's Anti-eviction Campaign. *International Feminist Journal of Politics* 8.2:194–218.

Molokomme, Athaliah. 1991. Emang Basadi (Botswana). *Signs* 16.4:848–51.

Molzen, Inga, and Alan Mabin. 1990. Pulling the Plug on Township Councils. *Work in Progress* 68 (August): 29–30. http://www.disa.ukzn.ac.za.

Monga, Célestin. 1996. *The Anthropology of Anger: Civil Society and Democracy in Africa.* Boulder, CO: Lynne Rienner.

Morris, Stephen D., and John Passé-Smith. 2001. What a Difference a Crisis Makes: NAFTA, Mexico, and the United States. *Latin American Perspectives* 28.3:124–49.

Movement for the Survival of the Ogoni People (MOSOP). [1990] 1992. *Ogoni Bill of Rights.* Port Harcourt, Nigeria: Saros International.

Mueller-Hirth, Natascha. 2009. South African NGOs and the Public Sphere: Between Popular Movements and Partnerships for Development. *Social Dynamics* 35.2:423–35.

Murray, Martin. 1987. *South Africa: Time of Agony, Time of Destiny; The Upsurge of Popular Protest.* London: Verso.

———. 2008. *Taming the Disorderly City: The Spatial Landscapes of Johannesburg after Apartheid.* Ithaca, NY: Cornell University Press.

Mutagwaba, Benjamin. 2009. Government Expenditure and Income Inequality in Tanzania: A Policy Dimension. Paper prepared for the International Academy of African American Business Conference, Kampala, Uganda. In author's possession.

Nash, Julie. 1997. The Fiesta of the Word: The Zapatista Uprising and Radical Democracy in Mexico. *American Anthropologist* 99.2:261–74.

Ndegwa, Stephen N. 1996. *The Two Faces of Civil Society: NGOs and Politics in Africa.* West Hartford, CT: Kumarian Press.

Ndlovu, Tchaka. 2007. The Impact of Globalization on Poverty and Income Inequality: Evidence from 32 African Countries. Working Paper Series 20, Economic and Social Research Foundation, Dar El Salaam, Tanzania.

Nkosi, Dennis Thokozani. 1991. Civics and the ANC. *Mayibuye* 2.10 (November): 33. http://www.disa.ukzn.ac.za.

Ntabazalila, Eric. 2002. "Champions of the Poor" Target Home-Owners. *Cape Times*, November 8.

Nussbaum, Martha. 2006. Poverty and Human Functioning: Capabilities as Fundamental Entitlements. In *Poverty and Inequality*, edited by David Grusky and Ravi Kanbur, 47–75. Stanford, CA: Stanford University Press.

Nwajiaku, Kathryn. 1994. The National Conferences in Benin and Togo Revisited. *Journal of Modern African Studies* 32.3:429–47.

Nzimande, Blade, and Mpume Sikhosana. 1991. Civics Are Part of the National Democratic Revolution. *Mayibuye* 2.5 (June): 37–39. http://www.disa.ukzn.ac.za.

———. 1992a. Civil Society and Democracy. *African Communist*, 1st quarter: 37–51.

———. 1992b. Civil Society and Democracy: A Rejoinder. *African Communist*, 3rd quarter: 65–71.

———. 1992c. "Civil Society" Does Not Equal Democracy. *Work in Progress* 84 (September): 26–27. http://www.disa.ukzn.ac.za.

Oberschall, Anthony. 1996. Opportunities and Framing in the Eastern European Revolts of 1989. In *Comparative Perspectives on Social Movements: Political Opportunities,*

Mobilizing Structures and Cultural Framings, edited by Doug McAdam, John McCarthy, and Mayer Zald, 93–121. Cambridge: Cambridge University Press.

Obi, Cyril I. 2000. *The Changing Forms of Identity Politics in Nigeria under Economic Adjustment: The Case of the Oil Minorities Movement of the Niger Delta.* Research Report 119, Nordiska Afrikainstitutet, Uppsala, Sweden.

O'Donnell, Guillermo, and Phillipe Schmitter. 1986. *Transitions from Authoritarian Rule: Tentative Conclusions about Uncertain Democracies.* Baltimore: Johns Hopkins University Press.

Offe, Claus. 1985. New Social Movements: Challenging the Boundaries of Institutional Politics. *Social Research* 52:817–68.

Okere, Theophilus, Chukwudi Anthony Njoku, and René Devisch. 2005. All Knowledge Is First of All Local Knowledge: An Introduction. *Africa Development* 30.3:1–19.

Olavarría, Margot. 2003. Protected Neoliberalism: Perverse Institutionalization and the Crisis of Representation in Postdictatorship Chile. *Latin American Perspectives* 30.6:10–38.

Oldfield, Sophie, and Kristian Stokke. 2006. Building Unity in Diversity: Social Movement Activism in the Western Cape Anti-Eviction Campaign. In *Voices of Protest: Social Movements in Post-Apartheid South Africa*, edited by Richard Ballard, Adam Habib, and Imraan Valodia, 111–32. Durban: University of KwaZulu-Natal Press.

Operation Khanyisa Movement. 2006. Poster. In author's possession.

Osaghae, Eghosa. 2005. The State of Africa's Second Liberation. *Interventions: The International Journal of Postcolonial Studies* 7.1:1–20.

Oxhorn, Philip D. 1995. *Organizing Civil Society: The Popular Sectors and the Struggle for Democracy in Chile.* University Park: Pennsylvania State University Press.

———. 2003. Social Inequality, Civil Society, and the Limits of Citizenship in Latin America. In *What Justice? Whose Justice? Fighting for Fairness in Latin America*, edited by Susan Eckstein and Thomas Wickham-Crowley, 35–63. Berkeley: University of California Press.

Paley, Julia. 2001. *Marketing Democracy: Power and Social Movements in Post-Dictatorship Chile.* Berkeley: University of California Press.

Pape, John, and David McDonald. 2002. *Cost Recovery and the Crisis of Service Delivery in South Africa.* Cape Town: Human Science Research Council.

Pateman, Carole. 1970. *Participation and Democratic Theory.* Cambridge: Cambridge University Press.

Pauw, Jacques. 1997. *Into the Heart of Darkness: Confessions of Apartheid's Assassins.* Johannesburg: Jonathan Ball.

Peruzzotti, Enrique. 2005. Demanding Accountable Government: Citizens, Politicians and the Perils of Representative Democracy in Argentina. In *Argentine Democracy: The Politics of Institutional Weakness*, edited by Steven Levitsky and María Victoria Murillo, 229–40. University Park: Pennsylvania State University Press.

Pickvance, Christopher. 1999. Democratization and the Decline of Social Movements: The Effects of Regime Change on Collective Action in Eastern Europe, Southern Europe and Latin America. *Sociology* 33.2:353–72.

Piper, Laurence, and Roger Deacon. 2008. Party Politics, Elite Accountability and Public Participation: Ward Committee Politics in the Msunduzi Municipality. *Transformation* 66/67:61–82.

Pithouse, Richard. 2006. Struggle Is a School: The Rise of a Shack Dwellers Movement in Durban, South Africa. *Monthly Review* 57.9:30–51.

———. 2008. A Politics of the Poor: Shack Dwellers' Struggles in Durban. *Journal of Asian and African Studies* 43.1:63–94.

Piven, Frances Fox, and Richard A. Cloward. 1979. *Poor People's Movements: Why They Succeed and How They Fail.* New York: Vintage Books.

Planact. 1989. The Soweto Rent Boycott. Report Commissioned by the Soweto People's Delegation. Planact files, Johannesburg, South Africa.

———. 1990a. The Crisis of Black Local Authorities in the Transvaal. Manuscript. Planact files, Johannesburg, South Africa.

———. 1990b. Local Level Negotiations in the Transvaal: An Overview. Document submitted to the TPA and Cast Joint Working Group, December 11. Planact files, Johannesburg, South Africa.

———. 1990c. Political Transition, Development, and the Role of Civil Society. Policy document. Planact files, Johannesburg, South Africa.

———. 1991a. Annual Report 1990/91. Planact files, Johannesburg, South Africa.

———. 1991b. Policy Issues Arising out of Local Level Negotiations. Discussion document. Planact files, Johannesburg, South Africa.

Pointer, Rebecca. 2004. Questioning the Representation of South Africa's "New Social Movements": A Case Study of the Mandela Park Anti-Eviction Campaign. *Journal of Asian and African Studies* 39:271–94.

Polletta, Francesca. 2002. *Freedom Is an Endless Meeting: Democracy in American Social Movements.* Chicago: University of Chicago Press.

Port Elizabeth Civic Organization (PEBCO). n.d. Constitution. In author's possession.

Posner, Paul W. 2004. Local Democracy and the Transformation of Popular Participation in Chile. *Latin American Politics and Society* 46.3:55–81.

Price, Robert M. 1991. *The Apartheid State in Crisis: Political Transformation in South Africa, 1975–1990.* New York: Oxford University Press.

Przeworski, Adam. 1991. *Democracy and the Market: Political and Economic Reforms in Eastern Europe and Latin America.* New York: Cambridge University Press.

Putnam, Robert D. 1993. *Making Democracy Work: Civic Traditions in Modern Italy.* Princeton, NJ: Princeton University Press.

———. 2000. *Bowling Alone: The Collapse and Revival of American Community.* New York: Simon and Schuster.

Raga, Kishore, and John Derek Taylor. 2005. An Overview of the Ward Committee System: A Case Study of the Nelson Mandela Municipality. *Politeia* 24.2: 244–54.

Ramírez-Saiz, Juan Manuel. 1990. Urban Struggles and Their Political Consequences. In *Popular Movements and Political Change in Mexico*, edited by Joe Foweraker and Ann L. Craig, 234–46. Boulder, CO: Lynne Rienner.

Republic of South Africa (RSA). 1996. *Constitution of the Republic of South Africa*. Act 108 of 1996. http://www.info.gov.za/documents.

Republic of South Africa (RSA), Presidency. 2009. Development Indicators 2009. http://www.thepresidency.gov.za/learning/me/indicators/2009/indicators.pdf.

Republic of South Africa (RSA), Cooperative Governance and Traditional Affairs. 2009. State of Local Government in South Africa. http://www.polity.org.za.

Reteng. 2008. Alternative Report Submitted to the Human Rights Council, July. Office of the High Commissioner for Human Rights, United Nations. http://www.unchr.org.

Riordan, Rory. 1992. Port Elizabeth and Uitenhage—Township Revolt and Political Development, 1976–1990. Paper prepared for the Port Elizabeth's Place in South African History and Historiography Conference, Port Elizabeth, September 24–25. In author's possession.

Roux, Andre, and Kirk Helliker. 1986. Voices from Rini: A Survey of Black Attitudes towards a Consumer Boycott in Grahamstown. Working Paper 23, Institute of Social and Economic Research, Development Studies, Rhodes University, Grahamstown, South Africa.

Salazar, Phillip Joseph. 2002. *An African Athens: Rhetoric and the Shaping of Democracy in South Africa*. Mahwah, NJ: Lawrence Erlbaum Associates.

Salman, Ton. 1994. The Diffident Movement: Generation and Gender in the Vicissitudes of the Chilean Shantytown Organizations, 1973–1990. *Latin American Perspectives* 21.3:8–31.

Saloojee, Cassim. 1987. The Role of the Extra-Parliamentary Opposition in the Democratization of South Africa: A United Democratic Front Perspective. Paper prepared for the International Conference on South Africa in Transition, White Plains, NY, September 29–October 2. In author's possession.

Sandi, Ntsokolo Daniel. 1993. Guidelines for Civic Committees, Anticrime Committees, and Community Courts at Yard, Street, Area, Branch, Local, Sub-regional, Regional and National Levels. Civic Information Consultants International (CICI) 1. In author's possession.

———. 1994. Profiles in Public Administration and Development: A Study of Local Government and Community Development and the Role of Civic Associations. MA thesis, Vermont College of Norwich University.

Schamis, Hector. 2002. Argentina: Crisis and Democratic Consolidation. *Journal of Democracy* 13.2:81–94.

Schedler, Andreas. 1998. What Is Democratic Consolidation? *Journal of Democracy* 9.2:91–107.

Schmidle, Nicholas. 2009. The Hostage Business. *New York Times*, December 4.

Schneider, Cathy Lisa. 1995. *Shantytown Protest in Pinochet's Chile*. Philadelphia: Temple University Press.

Schock, Kurt. 2005. *Unarmed Insurrections: People Power Movements in Nondemocracies*. Minneapolis: University of Minnesota Press.

Schumpeter, Joseph Alois. 1947. *Capitalism, Socialism and Democracy*. New York: Harper.

Scott, James C. 1998. *Seeing like a State: How Certain Schemes to Improve the Human Condition Have Failed*. New Haven, CT: Yale University Press.

Scott, Sally J. 2001. Not a Circle but a Spring: A Case Study of Civil Society in the Republic of Benin. PhD diss., Johns Hopkins University.

———. 2003. From Benin to Baltimore: Civil Society and Its Limits. *International Journal of Not-for-Profit Law* 6.1. http://www.icnl.org.

Seekings, Jeremy. 1988. The Origins of Political Mobilization in PWV Townships. In *Popular Struggles in South Africa*, edited by William Cobbett and Robin Cohen, 59–76. Trenton, NJ: Africa World Press.

———. 1989. People's Courts and Popular Politics. In *South African Review 5*, edited by Glenn Moss and Ingrid Obery, 119–35. Johannesburg: Ravan Press.

———. 1992a. Civic Organizations in South African Townships. In *South African Review 6: From Red Friday to Codesa*, edited by Glenn Moss and Ingrid Obery, 216–38. Johannesburg: Ravan Press.

———. 1992b. The Revival of "People's Courts" Informal Justice in Transitional South Africa. In *South African Review 6: From Red Friday to Codesa*, edited by Glenn Moss and Ingrid Obery, 186–200. Johannesburg: Ravan Press.

———. 2000. *The UDF: A History of the United Democratic Front in South Africa, 1983–1991*. Athens: Ohio University Press.

———. 2007. Poverty and Inequality after Apartheid. Working Paper 200, Centre for Social Science Research, Cape Town, South Africa.

Seekings, Jeremy, and Nicoli Nattrass. 2005. *Class, Race, and Inequality in South Africa*. New Haven, CT: Yale University Press.

Seekings, Jeremy, Khehla Shubane, and David Simon. 1993. An Evaluation of the European Community/Kagiso Trust Civic and Advice Centre Programme. Final report. In author's possession.

Seely, Jennifer. 2009. *The Legacies of Transition Governments in Benin and Togo*. New York: Palgrave Macmillan.

Selolwane, Onalenna. 2000. Civil Society, Citizenship and Women's Rights in Botswana. In *International Perspectives on Gender and Democratisation*, edited by Shirin M. Rai, 83–99. London: Macmillan.

Sen, Amartya. 2006. Conceptualizing and Measuring Poverty. In *Poverty and Inequality*, ed. David Grusky and Ravi Kanbur, 30–46. Stanford, CA: Stanford University Press.

Shaw, Mark. 2002. *Crime and Policing in Post-Apartheid South Africa: Transforming under Fire*. Bloomington: Indiana University Press.

Shubane, Khehla. 1989. Soweto Rent Boycott: The Debate Continues. *Work in Progress* 61 (September): 37–42. http://www.disa.ukzn.ac.za.

———. 1991. Soweto. In *All, Here, and Now: Black Politics in South Africa in the 1980s*, edited by Tom Lodge and Bill Nasson, 255–72. New York: Ford Foundation.

———. 1992. Civil Society in Apartheid and Post-Apartheid South Africa. *Theoria* 79: 33–42.

Shubane, Khehla, and Pumla Madiba. 1992. *The Struggle Continues? Civic Associations in the Transition*. Centre for Policy Studies Transition Series 25. Johannesburg: Centre for Policy Studies.

Simkins, Charles. 2004. What Happened to the Distribution of Income in South Africa between 1995 and 2001? Manuscript, November 22. http://www.sarpn.org.za/documents/d0001062/index.php.

Sinwell, Luke. 2009. Participatory Spaces and the Alexandra Vukuzenzele Crisis Committee (AVCC): Reshaping Government Plans. *Social Dynamics* 35.2:436–49.

Sinwell, Luke, Joshua Kirchner, Kgopotso Khumalo, Owen Manda, Peter Pfaffe, Comfort Phokela, and Carin Runciman. 2009. Service Delivery Protests: Findings from Quick Response Research on Four "Hot Spots"—Piet Retief, Balfour, Thokoza, Diepsloot. Centre for Sociological Research, University of Johannesburg, September 1. http://tinyurl.com/293eqz6

Sisk, Timothy D. 1995. *Democratization in South Africa: The Elusive Social Contract*. Princeton, NJ: Princeton University Press.

Skocpol, Theda. 1979. *States and Social Revolutions: A Comparative Analysis of France, Russia and China*. New York: Cambridge University Press.

Snow, D. A., E. B. Rochford Jr., S. K. Worden, and R. D. Beneford. 1986. Frame Alignment Processes, Micromobilization, and Movement Participation. *American Sociological Review* 51:464–81.

Solway, Jacqueline. 2009. Human Rights and NGO "Wrongs": Conflict Diamonds, Culture Wars and the "Bushman Question." *Africa* 79.3:321–46.

South African Institute of Race Relations (SAIRR). 1952–84. *Survey of Race Relations*. Johannesburg: South African Institute of Race Relations.

———. 1984–95. *Race Relations Survey*. Johannesburg: South African Institute of Race Relations.

———. 1996–. *South Africa Survey*. Johannesburg: South African Institute of Race Relations.

South African National Civic Organization (SANCO). 1992. Constitution. In author's possession.

———. 1997a. Constitution. In author's possession.

———. 1997b. Membership flyer. In author's possession.

———. 1997c. Secretary's Report. In author's possession.

South African National Civic Organization, Port Elizabeth, Despatch, and Uitenhage (SANCO PEDU). 2000. Memorandum to SANCO National and Provincial Offices, July 14. In author's possession.

South African National Civic Organization (SANCO) and SANCO Investment Holdings (SIH). 1997. The South African National Civic Organization and SANCO Investment Holdings (Pty) Ltd.: An Overview. In author's possession.

Soweto Civic Association (SCA). 1984. A Watershed in Our History: Annual General Meeting, 1 December. Historical Papers, University of the Witwatersrand, Johannesburg, South Africa.

————. 1986. We Won't Pay Rent from 1 June! Flyer, Historical Papers, University of the Witwatersrand, Johannesburg, South Africa.

————. 1987. SCA News. April. Historical Papers, University of the Witwatersrand, Johannesburg, South Africa.

————. 1990. Soweto March. Flier, Historical Papers, University of the Witwatersrand, Johannesburg, South Africa.

————. n.d. Brief History of the Soweto Civic Association. Historical Papers, University of the Witwatersrand, Johannesburg, South Africa.

Sparks, Allister. 1990. *The Mind of South Africa.* New York: Alfred A. Knopf.

Speak Community Newspaper Project. 1982–86. *Speak: The Voice of the Community.* http://www.disa.ukzn.ac.za.

Stahler-Sholk, Richard. 2008. Resisting Neoliberal Homogenization: The Zapatista Autonomy Movement. In *Latin American Social Movements in the Twenty-first Century: Resistance, Power and Democracy,* edited by Richard Stahler-Sholk, Harry Vanden, and Glen Kuecker, 113–29. New York: Rowman and Littlefield.

Stahler-Sholk, Richard, Harry E. Vanden, and Glen David Kuecker. 2007. Introduction: Globalizing Resistance; The New Politics of Social Movements in Latin America. *Latin American Perspectives,* issue 153, 34.2:5–16.

Statistics South Africa (SSA). 2007. Labor force survey: September 2007. http://www.statssa.gov.za.

————. 2008. Income and Expenditure of Households 2005/2006: Analysis of results. http://www.statssa.gov.za.

————. 2010. Quarterly Labour Force Survey. Quarter 2. http://www.statssa.gov.za.

Stavrou, Paraskevi. 1992. *The Alexandra Community Crime Survey: A Study of the Perceptions and Fear of Crime of the Residents in an Area of Alexandra.* Johannesburg: Centre for the Study of Violence and Reconciliation, University of the Witwatersrand.

Steinberg, Jonny. 2000. A Place for Civics in a Liberal Democratic Polity? The Fate of Local Institutions of Resistance after Apartheid. In *From Comrades to Citizens: The South African Civics Movement and the Transition to Democracy,* edited by Glenn Adler and Jonny Steinberg, 175–204. New York: St. Martin's Press.

Swampa, Maristella, and Damían Corral. 2006. Political Mobilization in Neighborhood Assemblies: The Cases of Villa Crespo and Palermo. In *Broken Promises? The Argentine Crisis and Argentine Democracy,* edited by Edward Epstein and David Pion-Berlin, 117–39. Lanham, MD: Lexington Books.

Swilling, Mark. 1988. The United Democratic Front and Township Revolt. In *Popular Struggles in South Africa,* edited by William Cobbett and Robin Cohen, 90–113. Trenton, NJ: Africa World Press.

————. 1992a. Quixote at the Windmills: Another Conspiracy Thesis from Steven Friedman. *Theoria* 79:97–104.

————. 1992b. Socialism, Democracy and Civil Society: The Case for Associational Socialism. *Theoria* 79:75–82.

————. n.d. Interpretations of Crowd Behavior, Protests and "Riots": Some Thoughts on the Vaal Uprising. Defense Material, Delmas Treason Trial. Historical Papers, University of the Witwatersrand, Johannesburg, South Africa.

Swilling, Mark, William Cobbett, and Roland Hunter. 1991. Finance, Electricity Costs and the Rent Boycott. In *Apartheid City in Transition*, edited by Mark Swilling, Richard Humphries, and Khehla Shubane, 186–200. Cape Town: Oxford University Press.

Swilling, Mark, and Khehla Shubane. 1990. Negotiating Urban Transition: The Soweto Experience. Manuscript, Planact files, Johannesburg, South Africa.

Swords, Alicia C. S. 2008. Neo-Zapatista Network Politics: Transforming Democracy and Development. In *Latin American Social Movements in the Twenty-first Century: Resistance, Power and Democracy*, edited by Richard Stahler-Sholk, Harry Vanden, and Glen Kuecker, 291–305. New York: Rowman and Littlefield.

Tarrow, Sidney. 1989. *Democracy and Disorder: Protest and Politics in Italy, 1965–1975.* Oxford: Oxford University Press.

———. 1994. *Power in Movement: Social Movements, Collective Action and Politics.* New York: Cambridge University Press.

———. 1996. States and Opportunities: The Political Structuring of Social Movements. In *Comparative Perspectives on Social Movements: Political Opportunities, Mobilizing Structures, and Cultural Framings*, edited by Doug McAdam, John D. McCarthy, and Mayer N. Zald, 41–61. New York: Cambridge University Press.

Taylor, Helen, and Robert Mattes. 1998. *Public Evaluations of and Demands on Local Government.* Idasa Public Opinion Service (POS) Report 3. Cape Town: Institute for Democracy in South Africa.

Taylor, Ian. 2003. As Good as It Gets? Botswana's "Democratic Development." *Journal of Contemporary African Studies* 21.1:215–31.

Taylor, Rupert. 2002. Justice Denied: Political Violence in KwaZulu-Natal after 1994. *African Affairs* 101.405:473–508.

Taylor, Rupert, and Mark Shaw. 1998. The Dying Days of Apartheid. In *South Africa in Transition: New Theoretical Perspectives*, edited by Aletta Norval and David Horwath, 13–30. New York: St. Martin's Press.

Teichman, Judith. 2009. Competing Visions of Democracy and Development in the Era of Neoliberalism in Mexico and Chile. *International Political Science Review* 30.1:67–87.

Terreblanche, Sampie. 2008. The Developmental State in South Africa: The Difficult Road Ahead. In *State of the Nation: South Africa 2008*, edited by Peter Kagwanja and Kwandiwe Kondlo, 107–30. Cape Town: HSRC Press.

Thipanyane, Tseliso. 2005. Human Dignity and Democracy: Can Socioeconomic Rights Be Realised without Human Rights? In *Democracy in the Time of Mbeki*, edited by Richard Calland and Paul Graham, 211–47. Cape Town: Institute for Democracy in South Africa.

Thompson, E. P. 1971. The Moral Economy of the English Crowd in the Eighteenth Century. *Past and Present* 50:76–136.

Thompson, Leonard. 2000 *A History of South Africa*. New Haven, CT: Yale University Press.

Tibaijuka, Anna Kajumulo. 2005. Report of the Fact-Finding Mission to Zimbabwe to Assess the Scope and Impact of Operation Murambatsvina. July 18. http://ww2.unhabitat.org/documents/ZimbabweReport.pdf.

Tilly, Charles. 1978. *From Mobilization to Revolution*. Reading, MA: Addison-Wesley.

———. 1986. *The Contentious French*. Cambridge, MA: Harvard University Press.

———. 1993–94. Social Movements as Historically Specific Clusters of Political Performances. *Berkeley Journal of Sociology* 38:1–30.

———. 1998. *Durable Inequality*. Berkeley: University of California Press.

———. 2004. *Contention and Democracy in Europe, 1650–2000*. New York: Cambridge University Press.

Tilly, Charles, Louise Tilly, and R. Tilly. 1975. *The Rebellious Century, 1830–1930*. Cambridge: Cambridge University Press.

Tocqueville, Alexis de. [1835] 2003. *Democracy in America: And Two Essays on America*. London: Penguin Books.

Toronto Committee for the Liberation of Southern Africa (TCLSAC) (later Toronto Committee for Links between Southern Africa and Canada). 1985–2000. *Southern Africa Report*. http://www.africafiles.org/sar.asp.

Touraine, A. 1981. *The Voice and the Eye: An Analysis of Social Movements*. Translated by Alan Duff. Cambridge: Cambridge University Press.

Treatment Action Campaign (TAC). 2003. TAC Civil Disobedience Campaign. In author's possession.

Ukiwo, Ukoha. 2007. From "Pirates" to "Militants": A Historical Perspective on Anti-state and Anti-oil Company Mobilization among the Ijaw of Warri, Western Niger Delta. *African Affairs* 106:587–610.

United Democratic Front (UDF). 1983. UDF National Launch, Aug. 20, 1983. Pamphlet, Historical Papers, University of the Witwatersrand, Johannesburg, South Africa.

———. 1986–87. *Isizwe* (*The Nation*). http://www.disa.ukzn.ac.za.

United Nations Development Program (UNDP). 2003. South Africa Human Development Report 2003: The Challenge of Sustainable Development; Unlocking People's Creativity. http://hdr.undp.org/en/reports/nationalreports/africa/southafrica/name,3190,en.html

———. 2009. Human Development Report 2009: Overcoming Barriers; Human Mobility and Development. http://hdr.undp.org/en/reports/global/hdr2009/.

United Nations Habitat. 2008. State of the World's Cities 2008/2009: Harmonious Cities. http://www.unhabitat.org/pmss/listItemDetails.aspx?publicationID=2562.

USAID Center for Democracy and Governance. 1998. Democracy and Governance: A Conceptual Framework. http://www.usaid.gov/our_work/democracy_and_governance/publications/pdfs/pnacd395.pdf.

U.S. Census Bureau. 2001. Historical Income Tables: Income Inequality. http://www.census.gov/hhes/www/income/histinc/ie.6.html.

Vaal Civic Association. 1983. Asinamali Masinhlanganeni. Flyer, Historical Papers, University of the Witwatersrand, Johannesburg, South Africa.

Van Allen, Judith. 2001. Women's Rights Movements as a Measure of African Democracy. *Journal of Asian and African Studies* 36.1:39–63.

Van der Merwe, Hugo. 1994. Informal Justice: The Alexandra Justice Centre and the Future of Interpersonal Dispute Resolution. Working paper, Centre for Applied Legal Studies, Johannesburg, South Africa.

Van Dyke, Nella. 2003. Protest Cycles and Party Politics: The Effects of Elite Allies and Antagonists of Student Protest in the United States, 1930–1990. In *States, Parties and Social Movements*, edited by Jack Goldstone, 226–45. New York: Cambridge University Press.

Villalón, Roberta. 2007. Neoliberalism, Corruption, and Legacies of Contention: Argentina's Social Movements, 1993–2006. *Latin American Perspectives*, issue 153, 34.2:139–56.

Wada, Takeshi. 2006. Claim Network Analysis: How Are Social Protests Transformed into Political Protests in Mexico? In *Latin American Social Movements: Globalization, Democratization and Transnational Networks*, edited by Hank Johnston and Paul Almeida, 95–111. New York: Rowman and Littlefield.

Wade, Robert. 1992. *Governing the Market*. Princeton, NJ: Princeton University Press.

Wantchekon, Leonard. 2003. Clientelism and Voting Behavior: Evidence from a Field Experiment in Benin. *World Politics* 55:399–422.

Webster, David. 1987. Repression and the State of Emergency. In *South African Review 4*, edited by Glenn Moss and Ingrid Obery, 141–72. Johannesburg: Ravan Press.

Welch, Claude. 1995. The Ogoni and Self-Determination: Increasing Violence in Nigeria. *Journal of Modern African Studies* 33.4:635–649.

Wolff, Jonas. 2009. De-idealizing the Democratic Civil Peace: On the Political Economy of Democratic Stabilization and Pacification in Argentina and Ecuador. *Democratization* 16.5:998–1026.

Woo-Cumings, Meredith, ed. 1999. *The Developmental State*. Ithaca, NY: Cornell University Press.

Wood, Elisabeth. 2000. *Forging Democracy from Below: Insurgent Transitions in South Africa and El Salvador*. New York: Cambridge University Press.

———. 2001. An Insurgent Path to Democracy: Popular Mobilization, Economic Interests, and Regime Transition in South Africa and El Salvador. *Comparative Political Studies* 34.8:862–88.

Woolard, Ingrid, and Murray Leibbrandt. 2006. Towards a Poverty Line for South Africa: Background Note. Paper prepared for the National Treasury, February. Southern Africa Labour and Development Research Unit, University of Cape Town. http://www.treasury.gov.za/publications/other/povertyline/default.aspx.

World Bank. 1989. *Sub-Saharan Africa: From Crisis to Sustainable Growth*. Washington, DC: World Bank.

———. 2001. *World Development Report 2000/2001: Attacking Poverty*. Oxford: Oxford University Press.

———. 2004. *Inequality in Latin America and the Caribbean: Breaking with History?* Washington, DC: World Bank.

Wright, Gemma, Michael Noble, and Wiseman Magasela. 2007. *Towards a Democratic Definition of Poverty: Socially Perceived Necessities in South Africa.* Cape Town: HSRC Press.

Xali, Mthetho. 2002. "They Are Killing Us Alive": A Case Study of the Impact of Cost Recovery on Service Provision in Makhaza Section, Khayelitsha. In *Cost Recovery and the Crisis of Service Delivery*, edited by David McDonald and John Pape, 101–22. Cape Town: HSRC Press.

———. 2006. Seeking Trade Union and Community Linkages in the Cape Town Metropolitan Area: Possibilities for New Trade Unionism and New Social Movements. *Journal of Asian and African Studies* 42.1/2:123–47.

Yashar, Deborah, J. 1999. Democracy, Indigenous Movements, and the Postliberal Challenge in Latin America. *World Politics* 52.1:76–104.

Zdravomyslova, Elena. 1996. Opportunities and Framing in the Transition to Democracy: The Case of Russia. In *Comparative Perspectives on Social Movements: Political Opportunities, Mobilizing Structures, and Cultural Framings*, edited by Doug McAdam, John D. McCarthy, and Mayer N. Zald, 122–40. New York: Cambridge University Press.

Zikode, S'bu. 2006. The Third Force. *Journal of Asian and African Studies* 41.1/2: 185–89.

Zuern, Elke. 2001. South Africa's Civics in Transition: Agents of Change or Structures of Constraint? *Politikon: South African Journal of Political Studies* 28.1:5–20.

———. 2002. Fighting for Democracy: Popular Organizations and Post-Apartheid Government in South Africa. *African Studies Review* 45.1:77–102.

———. 2006a. Elusive Boundaries: SANCO, the ANC and the Post-Apartheid South African State. In *Voices of Protest: Social Movements in Post-Apartheid South Africa*, edited by Richard Ballard, Adam Habib, and Imraan Valodia, 179–201. Durban: University of KwaZulu-Natal Press.

———. 2006b. La Pauvreté en Débat: Marginalité et Démocratie Constitutionnelle en Afrique du Sud. *Politique Africaine* 103:27–45.

———. 2009. Democratization as Liberation: Competing African Perspectives on Democracy. *Democratization* 16.3:585–603.

Index

COSAS (Congress of South African Students), 34, 193n32
COSATU (Congress of South African Trade Unions), 141, 193n34, 203n15
CP (Conservative Party), 84
CRADORA (Cradock Residents' Association), 50, 73–74, 84
Cuba, 170

DA (Democratic Alliance), 142, *143*, 203n10
Dagnino, Evelina, 44
Dahl, Robert, 185
de Klerk, Frederik Willem, 54, 84
de Kock, Eugene, 103–4, 198n8
Delmas treason trial (1988), 35–38, 79, 193nn31–32
democracy: dominant party concept, 202n9; material demands and expansion of rights, 3–6, 10, 13–15, 19, 51–52, 56–57, 67–70, 75, 97, 124, 127, 173, 195n3, 197n18; people's power, 73–78; popular perceptions, xi–xiv, 18, 43, 176–78, 185–87, 190n8, 190n12; second liberation concept, 172; and socioeconomic conditions, xii, 6–11, 17–18, 20–21, 142–43, 163, 168–87, 189n4; substantive democracy concept, 184–87; Western liberal concepts, xi–xii, 6, 18, 76–77, 136–37, 165–73, 185. *See also* protest and contention
Desai, Ashwin, 42–43, 153
Diamandouros, P. Nikiforos, 135
Díaz-Barriga, Miguel, 13
Diepkloof Civic Association, 25
Dipaliseng Youth Forum (Balfour), 184
Ditshwanelo (Botswana), 161–62
Dlamini, Sam, 35
Dow, Unity, 160, 162
Duarte, Jessie, 140
Duduza Civic Association, 37
Duhalde, Eduardo, 163, 165

Ebrahim, Zohra, 106
Economist (London), 7
Ecuador, 6, 189n5
Ekeh, Peter, 171–72
Elimination and Prevention of Reemergence of Slums Act (2007), 152–53

Emang Basadi ("Stand Up, Women," Botswana), 160–61, 204n25
Emerald Resort and Casino, 115
environment, 94
Escobar, Arturo, 13, 44
escraches (Argentina), 163
ESKOM (Electricity Supply Commission), 61, 154–56
EZLN (Ejército Zapatista de Liberación Nacional, Zapatista Army of National Liberation). *See* Zapatista movement (Mexico)

Faku, Nceba, 59
Fazzie, Henry, 40
Federal Alliance (FA), *143*
Federation of Cape Civic Associations, 48, *49*, 192n20
First People of the Kalahari (Botswana), 161
Flores, Hugo, 129
Fluconazole, 146
Foweraker, Joe, xiii, 65–66, 190n9
France, 124
Freedom Charter (1955), 31–33, 40, 47–48, 62, 173, 191n11
Freedom House democracy ratings, 6, 11, 170–72, 189n1
Frei Ruiz-Tagle, Eduardo, 127
Friedman, Steven, 89
Friends of the Earth, 94
Fuchs, A. J., 143–44

Gamble, Barry, 202n4
GEAR (Growth, Employment, and Redistribution), 61, 145, 179
Gebengana, Isaac, 205n1
Germany, 136
Ghana, 178–79
Gilbreth, Chris, 91
Gini coefficient, 6, 8, 54, 159, 189n3, 189nn5–6, 190n15, 194n4, 204n24. *See also* income inequality
Goldstone Commission, 104
Gomati, Morgan, 144
Goniwe, Matthew, 73–74, 81
Goniwe, Mbulelo, 47, 50, 74, 79
Goodwin, Jeff, xiii

Critical Human Rights

Court of Remorse: Inside the International Criminal Tribunal for Rwanda
Thierry Cruvellier; translated by Chari Voss

Beyond Displacement: Campesinos, Refugees, and Collective Action in the Salvadoran Civil War
Molly Todd

The Politics of Necessity: Community Organizing and Democracy in South Africa
Elke Zuern

www.ingramcontent.com/pod-product-compliance
Lightning Source LLC
Chambersburg PA
CBHW061723270326
41928CB00011B/2088